I0027965

PEARLS

AND

PEARLING LIFE.

BY

EDWIN W. STREETER, F.R.G.S., M.A.I.

Gold Medallist of the Royal Order of Frederic,
Holder of a Gold Medal from H.M, the King of the Belgians,
Author of "PRECIOUS STONES AND GEMS," 4th Edition,
"GREAT DIAMONDS OF THE WORLD,"
"GOLD: Its Legal Regulations and Standards," &c., &c.,

Illustrated,

Copyright © 2018 Read Books Ltd.
This book is copyright and may not be
reproduced or copied in any way without
the express permission of the publisher in writing

British Library Cataloguing-in-Publication Data
A catalogue record for this book is available from
the British Library

"For me the balm shall bleed and Amber flow,
The Coral redden, and the Ruby glow,
The Pearly shell its lucid globe infold,
And Phœbus warm the ripening ore to Gold."

Pope's "Windsor Forest."

AN INTRODUCTORY EXCERPT CHAPTER

BY

GEORGE FREDERICK KUNZ,

"THE BOOK OF THE PEARL - THE HISTORY, ART, SCIENCE
AND INDUSTRY OF THE QUEEN OF THE GEMS" 1908

PEARL-CULTURE AND PEARL-FARMING

> Some asked how pearls did grow, and where,
> Then spoke I to my girl,
> To part her lips, and show them there
> The quarelets of pearl.
> HERRICK, *The Quarrie of Pearls.*

THE great profit that would accrue from an increased output of pearls has long directed attention to the problem of bringing this about by artificial means.

In his life of Apollonius of Tyana, Philostratus, a Greek writer of the third century, repeats a story afloat at the time, which credited the Arabs of the Red Sea with possessing some method of growing pearls artificially. The story as it reached Greece was that they first poured oil upon the sea for the purpose of calming the waves, and then dived down and caused the oysters to open their shells. Having effected this, they pricked the flesh with a sharp instrument and received the liquor which flowed from the wounds into suitable molds, and this liquor there hardened into the shape, color, and consistence of the natural gems.[1]

While the description given by Philostratus is charged with many improbable details, and could scarcely develop belief, even in the most credulous, as to the exact method of procedure, it seems that the story may not have been wholly without foundation, and that attempts were made at that remote date to stimulate the growth of pearls.

In more modern times, the possibility of aiding or starting pearly formations in mollusks seems first to have been conceived by the Chinese about the fourteenth century. In 1736 there appeared in that storehouse of Oriental information, "Lettres édifiantes et curieuses écrites des missions étrangères,"[2] a communication from F. X. de Entrecolles, dated Pekin, 4th November, 1734, which set forth that there were people in China who busied themselves with growing pearls,

---

[1] Philostratus, "Vita Apollonii," *Lib.* III, c. 57, edit. Olearii, p. 139. Also see Konrad von Gessner, "Historiæ natura," *Lib.* IV, p.634.   [2] Vol. XXII, pp. 425-437.

and the product was not only vastly superior to the imitations manufactured in Europe, but were scarcely to be distinguished from the
genuine. From Father Entrecolles's very detailed quotation of his
unnamed Chinese authority, we condense this account. In a basin
one half full of fresh water, place the largest mussels obtainable, set
this basin in a secluded place where the dew may fall thereon, but
where no female approaches, and neither the barking of dogs nor the
crowing of chickens is to be heard. Pulverize some seed-pearls (*Yo
tchu*), such as are commonly used in medicine, moisten this powder
with juice expressed from leaves of a species of holly (*Che ta-kong
lao*), and then roll the moistened powder into perfectly round pellets
the size of a pea. These are permitted to dry under a moderate
sunlight, and then are carefully inserted within the open shells of
the mollusks. Each day for one hundred days the mussels are nour-
ished with equal parts of powdered ginseng, china root, *peki,* which
is a root more glutinous than isinglass, and of *pecho,* another medicinal root, all combined with honey and molded in the form of rice
grains.

Although extremely detailed in some particulars, the Chinese account omits much to be desired as to the method in which the shells
were opened to receive the pellets and the nourishment, and as to the
importance of seclusion from females and loud noises. Admitting
that it is "inaccurate and misleading," this letter seems to indicate very
clearly that the Chinese had some method of assisting nature in growing pearls in river mussels.

The first person in Europe whose suggestion of the possibility of
pearl-culture attracted general attention was Linnæus, the Swedish
naturalist (1707–1778). In a letter to Von Haller, the Swiss anato-
mist, dated 13th September, 1748, he wrote: "At length I have ascer-
tained the manner in which pearls originate and grow in shells; and in
the course of five or six years I am able to produce, in any mother-of-
pearl shell the size of one's hand, a pearl as large as the seed of the
common vetch."[1] There was much secrecy about Linnæus's discovery,
and even yet there is uncertainty as to the details of the method.

The Linnean Society of London apparently possesses some of the
very pearls grown by Linnæus, as well as several manuscripts which
throw much light on this subject. It appears from the latter that,
under date of 6th February, 1761, Linnæus wrote that he "possessed
the art" of impregnating mussels for pearl-production, and offered for
a suitable reward from the state to publish the "secret" for the public
use and benefit. A select committee of the state council of Sweden
was appointed to confer with him, and on 27th July, 1761, the

[1] Pulteney, "General View of the Writings of Linnæus," London, 1805.

naturalist appeared and verbally explained his discovery. After various meetings, the select committee approved the "art" and recommended a compensation of 12,000 dalars (about $4800). It does not appear that the award was paid, and the following year the secret was purchased by Peter Bagge, a Gothenberg merchant, for the sum of 6000 dalars. On 7th September, 1762, King Adolph Frederick issued a grant to this merchant "to practice the art without interference or competition."[1]

Peter Bagge was unable to exercise the rights which he had acquired, nor was he able to dispose of them to advantage. On his death the memorandum of the secret became lost, and it was not found until about 1821, when it was discovered by a grandson, J. P. Bagge. Under the date of 27th February, 1822, the King of Sweden confirmed to this grandson the privileges which his ancestor had purchased in 1762. Fruitless efforts were again made to dispose profitably of the rights either to individuals or to the Swedish government.

The details of Linnæus's "secret" have never been published authoritatively. In his "History of Inventions," Beckmann states that before the naturalist thought of the profits that might accrue from his discovery, he intimated the process in the sixth edition of his "Systema naturæ," wherein he states: "Margarita testæ excrescentia latere interiore, dum exterius latus perforatur."[2] "I once told him," says Beckmann, "that I had discovered his secret in his own writings; he seemed to be displeased, made no inquiry as to the passage, and changed the discourse."[3]

In the second volume of his edition of "Linnæus's Correspondence,"[4] Sir J. E. Smith remarks: "Specimens of pearls so produced by art in the *Mya margaritifera* are in the Linnean cabinet. The shell appears to have been pierced by flexible wires, the ends of which perhaps remain therein." Referring to this remark, J. P. Bagge comments: "This is the nearest I have seen any one come to truth, but still it will be remarked by reading the 'secret' that more information is required to enable persons to practice the art."

After a thorough examination of the manuscripts and other material, Professor Herdman concludes that the essential points of Linnæus's process are to make a very small hole in the shell and insert a round pellet of limestone fixed at the end of a fine silver wire, the hole being near the end of the shell so as to interfere only slightly with the mollusk, and the nucleus being kept free from the interior of the

[1] "Proceedings of the Linnean Society of London," October, 1905, p. 26.
[2] Pearl: an excrescence on the inside of a shell when the outside has been perforated.
[3] Beckmann, "History of Inventions," London, 1846, Vol. I, p. 263.
[4] London, 1821, p. 48.

shell so that the resulting pearl may not become adherent to it by a deposit of nacre.[1]

Shortly after Linnæus communicated with the Swedish government and before his death, it was learned in Europe that the art of producing "culture pearls" by a somewhat similar process had been practised by the Chinese for centuries.[2] They used several forms of matrices or nuclei, but principally spheres of nacre and bits of flat metal or molded lead, which were not infrequently in conventional outline of Buddha. In the spring or early summer, these were introduced under the mantle of the living mollusk after the shell had been carefully opened a fraction of an inch, and the animal was then returned to the pond or lake. The mollusk did its work in a leisurely way, like some people who have little to do, and many months elapsed before it was ready for opening and the removal of the pearly objects.

The most satisfactory description we have seen of this process appears to be that communicated nearly a century later to the London Society of Arts by Dr. D. T. Macgowan,[3] through H. B. M. plenipotentiary in China, from which this account is abridged and modified.

The industry is prosecuted in two villages near the city of Titsin, in the northern part of the province of Che-kiang, a silk-producing region. In May or June large specimens of the fresh-water mussels, *Dipsas plicatus,* are brought in baskets from Lake Tai-hu, about thirty miles distant. For recuperation from the journey, they are immersed in fresh water for a few days in bamboo cages, and are then ready to receive the matrices.

These nuclei are of various forms and materials, the most common being spherical beads of nacre, pellets of mud moistened with juice of camphor seeds, and especially thin leaden images, generally of Buddha in the usual sitting posture. In introducing these objects, the shell is gently opened with a spatula of bamboo or of pearl shell, and the mantle of the mollusk is carefully separated from one surface of the shell with a metal probe. The foreign bodies are then successively introduced at the point of a bifurcated bamboo stick, and placed, commonly in two parallel rows, upon the inner surface of the shell; a sufficient number having been placed on one valve, the operation is repeated on the other. As soon as released, the animal closes its shell, thus keeping the matrices in place. The mussels are then deposited one by one in canals or streams, or in ponds connected therewith, five or six inches apart, and where the depth is from two to five feet under water.

[1] "Proceedings of the Linnean Society of London," October, 1905, p. 29.

[2] See Grill, Abhandlungen der königlichen Schwedischen Akademie der Wissenschaften auf das Jahr 1772," Leipzig, Vol. XXXIV, pp. 88-90.

[3] "Journal of the Society of Arts," Vol. II, pp. 72-75.

If taken up within a few days and examined, the nuclei will be found attached to the shell by a membranous secretion; later this appears to be impregnated with calcareous matter, and finally layers of nacre are deposited around each nucleus, the process being analagous to the formation of calculary concretions in animals of higher development. A ridge generally extends from one pearly tumor to another, connecting them all together. Each month several tubs of night soil are thrown into the reservoir for the nourishment of the animals. Great care is taken to keep goat excretia from the water, as it is highly detrimental to the mussels, preventing the secretion of good nacre or even killing them if the quantity be sufficient. Persons inexperienced in the management lose ten or fifteen per cent. by deaths; others lose virtually none in a whole season.

In November, the mussels are removed from the water and opened, and the pearly masses are detached by means of a knife. If the matrix be of nacre, this is not removed; but the earthen and the metallic matrices are cut away, melted resin or white sealing-wax poured into the cavity, and the orifice covered with a piece of shell. These pearly formations have some of the luster and beauty of true pearls, and are furnished at a rate so cheap as to be procurable by almost any one. Most of them are purchased by jewelers, who set them in various personal ornaments, and especially in decorations for the hair. Those formed in the image of Buddha are used largely for amulets as well as for ornaments. They are about half an inch long, and while in the shell have a bluish tint, which disappears with removal of the matrix. Quantities of them are sold as talismans to pilgrims at the Buddhist shrines about Pooto and Hang-chau.

In some shells the culture pearls are permitted to remain by the Chinese growers, for sale as curios or souvenirs; specimens of these have found their way into many public and private collections of Europe and America. These shells are generally about seven inches long and four or five inches broad, and contain a double or triple row of pearls or images, as many as twenty-five of the former and sixteen of the latter to each valve. That the animal should survive the introduction of so many irritating bodies, and in such a brief period secrete a covering of nacre over them all, is certainly a striking physiological fact. Indeed, some naturalists have expressed strong doubts as to its possibility, supposing the forms were made to adhere to the shell by some composition; but the examination of living specimens in different stages of growth, with both valves studded with them, has fully demonstrated its truth.

It is represented that in the northern part of the Che-kiang province about five thousand families are employed in this work in connection

19

with rice-growing and silk-culture. To some of them it is the chief source of income, single families realizing as much as 300 silver dollars annually therefrom. In the village of Chung-kwan-o, the headquarters for culture pearls in China, a temple has been erected to the memory of the originator of this industry, Yu Shun Yang, who lived late in the thirteenth century, and was an ancestor of many persons now employed thereby.

The method in vogue in China for so many centuries has been the starting-point for similar attempts in various other countries. During the New Jersey pearling excitement in 1857, there were found several spherical pieces of nacre which had been introduced into Unios apparently for experimental pearl-culture; and in the collection of shells bequeathed to the United States National Museum by the late Dr. Isaac Lea, is a hemispherical piece of candle grease partly coated with pinkish nacre. Kelaart applied the Chinese method to the Ceylon pearl-oysters with much success in 1858. At the Berlin Fisheries Exhibition, in 1880, appeared the results of experiments in growing culture pearls in the river mussels in Saxony. Small foreign bodies had been introduced in the mantle, and others had been inserted between the mantle and the shell. These nuclei consisted of shell beads, unsightly pearls from other mussels, etc.; but unfortunately the shape of these was such that the mantle could not fit closely around them, consequently the result was so irregular as to be of no value except to show that German Unios as well as those of China could be made to cover foreign objects with pearly material.

Professor Herdman notes that, between 1751 and 1754, an inspector named Frederick Hedenberg received an annual salary "to inoculate the pearl mussels of Lulea (in the northern part of Sweden) with 'pearl-seeds' which he manufactured, and then to replant the mussels. Certain pearls were produced by the inspector, which it is recorded were sold for some 300 silver dollars."[1]

As noted by Broussonnet, in Finland artificial pearls were produced by inserting a round piece of nacre between the inner face of the shell and the mantle. The owner of the pearl fisheries at Vilshofen has succeeded in producing pearly figures by introducing into the mollusk flat figures of pewter, most of them representing fish in form.

In 1884, Bouchon-Brandely made experiments in pearl production at Tahiti. Gimlet holes about half an inch in diameter were drilled through different places in the shells of pearl-oysters, and through each of these holes a pellet of nacre or of glass was inserted and held by brass wire passing through a stopper of cork or burao wood, by means of which each opening was hermetically closed, so that the

---

[1] "Proceedings of the Linnean Society of London," October, 1905, p. 28.

pellet was the only foreign substance protruding on the inside of the shell.[1] The oysters were returned to the sea without further injury, and after the lapse of a month the pellets were found covered with thin layers of nacre.

Experiments in growing pearls in the abalone or Haliotis were made in 1897 by Louis Bouton, an account of which was given at the meeting of the Paris Académie des Sciences in 1898.[2] The tenacity of life in this mollusk makes it especially desirable for experiments of this nature. Through small holes bored into the shell, pellets of mother-of-pearl were inserted and placed within the mantle, the small holes being afterward closed up. Other nacreous pellets were introduced directly into the bronchial cavity. The objects were soon covered with thin, pearly layers, resulting in a few months in spheres of much beauty, resembling somewhat the pearls naturally produced by this mollusk. In six months, according to M. Bouton, the layers became of sufficient thickness to be attractive. Within limitations, the size of the pearl produced is in proportion to the length of time it is allowed to remain within the mollusk. The results of the experiments seem to encourage further efforts in this line, and possibly in course of time there may be a profitable business in growing pearls in abalones on the Pacific coast of the United States. Indeed, the experiments in transplanting and cultivating the pearl-oyster in Australia leads one to fancy that the culture of that species in the warm coastal waters of America is by no means an impossibility.

Many other experiments along similar lines have been made more recently. An interesting feature of attempts made by Mr. Vane Simmonds of Cedar Rapids, Iowa, in 1896–1898, is that in order to avoid straining the adductor muscles by forcibly opening the shell while the mollusk resisted the intrusion, each selected Unio was exposed in the open air and sunshine until the valves opened; then a wooden wedge was carefully inserted in the opening, and the mollusk immediately immersed in water to revive it or to sustain life. After a few moments of immersion, the operator carefully raised the mantle from the shell, inserted the pellet of wax or other small article to be covered with nacre, drew the mantle to its normal position, removed the wedge, and returned the mollusk to a selected place in the stream at sufficient depth to avoid danger of freezing in winter.

Probably it would be more satisfactory to stupefy the mollusks by means of some chemical in order to insert the pellets. Marine mollusks have been successfully stupefied by slowly adding magnesium sulphate crystals to the sea water until the animals no longer respond

[1] "La Pêche et la Culture des Huitres Perlières à Tahiti," Paris, 1885.

[2] "Comptes Rendus de l'Académie des Sciences," Vol. CXXVII, pp. 828-830.

to contact. If treatment is not too prolonged, they may be returned to normal sea water with good prospects of recovery. To stupefy fresh-water mollusks, either chloral hydrate or chlorosone may be employed, although the latter is expensive to use in great quantity. Dr. Charles B. Davenport, of the Carnegie Institution, suggests that it might be well to experiment with pouring ether or chloroform over them.

In Japan the production of these pearly formations in *Margarit-ifera martensi,* which is closely related to the Ceylon oyster, has developed into some prominence since 1890, and the results have been well advertised. The industry is located in Ago Bay, near the celebrated temple of Ise in the province of Shima, and gives employment to about one hundred persons. It is stated that the proprietor, Kokichi Mikimoto, has leased about one thousand acres of sea bottom, on which are a million oysters of this species, which yield from 30,000 to 50,000 culture pearls annually.

As described by Dr. K. Mitsukuri, the shoal portions of this area are used for breeding the oysters and raising them to maturity, and in the deeper parts—covered by several fathoms of water—the oysters are specially treated for producing the culture pearls. In the former, the spat is collected on small stones, weighing six or eight pounds each, placed during May or June. The following November these stones, with the attached spat or young, are removed, for protection from cold, to depths greater than five or six feet, where they remain for about three years. At the end of that period, the growing oysters are taken from the water, the shells opened slightly, and rounded bits of pearl shell or nacre are introduced under the mantle without injury to the mollusks. About 300,000 are thus treated annually, and placed in the deeper water at the rate of about one to each square foot of bottom area. After the lapse of about four years more, the oysters are removed from the water and opened, when a large percentage of the pellets are found covered on the upper or exposed surface with nacre of good luster.

Most of these culture pearls are button-shaped and weigh two or three grains each. Although somewhat attractive and superior to the culture pearls of China and other fresh waters, they by no means compare favorably with choice pearls. They are rarely, if ever, spherical, and only the upper surface is lustrous; consequently they serve only the purpose of half-pearls. A cross section shows the nacreous growth in a thin concentric layer, forming a fragile hemispherical cap, the concave wall of which is covered with a brownish granular secretion which prevents perfect adhesion. Compared with choice pearls, they are not only deficient in luster, but are fragile, and are beautiful only on the upper surface, and not available for necklaces. Good specimens sell for several dollars each, and some individuals reach $50 or more. Specimens exhibited at the Paris Exposition in 1900 were awarded a silver medal; at the St. Petersburg Exhibition in 1902 they were awarded a gold medal; at the Tokio Exhibition a grand prize, and a medal at the St. Louis Exposition in 1904. The awards were given in the fisheries, and not the gem divisions.

The work of Mikimoto is not the only attempt now being made in Japan to produce pearls. A letter from Dr. T. Nishikawa, of the Tokio Imperial University, states: "It is a great pleasure for me to tell you that I am studying pearl formation and pearl-oyster culture in the university laboratory, and recently I have got my pearl laboratory at Fukura, on the Island of Awaji, where I began the pearl culture work this summer (1907). Fortunately, I found the cause of Japanese pearl formation, *i.e.*, the reason why and how the pearl is produced in the tissue of an oyster. I made practical application of this theory with great prospects for producing the natural and true pearls at will."

Among the most interesting of the pearl-culture enterprises are those of the Compañia Criadora de Concha y Perla, under the direction of Sr. Gaston J. Vives, in the Gulf of California. This company has an extensive station at San Gabriel, near La Paz, where breeding oysters are placed in prepared chests or cages for collecting the spat on trays. After remaining there for several weeks or months, the young mollusks are removed to prepared places (*viveros*) for further growth. Experiments are now made in depositing them between a series of parallel dams alternately touching each shore of a lagoon, thus developing a current of water over the oysters for conveying food to them, and thus hastening their growth.

In efforts to increase the output of pearls, attention has been given to the possibilities for extending the area and production of the reefs, and for stocking new areas and replenishing exhausted ones, thus bringing the pearl-bearing mollusks to maturity in greater abundance.

Although theoretically it does not seem a very difficult undertaking to cultivate the pearl-oysters by methods somewhat similar to the cultivation of edible oysters and clams, in no part of the world has this been successfully done on an extensive scale. While in certain minor cases, the areas of some species of pearl mollusks have been extended indirectly through man's agency—as the range of the Red Sea pearl-oyster into the Mediterranean since the Suez Canal was opened—there is no well-known instance in which new areas have been abundantly populated through direct efforts.

In the chapter on the pearl fisheries of Asia are noted the hitherto unsuccessful efforts made in Ceylon and India to preserve the young and immature oysters on the storm-swept reefs by removing them to less exposed areas. This has received close attention from the Ceylon authorities during the last two years. Other practical measures which are recommended for that region include "cultching," or the deposit of suitable solid material, such as shells or broken stone, to which the young oysters can attach themselves; thinning out overcrowded reefs, and cleaning the beds by means of a dredge, thereby removing starfish and other injurious animals. The attempts made by individuals and associations to extend the range of the reefs on the coast of Australia, among the Tuamotu Islands, in the Gulf of California, and some other localities, are noted in the appropriate chapters. But it may be stated that in most instances lack of adequate police protection has been not the least of the difficulties with which these experiments have had to contend.

Nor has much greater success followed upon efforts to prevent the exhaustion of the reefs and productive grounds through overfishing, except in those instances in which the government exercises a proprietory interest and determines the season, the area to be fished, and the quantity of mollusks to be removed. The most prominent instance of this is in Ceylon, where the fishery has been restricted to such seasons and periods as appeared to insure the maximum yield of pearls. Without restriction upon the fishery, the pearl-oyster in that populous region would doubtless become almost extinct in a few years. Another instance of proprietory interest on the part of the government is in some of the German States, where pearl fishing has been regulated and restricted for centuries. But there the sewage from cities and factories has accomplished almost as effectively, if less rapidly, what unrestricted fishing would have done.

Much attention has been given to the subject of pearl-culture in Bavaria, where the government has granted a small subsidy to encourage this industry, and a model pearl-mussel bank has been established in one of the brooks for the rational culture of the mussels.

On the Australian coast, the only theoretical protection of consequence is the restriction on taking small or immature oysters; but, owing to the great area over which the fisheries are prosecuted there, it has not been possible to enforce the regulations. At some of the Pacific islands and elsewhere, interdictions exist as to use of certain apparatus of capture, but this is intended for the purpose of reserving the industry to dependent natives rather than for protecting the reefs. Several efforts have been made to insure adequate protection for the Unios in our American rivers, but nothing in this direction has yet been accomplished by legislative enactment, except in Illinois.

Reference has already been made to the parasitic stage of Unios.[1] The attachment of the newly-hatched mollusks to the gills or fins of a fish is entirely a matter of chance, and unless this takes place they die within a few days. Under natural conditions the fish thus infected will rarely be found carrying as many of the parasitic Unios as they can without serious injury. If the fish are placed in a tank or a pond containing large numbers of newly-hatched Unios, it is possible to bring about the attachment of hundreds of them for every one that would be found there by chance of nature. A fish six inches in length may thus be made to carry several hundred parasitic Unios, and thus a thousand fish artificially infected may do the work of several hundred thousand in a state of nature. Experiments with small numbers of fish under observation in the laboratory indicate that their infection on a large scale is entirely possible, and the experiment by· Messrs. Lefevre and Curtis now in progress at La Crosse, Wisconsin, in which over 25,000 young fish have been infected, gives every indication that such work may be begun even with the scanty knowledge now possessed.

Since it has already been shown that the production of pearls is an abnormal condition, it does not follow that an increase in the quantity of mollusks would necessarily result in a corresponding increase in the yield of pearls. Indeed, it might even be that the artificial conditions bringing about an enhanced prosperity and abundance of the mollusks would result in a corresponding decrease in the product of gems, the improved surroundings impairing if not destroying the conditions to which the pearls owe their origin. This has resulted in directing efforts toward abnormally increasing the abundance of pearls in a definite number of mollusks.

The development of the parasitic theory of pearl formation has naturally invited attention to the possibilities of increasing the yield of pearls by inoculating healthy mollusks with distomid parasites. It does not appear that this has yet advanced beyond the experimental stage, and virtually all that has been accomplished has been set forth in the chapter on the origin of pearls. It seems that there are great possibilities in the artificial production along these lines; and that under skilful management it could be made a profitable industry, especially if carried on concurrently with the systematic cultivation of mother-of-pearl shells.

Although there is scientific basis for the belief that it may be possible in time to bring about pearl growth in this manner, the public should not be too hasty in financing companies soliciting capital for establishing so-called "pearl farms." Every once in a while announcement is made in the public press of wonderful success which has been attained by some investigator, who surrounds his discovery with as much mystery as enveloped the Keeley motor, and who is as anxious to sell stock as was the owner of that mythical invention. A prospectus of one of these "pearl syndicates," which is now before us, claims to "increase and hasten pearl production by forcing the oyster, through doctoring the water in which it is immersed and also by irritating the mollusk itself." So far as the writers are aware, aside from the inexpensive but somewhat attractive culture pearls, no commercial success has yet followed the many attempts at artificial production.

This chapter should not close without reference to the so-called "breeding pearls," probably the most curious of all theories of pearl growth, regarding which many inquiries have been made. Throughout the Malay Archipelago there exists a generally accepted belief that if several selected pearls of good size are sealed in a box with a few grains of rice for nourishment they will increase in number as well as in size. If examined at the expiration of one year, small pearls may be found strewn about the bottom of the box, according to the theory; and in some instances the original pearls themselves will be found to have increased in size. If again inclosed for a further period of a year or more, the adherents of the theory say, the seed-pearls will further increase in size, and additional seed-pearls will form. Furthermore, the grains of rice will present the appearance of having been nibbled or as though a rodent had taken a bite in the end of each.

It is claimed that the breeding pearls are obtained from several species of mollusks, mostly from the Margaritifera, but also from the Tridacna (giant clam) and the Placuna (window shell). While cotton is the usual medium in which the pearls and rice are retained, some collectors substitute fresh water and yet others prefer salt water. It seems that rice is considered essential to success.

The earliest account we have seen of this extraordinary belief was given by Dr. Engelbert Kæmpfer,[1] who was connected with the Dutch embassy to Japan from 1690 to 1696, and since that time it has been referred to by many travelers in the Malay Archipelago.

A correspondent in the time-honored "Notes and Queries," 20th September, 1862, writes:

Nearly five years ago, while staying with friends in Pulo Penang (Straits of Malacca), I was shown by the wife of a prominent merchant five small pearls, which had increased and multiplied in her possession. She had set them aside for about 12 months in a small wooden box, packed in soft cotton and with half a dozen grains of common rice. On opening the box at the expiration of that time, she found four additional pearls, about the size of a

[1] Kæmpfer, "History of Japan," London, 1728, Vol. I, pp. 110-112.

small pinhead and of much beauty, which I saw and examined not long after the lady made the discovery. While my story may be received with laughter, I can most solemnly assure you of the truth of my having seen these pearls, and I have not the slightest doubt of the perfect truthfulness of the lady who possessed them. I questioned an eminent Malay merchant of Penang on this subject, and he assured me that one of his daughters had once possessed a similar growth of pearls. [1]

Notwithstanding the apparent absurdity of this pearl-breeding theory, belief in it appears to be not only sincere but wide-spread; as can be attested by any one familiar with affairs in the archipelago. A critical examination into the matter was made in 1877 by Dr. N. B. Dennys, curator of the Raffles Museum at Singapore, the result of which was communicated to the Straits branch of the Royal Asiatic Society, 28th February, 1878. [2] From his numerous quotations of persons who gave the results of their experiences we extract two instances. One gentleman had 120 small pearls in addition to the five breeding ones with which the experiment had started twenty years before, and during the entire period the box had not been molested except that it was opened occasionally for inspection by interested persons. Another experimentor inclosed three breeding pearls with a few grains of rice on 17th July, 1874; on opening the box on 14th July, 1875, nine additional pearls were discovered, and the three original ones appeared larger.

The belief has many curious variations. It is stated that in Borneo and the adjacent islands, many of the fishermen reserve every ninth pearl regardless of its size, and put the collection in a small bottle which is kept corked with a dead man's finger. According to Professor Kimmerly, nearly every burial-place along the Borneo coast has been desecrated in searching for "corks" for these bottles, and almost every hut has its dead-finger bottle, with from ten to fifty "breeding pearls" and twice that number of rice grains. [3] A correspondent at Sandakan, North Borneo, writes that at the time of his death at Hongkong in 1901, Dr. Dennys had in his possession a small box containing "breeding pearls"; but these disappeared after his death, and his brother, the crown solicitor, was unable to find them. This correspondent also states that the Ranee of Sarawak, a British protectorate in western Borneo, has a collection of "breeding pearls" numbering about two hundred, and that this is the only large collection known at present.

[1] "Notes and Queries," 3rd Series, Vol. II, p. 228.
[2] "Journal of the Straits Branch of the Royal Asiatic Society," Singapore, 1878, Vol. I, pp. 31-37.
[3] "Jewelers' Review," May 10, 1892.

As contrasted with abundant and unquestionably sincere testimony that pearls do "breed," it may be stated that absolutely no result has followed one or two native experiments made under supervision. While it must be admitted that negative evidence is always weaker than positive, and twenty failures would be outweighed by one successful experiment, yet the scientific objections to the possibility of pearls "breeding" cannot be overcome. The phenomenon is doubtless one of those curiosities of natural history in which some important factor has been overlooked.

Another curious theory is that peculiar pearls continue to grow after removal from the mollusk in which they originate. Quite recently it was reported from New Durham, North Carolina, that a pearl found there in 1896 had been growing continually since it was found and removed from the water. Unfortunately, it was weighed only when the last observation was made, and its increased size doubtless existed only in the imagination of its possessor.

OPENING OYSTER-SHELLS, COLLECTED BY THE PEARLING FLEET AND SEARCHING FOR THE PEARLS ON BOARD MR. STREETER'S SCHOONER, THE "SREE PAS-SAIR."

CONTENTS.

———

LIST OF ILLUSTRATIONS.

LIST OF FIGURES IN TEXT.

PREFACE.

T is strange that although Pearls have been highly valued in all ages as objects of personal adornment, there should not exist in the English language a single book entirely devoted to their history. There are, it is true, many notices of Pearls—more or less complete—in various works on Precious Stones, and in others on the Mollusca, or on the products of the sea in general. In like manner there are numerous articles on the subject, scattered throughout our periodical literature, or enshrined in the proceedings of our learned societies. But the fact remains that, so far as my knowledge extends, there exists no work in which the subject of Pearls is treated with fulness, much less with any approach to exhaustion, and to which the reader may confidently turn for information on any point connected with these lovely productions of the sea.

In the earlier editions of my work on " Precious

Stones and Gems," I introduced a chapter on Pearls. But within the last few years so much information has accumulated, that I felt it impossible to do justice to the Pearl in any other way than in a separate volume. Moreover, the fact that a Pearl, although composed mainly of carbonate of lime, is after all an organic product, renders it desirable to remove it from association with true minerals. Accordingly in the fourth edition of " Precious Stones and Gems," I was induced to omit the description of Pearls, and to promise that the subject should be separately dealt with in a special work. That promise I have now the satisfaction of fulfilling.

When I first took the matter in hand, I had no idea of the amount of labour which would be involved in the production of such a work. The study has, however, been a source of much pleasure to myself, and I trust that the perusal of the results set forth in this volume, will be equally a source of gratification to the reader. Although I cannot for a moment hope that the work is anything like complete in all its details, yet I may venture to remark that I have spared no pains in collecting and arranging my materials, and that my information has in many cases been derived from original sources. At the same time, the work is not put forth as a scientific treatise, but rather as a practical guide, either for those engaged in the trade, or for such of the public as may desire to acquire a knowledge of the history, formation and uses of Pearl and Pearl-shell.

It may be useful here to give a brief explanation of the general arrangement of the book. After a short introductory chapter, the subject of Pearls is discussed historically, and reference made to the use of Pearls by the principal nations of antiquity.

The historical chapter is followed by one in which I have sought to give a fair notion of the views of ancient writers on the origin and virtues of Pearls. The fanciful theories which were current in pre-scientific ages—some of which are not quite exploded at the present day—I hope will be found to furnish many subjects of interest. Not only the occult virtues of the Pearl, but its reputed medical properties claim consideration; while the curious notion, still current in certain quarters, as to the self-generation of Pearls, is too strange a subject to be passed over, and hence a section is devoted to the so-called " Breeding Pearls."

Having thus described most of the fallacies and fancies connected with Pearls, I proceed to treat the subject from a natural-history point of view. The various Pearl-bearing Molluscs, both marine and fluviatile, are described; and attention is then directed to the composition and physical properties, first of Mother-of-Pearl, and afterwards of the Pearl itself. The opinions of modern authorities are freely quoted, and it is hoped that my views may contribute in some measure to the elucidation of the vexed question of the formation of Pearls.

The principal localities producing Pearls are next given, the description commencing with the Sooloo Archipelago, and proceeding thence to the fisheries off the coast of North-Western Australia and in Torres Straits. For several years I have had a fleet engaged in Pearl-fishing in these regions, and I have consequently been able to introduce a considerable amount of information which has never before been published.

Few have any idea of the many dangers and difficulties experienced by pearlers, and by those engaged in the trade of collecting Pearls and Pearl-shell. I was horrified to notice in *The Times* of the 2nd November, the following paragraph :—

MURDER OF PEARL DIVERS.

MELBOURNE, Nov. 1

Captain Craig, of the ketch Emily, and a party of pearl divers, of whom two were Englishmen and six Malays, have been murdered at Johannes Island, near New Guinea.

The troubles of the Pearl-seeker are not confined,

however, to encounters with semi-savages. For instance, the houses which my men had erected in the Sooloo Archipelago—of which a sketch will be found opposite to page 142,—were wantonly pillaged and wrecked in March, 1884, by the Spaniards, when at war with the late Sultan of Sooloo. Not only was my property destroyed, but the town of Lamenusa was entirely burnt, and many of the population were taken captive and sold into slavery.

On my behalf the English Government has applied to the Spanish Government for redress, but I regret to say that as yet I have only received an acknowledgement of my complaint.

Such difficulties as that just instanced, shew the necessity for more adequate protection of the interests of British trade in the Pacific. This question is ably treated by Mr. C. Kinloch Cooke, in the November number of the *Nineteenth Century*, and I should like to see his suggestion for establishing a system of Pacific Commercial Agents carried into effect. Nor are our troubles confined to dealings with foreign countries. A letter just received from Mr. Haynes, in Western Australia, sets forth another grievance against the Government of that Colony, in respect to many vexatious restrictions.

In order to give a vivid picture of the life led by the Pearl-fishers in the prosecution of their exciting labours, a chapter is introduced on "Pearling Life at the Present Day." It may here be mentioned that an important improvement in recent fishing, is the use of the diving dress ; and as the fishers have to go deeper in search of shell,—the waters becoming cooler—the employment of the dress must become more and more extended.

Although the Pearls and Pearl-shell of the Sooloo seas and the Australian waters have of late years taken a most important place in commerce, the older fisheries have by no means been neglected in this volume. The fisheries off Ceylon, which have been worked more or less interruptedly from time immemorial, are fully described ; and it is hoped that the experience of my agent at the last great Ceylon fishery, will add freshness and life to this chapter. The ancient fisheries in the Persian Gulf and in the Red Sea, are next noticed, and attention is then directed to the American fisheries. I expected to receive some original information respecting the Mexican and Panama fisheries, and the publication of the work has been consequently delayed, but it is hoped that the anticipated information may be available if a second edition should be called for.

Fresh-water Pearls, though of far less importance than marine Pearls, claim a chapter to themselves.

Here the reader may learn something about the Pearls occasionally found in certain streams in England and Wales, Scotland and Ireland, various parts of Europe, the United States, Canada and China.

Those exceptional Pearls which possess a colour sufficiently marked to render them attractive, are next described, and it is hoped that my own experience in connexion with black and pink Pearls, may be of some interest. The book would have been incomplete without a notice of those famous Pearls which have figured in history. A chapter is consequently devoted to this subject, and another to that remarkable cluster of Australian Pearls, known as "The Southern Cross," which attracted so much attention at the Colonial and Indian Exhibition.

It only remains to tender my thanks to those who have been good enough to assist me in the preparation of this work. To the Earl of Crawford and Balcarres, I am indebted for a description of the constellation of the Southern Cross; and to Mr. F. W. Rudler and Dr. MacLarty for much valuable assistance on various scientific matters. Above all, however, I desire to thank Mr. T. H. Haynes, a gentleman who, in connexion with my Pearling operations, has been through the Sooloo Archipelago, and neighbouring islands, and along the coast of New Guinea and Northern and Western Australia.

For nearly seven years, Mr. Haynes has been assiduously collecting information for this work, and to his pen is due the chapter on "Pearling Life," not to mention important contributions to many other chapters.

I have also to acknowledge the valuable services rendered me by the late Capt. Chippindall, R.N., who for nearly seven years commanded my Pearling fleet in these waters, and to whose unwearied exertions and faithful discharge of duty, the fleet has been brought to its present state of efficiency. Nor can I omit mention of my son, the late Harry Edwin Streeter, who was the first to discover shell in Port Darwin, and who passed away in the flower of his life while Pearling in the waters of the Southern hemisphere.

Edward H. Streeter

London, December, 1886.

AUCTION OF PEARL OYSTERS IN CEYLON.

CHAPTER I.

INTRODUCTORY.

"Errors like straws upon the surface flow,
He who would search for *Pearls* must dive below."
Dryden.

THERE is perhaps, no instinct implanted in the human breast more powerful than the love of admiration ; there is certainly none more ancient and universal. It is a passion more or less strongly developed in every one of us—in the savage who rejoices in his tattooing, and barters his gold for beads and ostrich feathers ; in the Red Indian, who regards the ring in his nose as the highest emblem of nobility ; and equally in the fashionable lady, arrayed in all the beautiful creations of Parisian millinery.

To furnish becoming material wherewith to

gratify this passion, every realm of Nature has been put under contribution. Earth has been mined and seas have been explored, and both have yielded lavishly of their bounty. Among all the products which have been contributed by the latter, the PEARL stands pre-eminent and unrivalled for native beauty. Indeed, we find that from the very earliest times, Pearls have attracted the regard of man, and have been employed by him for purposes of personal adornment.

In whatever light Pearls may be regarded by the naturalist or man of science — whether as redundant deformities, the result of special and fortuitous circumstances, with which the Pearl-bearing oyster may be surrounded, or as the legitimate production of a function inherent in the mollusc—they are undoubtedly ranked by those skilled in precious stones, as costly products rivalling in value and surpassing in beauty the choicest gems of rock or water-course. By the fortunate possessors of wealth and beauty, they are highly esteemed as a means of judiciously investing the one, and of chastely yet elegantly heightening the charms of the other.

Poets and philosophers too, have in all ages, recognized in Pearls the emblems most fitted to represent whatever they regarded as of surpassing purity, or of exceeding worth. The high estimation in which they have always been held cannot be attributed to any hereditary idiosyncrasy or commercial bias ; indeed, the love of these "delicate gems of the ocean " appears to be more strongly rooted in the instincts of the human race, the deeper we enquire into it. In some instances we find the passion for them has been communicated by the conquerors to the conquered, as in the case 'of the Persians and the Greeks ; but nations that have never come in contact with each other, and have originated from entirely different root - stocks of the human family, are yet found to have cherished the same unaccountable love for the Pearl. In the New World, the Aztecs, and in the Old World, the Aryan and. Semitic races, appear to have been equally charmed with them'; and where we have failed to find authentic historic records, legends have come to us teeming with allusions to them. No nation can boast a history in which place and favour have not been bought or sold by Pearls ; and scarce a religion or sacred literature has existed in which they have not borne some venerable significance.

It is possible that the Pearl may be referred to,

in connection with the introduction of man upon
earth, as recorded in the opening chapters of the
Old Testament.* But be this as it may, it is
certain that when the ideal state is revealed in
the closing chapters of the New Testament, we
have presented to us, in the sublime Apocalyptic
vision, the city whose "Twelve gates were twelve
pearls," while throughout "The Book" they are
alluded to by various inspired writers.

So great was the importance attached to Pearls,
and such the high estimation in which they were
held at all times and in all countries, that we can
hardly wonder that their origin should have been
the subject of much speculation and even wild
conjecture. From a very early period in their
history, when a belief existed that they were formed
from drops of rain which fell into the open oyster-
shell, down to our own time, when science has busied
itself with enquiring into their origin, numerous

---

* The word *Bdellium* (Heb.; *"Bedolach"*) mentioned in Genesis ii. 12,
as one of the products of the land of Havilah, is considered by
many ancient interpreters to mean a costly aromatic gum, and
this opinion is held by the majority of modern commentators.
The Rabbinic interpreters, however, reject this explanation on
the ground that the aromatic gum *Bdellium* was not so valuable
a product as to deserve mention along with gold and precious
stones; they understood it to mean "Pearls," and Gesenius,
following Bochart, concurs in this rendering.—See Smith's *Dictionary of the Bible*, vol. i., p. 173.

theories, many of them fanciful and poetic, have been advanced to account for their production.

In the following pages, an attempt will be made to submit some of these theories to the reader, together with such fragments of history as will tend to show what an important part these "un-ostentatious little globules" have sometimes played in the progress of the world and the development of civilization. We have endeavoured to rescue the Pearl, if possible, from the superstition and confusion in which its origin has frequently been enveloped, and to set its true nature in a clearer light; to specify the conditions under which Pearls are produced, and the different species of mollusc producing them; to offer a few observations on their value and importance; and finally to describe those Pearl fisheries, which have been more recently opened up, and give some idea of the modes employed in pursuing this fascinating industry. Upon these subjects the author has had exceptional opportunities of obtaining the most accurate, and recent information. In addition to his experience gained in the Ceylon fisheries, he equipped and sent out in January, 1882, an expedition to examine and report upon the Mother-of-pearl, and Pearl fisheries of the Sooloo Archipelago, and of Australia. This expedition was commanded by the late Mr. E. C. Chippendale, R.N., and Mr. T. H. Haynes, who were

Pearls.

afterwards joined by the late Mr. Harry E. Streeter.
Mr. Haynes is still at work, pearling in the Eastern
Seas, and his researches combined with those of
his former comrades, have furnished us with much
valuable information, which is embodied in some of
the later chapters of this work.

CHAPTER II.

HISTORICAL.

" The sea-born shell conceals the *Unio* round,
Called by that name, as always single found,
One in one shell, for ne'er a larger race .
Within their pearly walls the valves embrace.
                                        Marbodus.

India.

IN the East, Pearls have always been highly prized, not only for personal decoration, but for the trappings of elephants and the embellishment of popular divinities. In very early times, Pearls ranked next to the most valued gems, and took their place with ivory, precious metals and the sweet smelling spices of Arabia. Pearls are frequently mentioned in Indian mythology, where their discovery is attributed to the god Vishnu, who is said to have searched the ocean for these jewels, and then to have taken them to India as a

wedding gift to his daughter Pandaïa. The Pearl
was considered no unbecoming ornament for the
great Gautama himself, for we are told that, during
the festivities on the occasion of the birth of his
son, being much pleased with the beauty of a particular serenade, he removed his necklace of Pearls,
and as a mark of appreciation, presented it to the
minstrel.

Pearls like most precious stones, being indi-
genous products of India, may certainly be classed
among the most ancient objects of Hindu luxury
and commerce ; yet it is curious that in the works
of the ancient Hindus which have come down to
us, there is no allusion to the Pearl fisheries. That
they existed before the time of Alexander the
Great, is certain, from their being mentioned by his
companions. The author of the " Periplus," who wrote
about the middle of the second century, A.D., mentions
that Pearls were found near Manaar. The principal
market for Pearls at that time was the town of
Nelkynda or Nelicurand.

Accounts of the natural history of the pearl-
oyster as known to the Ancients are given by
Athenæus and by Chares of Mitylene, from whose
writings we learn that, in their day, the pearl-bearing
oyster was found in the Indian Sea and in the
Persian Gulf. Every ancient Indian deity is

represented as being adorned with Pearls, arrayed in all conceivable forms of ornament. According to the Indian astronomer, Varahamihira, the statue of the Sun-god Mithra wore a crown upon his head, and was decked with chain-work of Pearls, and earrings of Pearls. Pearls and diamonds were employed in India as eyes for images of the gods : they shone upon the beautiful box which held Buddha's sacred tooth, and they also decorated the interior of his tomb. Distinguished Indian women wore purple draperies ornamented with Pearls, and on great public occasions their arms were covered with them ; and they even wove Pearls into their hair. When the French jeweller, Jean Baptiste Tavernier (born 1605 ; died, 1689), visited India, about the middle of the seventeenth century, he noticed that the women, both high and low, generally wore in each ear a Pearl between two coloured stones, more or less costly, according to their means. It is still a custom in India, at a wedding, to bore a fresh Pearl, as an emblem of maiden purity. Tavernier was allowed in 1665, to see the throne of the Grand Mogul, Aurungzeb, the most powerful sovereign of Hindustan, and he has given a very elaborate account of this throne in his *Voyages*. " The arched roof of the throne," he says, " is entirely ornamented with diamonds and Pearls, and all round is a fringe of Pearls. Over the same stands a peacock, with its outstretched tail of

blue sapphires and other coloured stones; its body is
of gold, ornamented with stones; and on its breast
sparkles a great ruby, from which hangs a pear-
shaped Pearl of a yellowish colour, about 200 grains.
But the most costly part of this wonderful throne
is the pillars which support the roof. Round these
are twined rows of Pearls of splendid quality, one
of which weighs from six to ten carats. Four feet
from the throne stand, on either side, two sun
umbrellas of red velvet, embroidered in Pearls and
with a Pearl fringe; the umbrellas stand seven or
eight feet high, and their sticks glitter with diamonds,
rubies and Pearls."

Pearls were used in the East as tributes of war
paid by the conquered to the conquerors. We are
told that king Partab Chund, (A.D. 500) after he had
conquered and ravaged the countries of Cabul and the
Punjaub, brought, amongst other things, as tribute
to Chosroes II. of Persia, 1000 lbs of aloe-wood and
a box full of the most costly Pearls. Malik Allah,
captured in 1290, at Deogiri, (now called Dowlatabad)
15,000 lbs of gold, 175 lbs of Pearls, and 50 lbs of
other beautiful jewels.

In the Hindu drama called the " Mrichchakati,"
written by the royal author, Sudraka, who lived about
the first century (B.C. or A.D.), there is an account
of a fierce elephant, which had broken loose and

ran about the streets, to the terror and horror of
the inhabitants, who in their fright tore off their
girdles and anklets, scattering their Pearls and diamonds upon the ground in all directions. In the
same drama, there is a description of the jewellers'
court, the entrance to which was through a gateway
of gold and many-coloured gems, on a ground of
sapphires, while inside were skilled artists examining
Pearls, topazes and other jewels ; some setting rubies
in gold, and some stringing Pearls.

China.

It appears, from information collected by Mr. F.
Hague, that as early as 22½ centuries before the
commencement of the Christian era, Pearls were used
as a tribute or tax in China. In the " *Bh-'ya,*" the
oldest Chinese dictionary, compiled more than a
thousand years B.C., Pearls are mentioned as precious
products of the western part of the empire. At
first, the Chinese used only fresh-water Pearls. The
Emperor Wuti, who lived 140 — 86, B.C., sent ships
to the Indian Ocean for the purpose of procuring
Pearls. After the introduction of Buddhism, "moni-
Pearls " are often mentioned in Buddhist writings. It
is related that in the middle of the 11th century, A.D.,
an embassy was sent by an Indian king to the
Court of the Chinese emperor, to pay tribute to
him. According to the custom of their country, the

ambassadors knelt at the door of the audience-chamber, bearing in their hands a golden tray full of Pearls and gold work. On approaching the throne, they threw the contents of the tray at the feet of the emperor; much to the delight of the courtiers, who were permitted to gather them up, and divide them amongst themselves.

Marco Polo, in his work on China, tells us that Kubla Khan, the founder of the 20th Chinese dynasty, who died in 1294, A.D., always presented his followers at great public festivals, with robes embroidered in gold, Pearls, and other jewels. Mingti, another Chinese ruler, notorious for his lavish expenditure, is said to have had his throne, his furniture, horses' trappings, carriages, and his own and his courtiers' robes, so profusely covered with Pearls, that after public processions the ground was often literally strewn with them. The Chinese Emperor, Kanghi (1661—1722), presented to the Temple of the Goddess of Grace, on the Buddhist island of Poets, an image of herself, finished in gold. It was five inches high, and the torso consisted of a single beautiful Pearl.

The repeated mention of Pearls in the history of China, and the use made of them to decorate idols, and as tribute, show the honour in which the Chinese have always held these jewels. In our own day,

Pearls are still very highly prized among the Chinese. The Emperor wears upon his cap, three golden dragons, embroidered and crowned with Pearls. Pearl buttons decorate the caps of the Mandarins and denote their rank. Chinese ladies are particularly fond of Pearl-embroidered shoes, in which to encase their tiny feet. In the sacking of the Summer Palace, or Yuen-Min-Yuen in 1860, the Allied forces found treasures of exquisitely carved jade, gold and silver, Pearls, precious jewels of jade and rubies, carved lapis-lazuli, priceless furs and the richest silks; such treasures indeed as could only have been accumulated by a long dynasty of Celestial rulers. The French taking advantage of a circuitous approach, at once proceeded to sack the palace ere the British soldiers guessed their intention. Consequently when the latter were allowed to join in the work of devastation and indiscriminate plunder, all the most obviously valuable treasures had already been removed, while the floors were strewn knee-deep with broken fragments of priceless china, and every sort of beautiful object, too cumbersome or too fragile for rough-and-ready removal, and therefore ruthlessly smashed with the butt ends of muskets. From 100 to 150 of the large Pearls were brought to England, their average weight being about 35 grains each—but they were of a yellowish hue, and were spoiled by having large holes drilled through them. They had been obtained from the troops in exchange, and still had pieces of gold hanging from them, just as they had been snatched from the idols which they had decorated. The value of these Pearls was about £20,000.

Persia.

The passion for Pearls, which at all times was strongly marked among the Medes and Persians, probably reached its zenith after the victory over Crœsus. Pearls were prized by the Persians more highly than gold, or any other article of adornment. All the early Queens of Persia are represented as wearing ear-rings composed of three Pearls graduated in size, one above the other, the largest being at the bottom. The portraits of Sassanian kings, shew a Pearl of great size, pendant from the right ear. The Persian nobles also wore in the right ear a golden ornament, containing Pearls—a fashion which also prevailed at a later period in Athens, amongst youths of noble birth. The women even wore a ring through the left nostril, upon which were strung three Pearls, and round their head a band, from which hung pendants of jewels or Pearls. The kings of the Medes and Persians wore splendid bracelets and necklaces of Pearls ; Pearls too were lavishly employed in their trappings and equipages, and to this day Pearls play a prominent part in all great festivals in Persia. At the enthronement of a new king, it is said to be the custom to shower Pearls upon him.

The unrivalled Pearl which king Perozes tore from his right ear at the moment of falling into the horrible pit-fall prepared for him and his army by the Ephthalite Huns, and which he cast into the abyss before him, was lost for ever. The story is told by the old Greek historian, Procopius, who adds that, although the Emperor Anastasius promised the finder of the Pearl five hundred-weight of gold pieces, the search was in vain.

Babylonian dignitaries and priests wore strings of beautiful Pearls. Most of these Pearls were, no doubt, derived from the fisheries in the Gulf of Persia, but possibly some may have come from more distant sources.

Huren, in his "Historical Researches," vol. ii. tells us that there can be no doubt that Pearls were obtained from Ceylon, and exchanged with the Babylonians for other merchandise, for we read of Indian Pearl fisheries as well as those of the Persian Gulf. Nearchus, in mentioning the latter of these adds, "Pearls are fished up here as well as in the Indian Sea." The best ancient account

of the Pearl fisheries of the Persian Gulf is given
by the Greek historian, Isidorus of Charace, in his
description of the Parthian empire.

Palestine, &c.

There can be but little doubt that the ancient
Hebrews valued Pearls, and used them for ornamental purposes. Probably they obtained them by
commerce with the neighbouring nations, especially
the Phœnicians. Yet it is notable that the Hebrew
word, *gabish*, translated "Pearl" in our English
version, occurs only once in the Old Testament.
"No mention shall be made of coral, or of *Pearls*,
for the price of wisdom is above rubies," (Job
xxviii., 18). Even here it is highly probable that
the word rendered as Pearl really applies to rock-
crystal, or some other substance than Pearl.

The Talmud contains many references to
Pearls, and we may quote one legend showing that
at that time there was but one object in nature
worthy to be ranked higher than Pearls.

On approaching Egypt, the patriarch Abraham,
aware of the fascinating beauty of his wife, Sarah,
hid her in a chest, that none might behold her
charms. But when he was come to the place of
paying custom, the officer said "Pay custom," and
he answered, "I will pay thee custom." Then they

tried to discover what this box contained, and suggested clothes, gold, fine silk, and at last as the most costly thing, *Pearls*, to all of which he replied that he would pay custom for them. Then they said, "It cannot be, but, thou open the box, and let us see what is therein." So they opened the box, and the whole land of Egypt was illumined by the brilliancy of Sarah's beauty, transcending even that of Pearls.

The New Testament shews us best how much the Pearl was prized among the Jews. The parable of "the Pearl of great price" (Matt. xiii., 45), and our Lord's allusion to casting Pearls before swine, (Matt. vii., 6), are familiar references to the high value set upon Pearls. In the time of the apostles, Hebrew women were notorious for their extravagance, and fastened their hair with strings of Pearls. The author of the Apocalypse ornaments his brides with the most costly jewels, among which Pearls are not forgotten ; and finally, he describes the twelve gates of the Heavenly city as formed of twelve Pearls, (Rev. xxi. 21).

Egypt.

It is probable that Pearls, like other Indian products, were at first brought to Egypt from Arabia ; but it is known that in later times Egyptian

C

merchants were in the habit of visiting India and purchasing Pearls and other commodities. Pearls are represented on old Egyptian monuments, and from time to time, diadems of Pearls have been found in ancient sarcophagi.

It would seem that Egyptian women, from the earliest times, wore ear-rings ; generally simple hoops of gold, from which hung pendants of precious stones or Pearls. They wore, likewise, necklaces made of alternate rows of shells, coral, scarabei, precious stones and Pearls. One ornament worn by both sexes was the *gorget*, upon which Pearls were embroidered in every conceivable pattern.

Alexandria, a city which, under the Ptolemies, became the central point of the commerce of the old World, was the scene of the greatest luxury in Pearls. We have only to re-call Cleopatra's wonderful Pearls, to understand to what an extent this luxury was carried in Egypt in her day. The history of these remarkable Pearls will be duly narrated in the chapter on "Historical Pearls."

Greece.

The splendid victory which the Greeks gained over the Persians about 490 B.C., made them acquainted with the treasures of Asia. During the following time of peace, they gave themselves up

to the enjoyment of their riches and the extension
of commerce; but gradually their simple tastes became corrupted, and engendered a love of display.
Pearls came into requisition for purposes of decoration. Like the Persian nobles, Grecian men of
rank wore one Pearl ear-ring in the right ear, while
the women wore one in each ear. The women's
neck ornament, as depicted on Greek vases, consisted
of a string or gold wire hanging loosely round the
neck, with Pearls or precious stones strung upon it.
It is probable that Pearls are referred to by *Homer*,
in his description of the ear-ornaments of Hera, or
Juno:

> "In three bright drops,
> Her glittering gems suspended from her ears."
>
> *Iliad* xiv.

Theophrastus, the favourite pupil of Aristotle, writing about 300 B.C., mentions the Pearl under the
name of μαργαρίτης (*Margarites*). His notice however is very brief, and though aware that it was
produced by shell-fish, he classes it among precious
stones. In his day, Pearls were valued for necklaces
or bracelets, and in describing their size he compares
them to the eyes of rather large fish. Athenæus,
a learned Greek who lived about 230 A.D., gives a
short description of Pearls, though he represents
them as having been sold for their weight in gold;

a statement which must probably be accepted with some hesitation. His description is chiefly taken from the Periplus of India by Androsthenes.

Italy.

Pearls were probably among the merchandise brought to Italy from the East, in the very earliest times. We first hear of them in Rome, during the Jugurthan wars in the second century, B.C. Pliny tells us that the taste for Pearls dated from the return of Pompey, after his successful expedition against Mithridates, in whose palace a priceless collection of Pearls was found, which being carried off, formed the nucleus of a Museum in Rome. The same writer informs us that Pearls took precedence over all other gems, and commanded a higher price than even diamonds.

Perhaps one of the grandest displays recorded in ancient history was that presented in the triumph of Pompey after the third Mithridatic war (B.C. 61). The victor exhibited, among other rich trophies, thirty-three crowns made of Pearls; a temple of the Muses surmounted with a dial; a portrait of himself in Pearls, probably a kind of Mosaic, and thirty head-bands of Pearls, which were deposited in the Temple of Venus. In the same temple was also suspended, as an offering by the great Cæsar, a shield studded with British Pearls; and indeed, history has preserved the tradition that the quest of Pearls was one of the inducements that tempted the Romans to invade Britain. Tacitus however, who enumerates Pearls among the products of our island, describes them as being small and of inferior colour.

After this period the passion for Pearls became quite a *furore* in Rome. The philosopher Seneca, sharply rebuked the Roman women for wearing so many Pearls. He declared they would not bend nor yield obedience to their husbands until double or treble the value of their own settlements was dangling from their ears. Roman ladies wore necklaces of Pearls or sometimes one row of Pearls and two longer rows of either blue or green stones, having occasional Pearls of particular beauty mixed with them. A necklace of a single row of gems was called a *monile*, of two rows a *dilium*, of three a *trelium*. Clusters of Pearls worn as ear-drops were known as *Crotalia*, or rattles, because they tinkled together with the movement of the head.

Pliny, who wrote his famous *Historia Naturalis* in the first century of the Christian era, gives a graphic description of the Pearls and other ornaments of a Roman empress at a private party. The passage is translated by Holland in these quaint terms:—" I myselfe have seene Lollia Paulina (late wife and after widdow to Caius Caligula the Emperor), when shee was dressed and set out, not in

stately wise, nor of purpose for some great solem-
nitie, but only when she was to goe unto a wedding
supper, or rather to a feast when the assurance was
made, and great persons they were not that made
the said feast; I have seen her, I say, so beset
and bedeckt all over with Emeraulds and Pearles,
disposed in rowes, rankes, and courses one by
another, round about the attire of her head, her
cawle, her borders, her perruke of hair, her bon-
grace and chaplet; at her ears pendant, about her
neck in a carcanet, upon her wrest in bracelets, and
on her fingers in rings; that she glittered and
shone againe like the sun as she went. The value
of these ornaments she esteemed and rated at 400
hundred thousand sestertij (about £400,000 sterling
of our money); and offered openly to prove it out
of hand by her books of accounts and reckonings."

Pliny states that in his day, the love of Pearls
was so widely spread in Rome, that even women
of the poorer classes strove to secure the coveted
ornaments.

"Now adaies also it is growne to this passe,
that meane women and poore men's wives affect
to weare them, because they would be thought
rich; and a by-word it is among them, that a faire
Pearle at a woman's eare is as good in the street
where she goeth, as an huisher to make way, for

that every one will give such the place. Nay, our gentlewomen are come now to weare them upon their feet, and not at their shoe latchets onely, but also upon their startops and fine buskins, which they garnish all over with Pearle. For it will not suffice nor serve their turne to carie Pearles about with them, but they must tread upon Pearles, goe among Pearles, and walke, as it were, on a pavement of Pearles."

Pearls also decorated the altars in the Roman temples, and the furniture of the houses, while the arms and the trappings of the horses, and of war-chariots shone with them.

Nero offered to Jupiter Capitolinus the first cuttings of his beard in a golden vase decorated with beautiful Pearls.

Caligula wore them in profusion, and had his slippers embroidered with them.

An eye-witness, Philo Judæus, tells us that the couches upon which the Romans reclined at meal-times were ornamented with tortoise-shell and ivory, and shone with gold and Pearls. He adds further, that upon the couches lay purple coverings embroidered in gold or Pearls. Nero distributed them lavishly among his favourites, and to such an extent was the fashion carried, that a lady's position in society was estimated by the number and value of the Pearls she wore on any public occasion. Hence the *Margaritaria*, or Pearl merchants, drove a flourishing trade by the loan of Pearls. The relics of females exhumed from the ashes of Pompeii, have in some cases been found decorated with Pearl ear-rings.

Various sumptuary laws were issued under successive emperors for the purpose of stemming the tide of extravagance which threatened to ruin all classes. Julius Cæsar issued an edict, prohibiting the use of purple and of Pearls to all persons who were not of a certain rank, and these were only to wear them on occasions of public ceremonies. Unmarried women were forbidden to wear precious stones, gems or Pearls—an edict which led to a great increase in the number of marriages in every city throughout the empire.

The last of the sumptuary laws was passed by the Emperor Leo, in the year 460 A.D., and forbade all persons of whatever quality, to enrich their baldrics, or the bridles and saddles of their horses with Pearls, emeralds, or hyacinths.

In the dark ages which followed the ruin of the Roman Empire, the Oriental trade in Pearls, which had at one time threatened to exhaust the wealth of the West, ultimately dwindled into obscurity.

Europe in the Middle Ages.

Throughout the early part of the Middle Ages, the city of Constantinople, or the ancient Byzantium, the capital of the Eastern Empire, was the centre of all culture and art. This city was especially rich in Pearls. The crowns and diadems of the Eastern Emperors were wrought in the richest gold, decorated with Pearls, precious stones, and enamel. The most ancient crown known to us,—the Hungarian crown of St. Stephen, presented to him by the Pope in the year 1001 A.D., when Hungary became an empire—was obtained from Byzantium. This crown is richly ornamented with Pearls and jewels. When it was pledged by Queen Elizabeth of Hungary to the Emperor Frederic IV, it was described as containing 320 Pearls.

The German Imperial crown which dates from the time of Charlemagne, is ornamented with numerous Pearls, strung upon gold wire, and round it is written, in Pearls, "Chonradus Dei Gratia Romanorum Imperator Augustus."

In the time of Charlemagne, (born 742; died 814 A.D.), a favourite decoration consisted of large gold rings, set with precious stones and Pearls, worn on the neck and arms, and in the ears. The women interwove gold thread or strings of Pearls in their hair, and bound fillets round their heads, which were often richly decorated with precious stones and Pearls. The embroidered borders of their robes and their shoes too were richly worked in Pearls.

The 12th and 13th centuries, the age of chivalry, were particularly luxurious, and the coats of arms worn by the knights were made of gold or silver stuff, velvet or silk, and embroidered in gold, silver, Pearls or precious stones.

Pearls were used so extravagantly, not only by the nobles, but also among the middle classes, in rich towns, that certain laws were passed to put a limit to their use; Philippe le Bel of France, (born 1268; died 1314 A.D.) forbade the burgher classes to wear ornaments of gold, precious stones, or Pearls. The Council of Zurich, held in 1411, published an order forbidding women or girls to wear more than one Pearl head-band, which was not to weigh more than 6 oz. Many noble families having been ruined by their excessive expenditure on clothes, a council of knights was called before the 28th great Tournament at Würzburg, which decided that no gold or Pearl ornaments should be worn, unless hidden from view! Women also were not to have their

dresses embroidered in Pearls. In Saxony, even
imitation Pearls were forbidden, and in Hamburg
women so loaded themselves with gold and jewels
that a mandate was issued forbidding them to wear
more than one gold chain : copies of this mandate
were posted on the town wall and at the corners
of the principal streets. The church, too, preached
against luxury in dress, but all to no purpose : the
women continued to wear Pearls and precious gems
in spite of ecclesiastical denunciation. But the
greatest splendour of the Middle Ages was to be
seen at the Court of the great house of Burgundy,
from the time of Philip the Bold to that of Charles
the Bold. Their magnificence far outshone that of
the kings of France and the German Emperors.
Magnificent jewels that can be traced back to the
time of the last dukes of Burgundy are to this
day reckoned among the most valuable possessions
of the crowns of France and Austria. Charles the
Bold surpassed all other princes of his line in
magnificence. When, in 1473, he attended the Imperial Diet at Trèves, he wore a dress of cloth
of gold, richly embroidered with Pearls. At the
banquet which he gave to the Emperor Frederick III.,
the goblets shone with precious stones and Pearls.
When in the same year he went to Dijon, he was
resplendent with Pearls and diamonds ; and the
crown which he wore on his triumphal entry into

Nancy in 1475, was so covered with diamonds and Pearls as to be worth the value of a "whole duchy."

At the famous meeting between Henry VIII. and Francis I. on the Field of the Cloth of Gold (A.D. 1520), the banqueting chamber was hung with tissue raised with silver, and framed with cloth of silver raised with gold; while the seams were covered with broad wreaths of goldsmith's work, set with precious stones and Pearls. The foot carpet of the English Queen's Throne was also embroidered with Pearls. When Henry VIII. met his bride, Anne of Cleves, he wore, we are told, a coat of purple velvet, embroidered in gold and clasped with great buttons of diamonds, rubies, and Oriental Pearls; and a collar richly ornamented with Pearls and precious stones. Anne of Cleves' wedding dress was a gown of cloth of gold thickly embroidered with large flowers of Pearls. Queen Mary wore at her wedding a dress richly brocaded in gold, and a train magnificently bordered with Pearls and diamonds. The sleeves were turned up with clusters of gold set with Pearls and diamonds. Elizabeth wore at a tournament given in Mary's reign, on December 29th, 1554, a white satin dress decorated with large Pearls.

Queen Elizabeth had a perfect passion for ornaments, especially jewellery of all kinds, and her courtiers were constantly impoverishing themselves in order to minister to her foibles. The costly parure of Pearls belonging to the unfortunate Mary Queen of Scots, which Elizabeth bought for much less than its value, is thus described by the French ambassador at the English court : "There are six cordons of large Pearls strung as paternosters, but there are five and twenty separate from the rest, much finer and larger than those which are strung ; these are for the most part like black muscades."

The discovery of America brought fresh treasures of gems and Pearls to Europe. As in the Old World, so in the New, they were used to decorate the gods and their temples, and were also worn by the natives, high and low. The temple in which the Governor of Mexico, Montezuma, used to pray at night, had walls of beaten silver and gold, decorated with Pearls and precious stones. Among the presents which Ferdinand Cortez received from Montezuma, and which he sent to Europe to Charles V. (I. of Spain), were necklaces of rubies, emeralds and costly Pearls. Fernando de Soto, in his expedition against Florida (in 1539) found great quantities of Pearls, and the Cacique Ichioha presented him with a splendid string of Pearls long enough to go three times round his neck, and to reach to his waist. As in Cleopatra's time in Egypt,

so in Florida, the graves of the kings were decorated with Pearls. Soto's soldiers found in one of
their temples, great wooden coffins, in which the
dead lay embalmed, and beside them were small
baskets full of Pearls. The temple of Tolomecco,
however, was the richest in Pearls; its high walls
and roof were of Mother-of-Pearl, while strings of
Pearls, and plumes of feathers hung round the walls;
over the coffins of their kings, hung their shields,
crowned with Pearls, and in the centre of the temple
stood vases full of costly Pearls.

To return to the history of Pearls in Europe;
we find them much worn both by men and women
during the 16th and 17th centuries. Marie dé Medici,
wife of Henry IV. of France, wore at the christening
of her son (1601) a gorgeous dress ornamented with
3,000 diamonds and 32,000 Pearls, valued at 60,000
crowns.

The Elector Maximilian of Bavaria, in 1635,
sent his bride, the daughter of the Emperor
Ferdinand II., a present of a string of 300 selected
Pearls each of which cost 1,000 gulden (about £100).

Table decorations were also very magnificent
at that time, and Charles II. of Spain, in 1680, presented his wife with an ornament in the form of
a salad, in which the leaves were represented

by enormous emeralds, the vinegar by sparkling rubies, the oil by yellow topazes, and the salt by Pearls.

Notwithstanding the dire consequences of the Thirty Years' war, immense sums were expended during the 17th century upon ornaments and luxury of all kinds. Knightly orders, sword and hat knots, rings, shoe buckles, waistcoat buttons— all glittered with gems. The stomacher and the enormous collar and ruff, both richly trimmed with Pearls and jewels, were also introduced about this time. In the 18th century precious stones were less lavishly employed, especially after the French Revolution, and dress in general came to be characterized by greater simplicity.

CHAPTER III.

Ancient Ideas on the Origin and Virtues of Pearls.

" And precious the tear as the rain from the sky,
Which turns into *Pearl* as it falls in the sea."
—*Thomas Moore.*

F all subjects connected with the study of Pearls, none is more fascinating than that referring to the ideas which were entertained by ancient philosophers and poets, regarding the origin and occult virtues of these beautiful gems. Among the ancient Persians, by whom Pearls were very highly extolled, a solar origin was attributed to them—an idea which harmonized well with the sun and fire-worship of the followers of Zoroaster. Such an idea is expressed by the poet Sheikh Fizee, and is found in an inscription occurring on the obverse of the principal gold coin of the Shah Akbar; this has been translated as follows :—

> " The sun from whom the seven seas obtained *Pearls*,
> The black stone from his rays obtains the jewel ;
> The mine from the correcting influence of his beams obtains gold,
> And gold is ennobled by the impression of Shah Akbar."

It may be mentioned incidentally, that this same Shah " ennobled " a diamond by having his name engraved upon it, as duly recorded in the author's work on diamonds. See " The Great Diamonds of the World," chap. xxxvi., p. 232.

The most wide-spread notion respecting the origin of Pearls, as briefly mentioned in our introductory chapter, is that which regards them as formed by dew and rain received into the gaping shell of the Pearl-oyster. This explanation of their origin is well set forth by Pliny, whose passage on the subject is thus quaintly rendered into English by old Dr. Holland :—

" This shell-fish, which is the mother of Pearle, differeth not much in the manner of breeding and generation from the oysters, for when the season of the yeere requireth that they should engender, seeme to yawne and gape, and so doe open wide ; and then (by report) they conceive a certaine moist dew as seed, wherewith they swell and grow bigge ;

D

and when time commeth, labour to be delivered
hereof; and the fruit of these shell-fishes are the
Pearls, better or worse, great or small, according
to the qualitie and quantitie of the dew which
they received. For if the dew were pure and
cleare which went into them, then are the Pearles
white, faire, and orient; if grosse and troubled,
the Pearles likewise are dimme, foule and duskish;
pale (I say) they are, if the weather were close,
darke, and threatning raine in the time of their
conception. Whereby, no doubt, it is apparent
and plaine that they participate more of the aire
and skie, than of the water and the sea; for, according as the morning is faire, so are they cleare;
otherwise, if it were mistie and cloudie, they also
will be thicke and muddie in colour. If they may
have their full time and season to feed, the Pearles
also will thrive and grow bigge; but if in the time
it chaunce to lighten, then they close their shells
togither, and for want of nourishment are kept
hungrie and fasting, and so the Pearles keepe at a
stay and prosper not accordingly. But if it thun-
der withall, then sodainly they shut hard at once,
and breed onely those excrescences which be called
Physemata, like unto bladders puft up and hooved
with wind, ond no corporall substance at all; and
these are the abortive and untimely fruits of
these shell-fishes. Now those that have their full

perfection, and may be sound and good indeed, have many folds and skins wherein they be lapt, not unproperly as it may be thought, a thicke, hard, and callous rind of the bodie, which they that be skilfull doe pill and cleanse from them. Certes, I cannot chuse but wonder how they should so greatly be affected with the aire, and joy so much therein : for with the same they wax red, and loose their native whitenesse and beautie, even as the bodie of a man or woman that is caught and burnt with the sunne. And therefore those shells that keepe in the maine sea, and lie deeper than that the sun-beames can pierce unto them, keepe the finest and most delicate Pearles. And yet they, as orient as they be, waxe yellow with age, become riveled, and looke dead, without any lively vigor ; so as that commendable orient lustre (so much sought for of our great lords and costly dames), continueth but in their youth, and decayeth with yeeres. When they be old, they will proove thicke and grosse in the very shells, and sticke fast unto their sides, so as they cannot be parted from them, unlesse they be filed asunder. These have no more but one faire face, and on that side are round, for the back part is flat and plaine, and hereupon such are called *Tympania*, as one would say, Bell Pearles."

A similar notion as to the origin of Pearls is

poetically expressed in the following lines translated from the *Lapidarium* of Marbodus, a writer of the first century, A.D.—

> " At certain seasons do the oysters lie
> With valves wide gaping t' ward the teeming sky
> And seize the falling dews, and pregnant breed
> The shining globules of th' Ethereal seed."

The assumed connexion between the character of the Pearl and the atmospheric influences which ruled at the time of its formation, finds expression in the following couplet from the same poem :—

> " Brighter the offspring of the morning dew ;
> The evening yields a duskier birth to view."

Other writers again give rather fuller details of the process of Pearl formation, and inform us that—" On the sixteenth day of the month, Nisan, the oysters rise to receive the rain drops, which are afterwards made into Pearls."

This curious legend probably furnishes us with a clue to the nature of the gem translated *Bdellium*, mentioned in the description of the Garden of Eden, (Gen. ii., 12) and already alluded to in the introductory chapter of this work. Benjamin of Tolida, when writing of the Indian Seas in the vicinity of Kathipha (Ethiopia), says " The stone called *Bdellius* is found made by wonderful workmanship of nature, for on the twenty-fourth day of the month Nisan, a certain dew falleth down into the waters, which being gathered, the inhabitants wrap together, and being fast closed they cast it into the sea, that it may sink of its own accord to the bottom of the sea, and in the middle of the month Tisri, two men being let down by ropes unto the bottom, bring up certain creeping worms, which they have gathered, into the open air, out of which—being broken and cleft—these stones are taken."

It is worthy of remark that this rain or dew-origin of Pearls as we may call it—was found by Columbus to exist among the semi-savages of the New World :—

" The natives entertained the old fanciful idea which the earlier naturalists' did ; they supposed the Pearls formed from petrified dew-drops, in connexion with sunbeams. We can therefore well credit the astonishment of Columbus and his mariners when in the Gulf of Paria they first found oysters clinging to the branches of trees, their shells gaping open to receive the dew which was afterwards to be transformed into Pearls."

The oyster here alluded to is the *Dendrostrea* or " Tree Oyster," a mollusc which is to be found upon the roots or branches of mangrove trees overhanging the water, and may with its "shells gaping open to receive the dew" have been the innocent cause of this fanciful idea.

This dew-origin of Pearls affords such ample opportunities for the play of fancy, that it is not surprising that poets and moralists should have considered Pearls fit subjects for imaginative writing, using them not only as poetic metaphors, but to teach many moral lessons. The virtue of humility, as embodied in the Christian precept that "Whosoever humbleth himself shall be exalted," is forcibly inculcated in the following parable recorded in the " Bostan " by the Oriental poet, Sadi :—

"A drop of water fell one day from a cloud into the sea. Ashamed and confounded on finding itself in such an immensity of water, it exclaimed, 'What am I in comparison with this vast ocean ? my existence is less than nothing in this boundless abyss.' Whilst it thus discoursed of itself, a Pearl-shell received it into its bosom, and fortune so favoured it, that it became a magnificent and precious Pearl, worthy of adorning the diadem of kings. Thus was its humility the cause of its elevation, and by annihilating itself it merited exaltation."

The same sentiment, but in more modern

language, is poetically expressed in the following
verses by the late Archbishop Trench :—

> " A dew-drop falling on the ocean wave
> Exclaimed in fear 'I perish in this grave ;'
> But in a shell received, that drop of dew
> Unto a Pearl of wondrous beauty grew ;
> And happy now the grace did magnify,
> Which thrust it forth (as it had feared) to die;
> Until again, ' I perish quite,' it said,
> Torn by rude diver from its ocean bed.
> Vain apprehension ! soon it gleamed a gem,
> Chief jewel of a monarch's diadem."

We can well imagine that so chaste and
charming a gem as the Pearl should be deemed
worthy of a more sacred birth than that arising
from a drop of common rain or dew, and hence
arose the highly poetical idea that Pearls were
formed from tears wept by angels, or shed by
mortals under circumstances of peculiar trial. Thus,
in "The Bridal of Triermain," Sir Walter Scott
writes :—

> " See the Pearls that long have slept,
> These were tears by Naiâdes wept."

So Shakespeare finds a similar idea in the
following lines :—

> " The liquid drops of tears that you have shed,
> Shall come again transformed to Orient Pearl,
> Advantaging their loan with interest,
> Of ten times double gain of happiness."

The favorite poetical idea that Pearls were
" angels' tears " has been beautifully expressed in

Buckert's *Edelstein und Perle*, a translation of which
appeared in the " Foreign Monthly Review" for 1839.

> " I was the angel, who of old bowed down
>   From heaven to earth and shed that tear, O Pearl,
>   From which thou wert first fashioned in thy shell.
>
>   *   *   *   *   *   *
>
>   To thee I gave that longing in thy shell,
>   Which guided thee and caused thee to escape,
>   O Pearl, from the bewitching siren's song."

It is difficult to say when this dew-origin of
Pearls ceased to find supporters ; but as late as
1684, a member of a high Venetian family had a
medal struck, on the reverse of which is an open
oyster-shell receiving the drops of rain, with the
motto *Rore Divine*, " By the divine dew."

The old English traveller, Mandeville, writing
in the fourteenth century, quaintly argues as
follows :—

" For right as the fine Pearl congels and grows
great by the dew of Heaven, so doth the true
diamond. And right as the Pearl by its own
nature takes roundness, so the diamond by virtue
of God, takes squareness."

The presence of the Tree-oyster or *Dendrostrea*,
before alluded to, may have given rise to the dew-
origin of Pearls, in those localities in which this
oyster occurs. It is, however, to India that we must

look for the true home of the many other fanciful
ideas which have been entertained regarding the
origin of Pearls. Some of these have reached the
western world almost unchanged ; others have
received, in their march, such local colourings, additions, or alterations, as were prompted by the
philosophy of the countries through which they
passed. So extensive is the literature, and so many
and diverse are the superstitions recorded, that one
would think the ingenuity of even the Oriental
imagination must have been stretched to its utmost
limit in dealing with this subject. Not to weary
the patience of the reader with a mass of details,
we will content ourselves with merely glancing at
a few of the principal superstitions. Our information on this head has been derived chiefly from a
work entitled "Mani-Málá," that is "Chain of Gems,"
written by a native Indian Prince.

"It is generally believed," says this writer,
"that the Pearl originates in clouds, elephants,
boars, conch-shells, fish, serpents, oysters, and bam-
boos,—of which oysters bear the largest share in
their production." To treat them in the order here
mentioned, we will first deal with the reputed formation of Pearls by *Clouds.*

" The Pearl which originates in the water-drop
from the clouds, is a gem of the first rank and a

rarity ; the gods appropriate it from the sky . . .
Of cloud-begotten Pearls, those which resemble a
hen's egg, which are beautifully circular, substantial,
weighty, and bright as the sun, are enjoyable by
the gods, and cannot be obtained by men." The
Oriental imagination describes them as " Clad in
the mighty effulgence of the mid-day sun."

"A cloud-begotten Pearl is a blessing not only
to its owner, but it shoots its blessed influence a
hundred *yojanas,* (a yojana is said to be equal to
about one Europeon league), beyond the precincts
of the dominion of the king possessing it." As to its
value as a talisman, we read that " This world
ornamented by the four oceans, the home of the
most splendid gems of infinite variety, can scarcely
equal in value one cloud-generated Pearl, and if
by rare good fortune, a person belonging to the
very lowest order comes in possession of such a
Pearl, he shall reign paramount in this world, so long
as the gem is with him."

Clouds are produced by the union of three
things—water, energy, and air—and the resulting
Pearls are divided into three corresponding classes,
according to the preponderance of one or more of
these elements.

" Pearls that originate in the head of the *Elephants*
of Khambogia are large as the fruit of the *emblic*

Myrobalan, heavy, and more yellow, but not more lustrous than the other kinds." Persons who have studied the elephant with particular attention, have divided it into four classes, after the names of the four cardinal divisions of the Hindoos ; accordingly Pearls derived from elephants are classed under four heads, "and were believed to produce good fortune."

Pearls which originate in the head of the *Boar* are generally white, like the tusks of that animal, and "as boars are divided into four orders, after the four cardinal castes, even so are the Pearls which are produced by them." "A Boar-begotten Pearl is not to be obtained by a meritless individual."

A Pearl derived from the *Conch-shell* is of large dimensions, has the same colour as the inner surface of that shell-fish, and is productive of good fortune to its possessor. "There are twenty-seven kinds of Conch-shells ; accordingly, Pearls generated in them, being marked out by distinctive qualities, are divided into twenty-seven orders."

Pearls attained from the mouth of *Sea-fish* are singularly round, small, and light. Those which originate in whales are "agreeably round, but not highly lustrous." Fishes are divided into seven kinds, according to the preponderance of one, two, or all of their three vital properties—air, bile, and cold : consequently there are several kinds of Pearls in this class.

Pearls which originate in the crest of *Serpents*, are beautifully round, and are enbosomed in a blue halo of surpassing glory, like the flash of a polished sword. These, persons void of merit are denied the privilege of even looking at ; the serpents who bear them are the descendants of Vásuki, sovereign of the snakes, are not born everywhere, and are rarely seen by men in some sacred ground. These Pearls are divided into four classes, called after the names of the principal castes, while as regards their great value, we are told that, " The power which is attained by virtuous people, through the possession of innumerable gems and great wealth, through ordinary prosperity or through regal good fortune, is obtained by wearing one serpent-begotten Pearl. "

The Pearls which originate in water - drops falling upon *Oysters* when the sun rests upon the Swáti star, are flawless and bright, and in size are in strict concomitance with the size of the water-drops. In one particular oyster, which is very rare, the Pearls are white, transparent, and large as nutmegs : "they are much coveted." The fourfold division of caste holds also with oysters ; accordingly these Pearls are of four kinds.

Pearls which originate in the *Bamboo* are clear as the moon, and are like the kakkol fruit in shape. They are generally enjoyable by the gods—though some mortals, through rare merit, obtain possession of one or two. " There are five species of Bamboo, consequently these Pearls are classified under five distinct heads."

This elaborate account of the various ways in which different kinds of Pearl may be supposed to originate, by no means exhausts the possibilities of their formation, as recognized in the East. Thus a very prominent Indian belief—one indeed, which has retained a certain amount of credence even down to our own times—is that which makes the *head of the toad* one of the many laboratories in which Nature manufactures Pearls. The same Indian authority we have already referred to says : " In certain places Pearls are found on the head of frogs ; learned men class them with serpent-Pearls." This notion was at one time widely prevalent in this country, and we find Lupton, in his book of " Notable Things " proposing a crucial test, whereby the true " Toad-jewel " may be recognized. This idea too is immortalized in those familiar lines of Shakespeare—

> " Sweet are the uses of adversity,
> Which, like the toad, ugly and venomous,
> Wears yet a precious jewel in his head."

That this superstition had its origin in India there can be little doubt, though in later times the right of the Pearl to this place of honor has been called in question, and the rival claims of Amber, and other precious substances, have each found their respective supporters.

It is worth noting that in the Malay Archipelago certain Pearls are said to be found in *Cocoa-nuts.* They are of a light yellow colour, generally of the size of a small marble, and it is difficult to distinguish them from ivory, or from the yellow porcellanous Pearls that are produced probably by some uni-valve mollusc, and often seen in the East.

These Pearls, reputed to have had their birth in cocoa-nuts, are frequently offered for sale by the natives ; and Europeans are occasionally tempted to purchase them at high prices.

According to Chinese tradition, the origin of certain Pearls may be referred to animals which would hardly be classed by zoologists as true Pearl-producers.

By far the most ancient work that is known,

the "*Shan Hai King,*" supposed to have been written B.C. 2255, makes mention of the existence of Pearls. The 4th book of this work, or "The Classic of Mountains and Seas," refers to the Li river, one of the affluents of the Tung-Ting lake, which drains the north-west portion of Hunan. " In it are many Chu-pick fish " (or water animals). " These look like lungs, but have eyes and six feet, and they have *Pearls.* They taste sour but pleasant, and are not unwholesome." The existence of Chu-pick fish is confirmed in Lüshi's edition of the Book of Confucius, and they are probably cuttle-fish with six tentacles. The same book also states that wild animals were found which looked like sucking-pigs, but have *Pearls.*

Passing now to the significance which has been assigned by imaginative writers to Pearls, we may remark that from the earliest times they have been considered as emblems of purity, beauty, and no-bility. Among the Romans they came, besides, to be regarded as emblematical of conjugal bonds, and upon a very fine sardonyx, portraying the marriage of Cupid and Psyche, "the high contracting parties " are represented joined together by a string of Pearls, the ends of which are in the hands of the god Hymen.

In comparatively modern times, however, they

acquired a more pathetic significance, and became the symbol of tears, as already mentioned. Reference is frequently made to them in this connection by many of our English poets. In his Epigram on the Marchioness of Winchester, Milton says—

> " And those Pearls of dew she wears,
> Prove to be presaging tears."

Shakespeare in King John, makes Constance allude to tears as—

> " Those heaven-moving Pearls from his poor eyes,"
> Which heaven shall take in nature of a fee."

Indeed they form a frequent metaphor in many of Shakespeare's plays. In "The Two Gentlemen of Verona," for instance, they assist in making up a pleasing picture of Valentine's great wealth in the possession of Silvia's love—

> " Why man, she is mine own :
> And I as rich in having such a jewel
> As twenty seas, if all their sand were Pearls,
> The water nectar, and the rocks pure gold."

In Othello's last, and perhaps most frequently quoted address after the death of Desdemona, he prays that they might speak of him as—

> " Of one whose hand
> Like the base Indian, threw a Pearl away
> Richer than all his tribe."

Pearls have been employed from very ancient times in the East, in the interpretation of dreams, and as preservatives of virtue, the marvellous properties and talismanic virtues with which the Pearl was supposed to be endowed, have no doubt contributed in no small degree, to intensify that love and admiration which a magnificent Pearl cannot fail to excite.

The medicinal qualities of Pearls.

In India, China, and other Oriental countries, Pearls have for ages been supposed to possess valuable medicinal properties. Even in our own country, down to a period not very remote, they found a place in the *Materia Medica*, and are mentioned in many of the pharmaceutical works of the last century. Thus, in Lewis' "Experimental History of the Materia Medica" (4th ed., 1791), we read that— "The coarse rough Pearls and the very small ones which are unfit for ornamental uses, called *rag Pearl* and *seed Pearl*, are those generally employed in medicine." Pearls were prescribed as astringents and antacids, a use which would be naturally suggested by their chemical composition—carbonate of lime. Their therapeutic value however, must have been but slight; while their cost would preclude them from being universally adopted.

Oriental potentates are said to have burned Pearls and chewed the lime so produced, with

E

the betel nut and sirih. In the East they were
credited with the property of strengthening the eyes,
were considered efficacious in hemorrhages, and
were in general use for diseases of the heart, for
ague and indigestion. Though never now prescribed
or used medicinally in this country — for " Pearl
powders," and kindred preparations retain nothing
but the name—they are still in repute in China and
some other Eastern countries: large quantities of
seed Pearls are used in the composition of majooms
or electuaries, in the formation of which several
precious stones are sometimes employed. The ma-
joom in which there is a large quantity of Pearls
is much in use for its supposed stimulating and
restorative qualities. At the present time however,
the healing virtue of the Pearl is regarded with
less favour than formerly in the East, and it is
now recognised and even admitted by their own
writers that "there is nothing in the gems or in the
shells which can render any more beneficial service
than that done by chalk and other antacids."

We subjoin an extract on the Indian idea of
the supposed medicinal properties of Pearls, from
the Mani-Málá, written in 1881 by the Rajah
Sourindro Mohun Tagore: "The use of Pearls
conduces to contentment of mind and to strength
of body and soul. The burnt powder of this

gem if taken in with water, as sherbet, cures vomiting of blood of all kinds. It prevents evil spirits working mischief in the minds of men, takes off bad smell from the mouth, cures lunacy of all descriptions and all mental diseases, jaundice, and all diseases of the heart, intestines and stomach. Burnt Pearl mixed with water and taken into the nostrils, as a powder, takes away head-sickness, cures cataract, lachryma and swelling of the eyes, the painful sensation such as is caused by the entry of sand into them, and ulcers. It gives them increased lustre. Used as a dentifrice it strengthens the gums and cleans the teeth. Rubbed over the body with other medicines it cures leprosy and the white skin disease, known in Arabic as " Bahac," in Hindo as "Chhip" and in Bengali as "Chhuli." It cures all skin diseases. It stops bleeding from cuts and ultimately heals them up. Whether taken internally or externally it is a sure antidote to poison. It drives away all imaginary fears and removes all bodily pain. To prevent its tendency to affect the brain it should always be used with the burnt powder of Basud, and in its absence with that of white mother-of-pearl. The dose of the Pearl powder should not exceed 2¼ mashas."

" Kerábádin Kabir contains full instructions as to how Pearls can be burnt, assimilated and made into pills, powders, oils, and majooms. The following is one of the processes by which burnt Pearls can be assimilated with each other. Strain the burnt powder well, put this into a bottle with some lime juice, and cork it up. Fill up half of an earthen vessel (*handi*) with vinegar, and hang the bottle over it by means of strings from outside, so that it does not touch the liquid. Cover the vessel up with an earthen dish, and keep it under a heap of cow-manure for 14 days. Then take it up, and after opening it, the powder having been converted into water, becomes one congealed lump. According to some authorities, it is not necessary to pour vinegar into the vessel ; the result desired might be obtained by attending to the other conditions of the process."

It need scarcely be added that the therapeutic virtues of the Pearl, extolled in the foregoing quotation, are purely imaginary.

Breeding Pearls.

Amongst all the ideas which have been entertained, both in ancient and more modern times, with regard to Pearls—grotesque and fanciful though many of them may be—none appears more romantic than that of their reputed powers of re-production.

In 1878, the subject of " Breeding Pearls "

occupied the attention of the Royal Asiatic Society at Singapore, and was introduced to their notice in a paper read by Dr. N. B. Dennys.

In the Malay Archipelago, and especially on the coast of Borneo, the natives allege that "Breeding Pearls" exist, that is to say, there are Pearls which possess the power of reproduction or rather *germination.* It is asserted that if a few of these Pearls be placed in a small box with some grains of rice and a little cotton wool, and then sealed up, on opening it a few months afterwards, one or more additional Pearls are found within, and the original ones none the worse, but the grains of rice have their ends apparently nibbled off. Many native women claim to possess these Pearls, and set great store by them, though they never exceed the size of a pin's head, and are not worth, at most, more than sixpence each.

Credible European evidence was adduced ; *pros* and *cons* were strenuously maintained in the discussion that followed the reading of Dr. Dennys' paper. But, as usual, neither side convinced the other ; and spontaneous creation in the matter of Pearls still owns its supporters. For our own part, we cannot conceive it possible that one Pearl can be developed from another *de novo*; however much the "nibbled end" of the rice particle may give colour to the idea. Yet the author can testify that after having kept some rice and some Pearls together in a box for a long time, the grains of rice, though originally perfect, have suffered some change, whereby they present all the appearance of having been nibbled. While unable to explain this phenomenon, he does not for a moment believe—although the belief is entertained by many intelligent Europeans resident in the East—that it has any connexion with the reputed re-production of the Pearls: indeed, it need hardly be added that the Pearls placed with the rice have not increased either in number or in magnitude.

CHAPTER IV.

PEARL BEARERS;

Marine and Fresh-water.

" Rich honesty dwells like a miser, Sir, in a poor house; as your *Pearl* in your foul oyster.—*As You Like It*, Act v. Scene iv.

AVING shewn in the preceding chapters how universal is the love of Pearls, and what a prominent position they occupy in the fashionable world for purposes of decoration ; having alluded also to some of the ideas that have at various times prevailed with respect to their origin, virtues and significance, we are now led naturally to the consideration of the principal sources whence our supply of these valuable gems is derived.

Pearls may be defined, in scientific language, as calcareous concretions, produced by certain shell-fish or molluscs. The Pearl-bearers of the sea are commonly known as "Pearl oysters," though they present but little resemblance to our "native oyster." Indeed although popularly so called they are not oysters in the scientific acceptation of the word, but belong rather to the group of sea-mussels. The term, however, is so commonly employed and universally recognised, that it would be pedantry to abandon it or to attempt to introduce any other word as a substitute.

For our purpose the Pearl-bearing molluscs may be conveniently divided into two great groups, viz.—

I. The Marine.

II. The Fresh-water.

All Pearls, whether marine or fluviatile, are produced by organisms belonging to that great group of bivalve shell-fish which was termed by the famous French naturalist, Lamarck, the *Conchifera.* This name however is by no means well-chosen, inasmuch as it literally means "Shell-bearers" and might therefore with equal propriety be bestowed upon other molluscs that secrete shells, such as certain *cephalopods* and *gasteropods.* It has hence become usual to replace the old term Conchifera by the better chosen name *Lamellibranchiata,* a name which was originally proposed by another French naturalist, De Blainville, and though rather longer than the older word is certainly more distinctive. The term Lamellibranchiata simply means "Platy gilled," and has reference to the fact that in this class of shell-fish the function of respiration is effected by means of two lamellar gills, placed on each side of the body.

The Lamellibranchiata or Conchifera form the lowest group of the mollusca, and are characterized by the absence of any distinctly differentiated part that can represent a true head ; hence they are sometimes referred to as the group of *acephalous*, or headless, molluscs. They are familiar to every one, under the form of oysters, scallops, cockles and mussels, and are found on every coast and in every climate, ranging from low water mark to a depth of 200 fathoms.

All mollusca are, as their name implies, soft-bodied animals (*mollis*=soft) ; but this soft body is usually defended by an external shell, whence the popular name of "shell-fish," and whence too the old scientific term of *Testacea* (*testa*=shell.) The shell is composed mainly of carbonate of lime, or as modern chemists sometimes prefer to call it, carbonate of calcium or calcic carbonate ; but this mineral-substance is associated with more or less organic matter which serves as a uniting medium. In *nacreous* or pearly shells we find an intimate association of the two textures, often in the form of alternating layers of very thin animal membrane and carbonate of lime. If digested in weak acid the calcareous ingredient of such a shell is slowly removed in solution, while the membranous residue retains with fidelity the original form of the shell. The shell is secreted by the soft external integument of the mollusc known technically as the "mantle," since it forms a kind of cloak, enveloping the viscera or internal organs. The edge, and indeed the general surface of this delicate membrane, separates calcareous matter from the food of the mollusc and from the surrounding medium, and thus slowly builds up the texture of the shell. In some molluscs the shell is formed of only a single piece, or valve, and hence they are termed *Uni-valves.* The snail, the whelk, and the nautilus are familiar examples of such uni-valved mollusca. But in other cases the shell is composed of two parts, whence they are termed *Bi-valves.* It is to this group, as previously stated, that all the ordinary Pearl-bearers belong.

Marine Pearls.

The great *class* of the Lamellibranchiata, or Conchifera, including all the common bivalves, embraces a number of separate *families*, while these in their turn comprise numerous *genera*.

The family *Aviculidæ* embraces nearly all the true marine Pearl-bearers, or Pearl oysters. It takes its name from the genus *Avicula* ("a little bird") so named in consequence of the winged shape of the shell. The largest quantity of medium sized Pearls are derived from the *Meleagrina fucata* (Gould) but the largest Pearls and mother-of-pearl shell from the *Meleagrina margaritifera* (Linnæus.) *Meleagrina* is now commonly regarded as a sub-genus of *Avicula*, and the word is therefore often written within brackets following the name of the true genus, thus : *Avicula (Meleagrina) margaritifera.* Although a great number of Pearls are supplied by various other species, yet the larger quantity which the *Meleagrina fucata* produces, and the fine quality of Pearls as well as shell yielded by the *Margaritifera*, justify us in referring to them at some length, and adopting them as types of the Pearl-bearers. A description of them, therefore, will hold true of all the others, except in certain scientific points of difference, which are of more interest to the marine zoologist than to the lover of gems or to the general reader.

The Pearl-oyster, *Meleagrina fucata*, is much much smaller than the *M. margaritifera* ; seldom exceeding in size the palm of a man's hand, and though it exhibits the most brilliant nacre, and produces fine small Pearls, its shell has but little market value as mother-of-pearl, being worth only from 20*s.* to 30*s.* per ton. On the other hand, the *Meleagrina margaritifera* is considerably larger and thicker, and yields the most valuable mother - of - pearl, as well as the finest Pearls, although these are not numerous. Indeed so pronounced are the differences between the two species in this respect, that the former might, with propriety, be called the " Pearl," and the latter the "Shell" oyster.

The number of Pearl-producing molluscs, however, is by no means confined to the *Aviculidæ:* they are on the contrary members of a very large group, which frequently differ from each other in almost every other possible respect: indeed their general configuration is as varied, as their distribution is widespread; some delighting in a tropical heat, deep seas and coral reefs, and others in the cool water of more northern latitudes and temperate zones. It is with the Pearl oyster of the Eastern Seas however that we are at present more immediately concerned.

All true Pearl-bearers have one feature in common, namely, the close resemblance existing

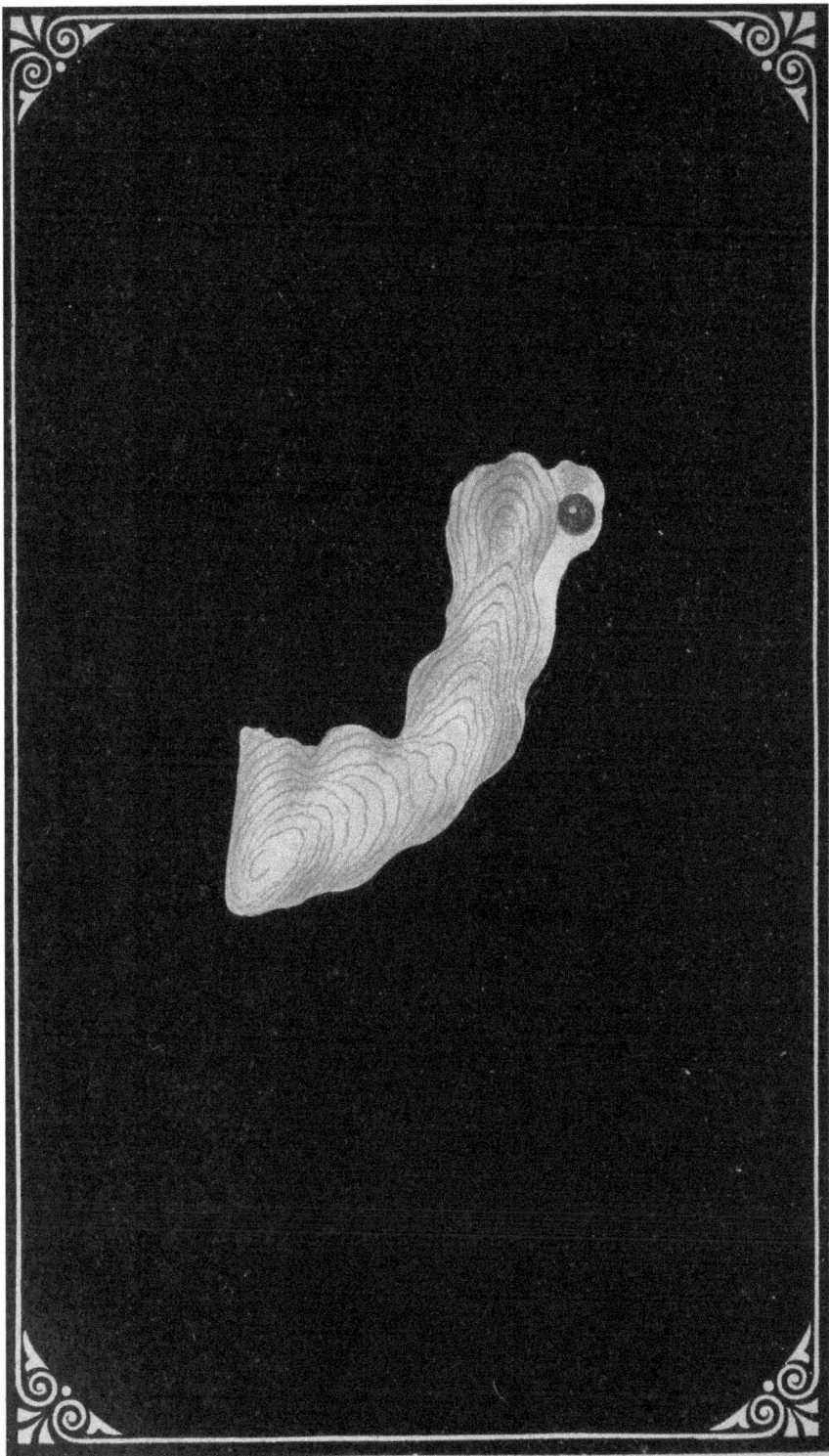

BLACK PEARL IN HAMMER-OYSTER   (Malieus).

between the Pearl itself and the shell of the mollusc producing it. The only shell however of true commercial value is what is known as mother-of-pearl shell, the substance of which, termed "nacre," is familiar to every one, and has been transformed into so many articles of ornament and utility from a period almost as remote as the introduction of the Pearl itself. A description of the shell forms the subject of a separate chapter.

Little need be said about the other marine shells, which subordinately yield Pearls. From the *Meleagrina Californica* Pearls are obtained in the Gulf of California and the Bay of Panama. Pearls are occasionally found in the curious *Malleus* or "Hammer Oyster;" in the *Pinna*, a wedge-shaped shell usually moored by a byssus or tuft of fibres ; in the delicate *Placuna* or "Window shell;" and even in the common edible oyster. But the last is rather a zoological curiosity than an object of commercial value or artistic interest.

It is perhaps worth mentioning that large white Pearls are occasionally found in the great clam shell, *Tridacna gigas.* These are always symmetrical and of some beauty, having a faint but pleasing sheen when looked at side-ways, but are of little or no value. The giant clam is probably the

largest shell in existence, and it is occasionally
used for church-fonts : a huge pair, used as *benitiers*,
in the church of St. Sulpice in Paris, were presented
to Francis I. by the Republic of Venice. The
clam is a bi-valve found buried up to the lips,
hinge downwards, in coral reef : it breathes with
siphons, but requires space to open its shell a few
inches. Instances are recorded of men having
stepped between the open valves, which have closed
immediately with the powerful adductor muscles,
and such an accident is almost certain death, either
by loss of blood, or by the rising tide.

Concretionary bodies commonly called Pearls,
but usually lacking the characteristic nacreous lustre,
are occasionally found associated with the shells of
certain gasteropods or univalves. They are of a
pink or rosy colour in the great conch shell of
the West Indies *(Strombus gigas)*, which is one of
the very largest known shells. Somewhat similar
pinkish concretions are yielded by another univalve
known as the *Turbinella Scolymus.*

Yellow Pearls from other shells are often
offered for sale in the East, where they are much
valued, but they are not yet appreciated in England.
They evidently come from a porcellanous shell
probably a gasteropod. The natives of the Sooloo

Archipelago assert that Pearls of a yellowish colour
have been taken from the Pearly Nautilus (*Nautilus
pompilius*), one of the group of cephalopodous molluscs ; but that they throw them away as they are
considered unlucky, adding that if a man fought with
a ring on, bearing such a Pearl, he would surely be
killed. Taking into consideration however the habits
and organization of this wonderful animal, and re-
membering the beautiful nacreous lining of its shell,
it may possibly be accepted as a true statement.
Indeed, Mr. Haynes, has a specimen in his possession which he considers an undoubted "Nautilus
Pearl."

Fresh-water Pearls.

As our principal supply of marine Pearls is
derived from the *Aviculidæ*, so our fresh-water Pearls
are mainly supplied by the great family of the
Unionidæ. The most important Pearl-bearer of
this family, and the one which chiefly concerns us,
as being the most productive, is the true European
Pearl-mussel, the *Unio margaritifera*. The word
unio is borrowed by conchologists, from Pliny, who
uses it to designate the Pearl, because as he tells
us no two Pearls were ever found exactly alike, so
that the task of matching a Pearl became one of
great difficulty. Each Pearl is in fact *unique* (*unio*).

The fresh-water Pearl-mussel is sometimes also called *Margaritana margaritifera;* the sub-genus *Margaritana* having been established by a German naturalist named Schumacher.

The Pearl-mussel is found inhabiting lakes and rivers in cool temperate zones, in almost all parts of the world. It occurs in mountain streams, not only in Great Britain and Ireland, but in all Northern Europe, in Bavaria and Saxony, and in the United States, and Canada. These Pearls are also occasionally produced by the *Anodon,* which although not included in the genus *Unio,* nevertheless presents less difference to the ordinary observer than really exists between many members of the genus *Unio* itself. There are about one hundred species of the *Anodon* distributed over North America, Europe and Siberia; while the genus *Unio* comprises upwards of 400 species.

The shell of the *Unio* is a more or less elongated oval, generally of a dark brown or almost black exterior, while its inside is slightly nacreous. Though very unlike the *Avicula* in outward appearance, yet in anatomical structure the two molluscs are very similar, being surrounded by a corresponding mantle, which secretes not only the shell but the Pearls contained in it. These however are greatly inferior to the marine Pearls in value and lustre, yet they have realized prices varying from £3 to £100.

It may be mentioned that in Japan, small Pearls are obtained from the fresh-water mussels, known to conchologists under the names of *Anadonta japonica* and *Cristaria spatiosa;* while in China the shell which yields many of the river Pearls has been termed *Dipsas plicata.* Nacreous concretions, more or less resembling true Pearls, are also occasionally secreted by other fluviatile mollusca. These facts are mentioned to shew that Pearls so far from being obtained from only one or two species, are really of wide occurrence. At the same time, the fact remains, that the finest Pearls, whether fresh-water or marine, are of very limited distribution, being confined to a narrow range of species ; and that the pearly concretions occasionally procured from other sources are fitted not so much for use as personal ornaments as to grace the cabinet of the conchologist.

The subject of river Pearls will be more fully discussed in a later chapter, where descriptions will be given of the Pearls of Great Britain, Europe and North America.

CHAPTER V.

MOTHER-OF-PEARL SHELL.

Fool: "Canst tell how an oyster makes his shell?"
— *King Lear.* Act I. Scene v.

THE principal sources of supply of Mother-of-Pearl shell are the Torres Straits and West Australian fisheries, and the trade-centres of Singapore and Macassar. Manila, situated on the Isle of Luzon and the capital of the Philippine Islands, was until quite lately the greatest centre of this trade in the East; and thus most of the shell from the surrounding seas has obtained, and still retains in the trade, the distinguishing name of "Manila shell." But the geographical advantages of Singapore, added to the enterprise of the Chinese steam-ship owners there, fostered by the far-seeing policy initiated by Sir Stamford Raffles, have transferred the whole of this trade from the Spanish port to the Straits' Settlements.

The innumerable islands of the North and South Pacific oceans, all contribute more or less to swell the supplies—notably the Tuamotus of the French colony Tahiti ; but the shell usually finds its way either to Sydney or to Auckland, and from its final port of shipment it receives its commercial nomenclature.

Three varieties are usually recognised in Commerce :—

    1. White

    2. Golden-Edged

    3. Black-Edged

The natives of the Sooloo Archipelago however, who raise the bulk of "Manila" shell, profess to distinguish four varieties of the golden-edged : namely, white or black backs, and either smooth or wrinkled. The meaning of these terms is not sufficiently clear, but it is not unlikely that they refer to the lines of horny substance sometimes seen radiating from the centre of the hinge of the shell to the circumference, produced by the successive layers of the lip in its growth from youth upwards; these lines however are not seen in old shell, as they are soon destroyed by decay.

Great differences are presented by the appear-ance of the oyster when opened, the outer edge of the " mantle " being in some cases black, and in others orange, speckled with either black or white spots. In fact the *Meleagrinæ* are subject to much local variation, and the appearance of the shell will generally allow a tolerably close conjecture as to whence it came. The black-edged variety is the most distinct both in the oyster and in the shell. In some shells the pallial line is more strongly marked than in others; in the Sooloo shell, the im-pressions of the adductor muscles are comparatively faint and almost smooth, whilst in the Australian shell a rough, uneven surface is more commonly found.

Mother-of-Pearl shells vary in weight, when clean and dry, from 400 to 4,000 pairs (*i. e.*, single oysters) to the ton, but occasional specimens have weighed as much as 14 lbs.

The valuable white shell is obtained chiefly from Tahiti and Macassar, the trade port of the Aru Islands, near New Guinea. It seems to exist in close proximity to the other varieties, without losing its distinctive peculiarity, for it is found year after year to the south side of Tapul, an island in the Sooloo Archipelago, without change, close to the golden-edged shell. The golden-edged is less infected with "worms" or "borers," such as the *Lithodomus*, (see Fig. 1) a small bivalve that eats into the shell, piercing it deeply.

Fig. 1.   LITHODOMUS.
(Natural size).

The horny lip of the shell is deep, and in some places the two valves are very similar in appearance.

On the Australian coast both golden and black-edged shells are found, but they are somewhat coarser and more worm-eaten, although as bright and lustrous as the best Sooloo shell. In all varieties, the horny lip is sufficiently flexible to make a tight joint when the shell is closed.

The sea bottom most favourable for shells is subject to wide variation. A reefy bottom near to mud is however generally considered as good holding ground as any, especially when there is a luxuriant growth of weeds, and more particularly coral cups, and a beautiful growth on the coral resembling coach whips, four or five feet in length.

The common Mother-of-Pearl shell consists of

two valves, the upper one rounded and the lower one flat. They are composed of consecutive layers of "nacre" secreted by the oyster, each layer trending away from the hinge and over the horny lip more than its fellow below; these layers are thicker at the hinge than at the lip, and they are continually in process of formation. This continued growth is necessary, in the first place to enlarge the young shell so as to accommodate the increasing dimensions of the owner, and secondly in order to renew and keep up the necessary thickness of the shell, which through external influences decays away; the nacre is also secreted in order to cover any foreign substance, such as mud or weed, that may drift into the shell, and being unable to escape may cause inconvenience to the delicately constructed mollusc; it likewise serves to arrest the progress of the "borers," which attack the shell and seek to effect an entrance. Conchologists assert, as stated in the preceeding chapter, that the nacre is secreted by the mantle, but it is probably that the adductor muscle itself contributes to the formation of that portion of the shell which bears the adductor impression.

The resplendent play of colour which the inner surface of the Pearl shell exhibits—a display that defies any attempt at artificial imitation — is not due to the presence of any material pigment or colouring matter, as might at first sight be supposed, but is referable to the action of light on its delicate structure. Like most other shells, the Mother-of-Pearl consists of carbonate of lime, with a little animal matter serving as a connective tissue or frame-work. In Dr. Watts' *Dictionary of Chemistry*, the Mother-of-Pearl is said to consist of 66 per cent. of carbonate of lime, 2.5 of organic matter, and 31.5 of water. The chemical composition, however, offers no explanation of the cause of the exquisite pearly lustre, and science is indebted to the late Sir David Brewster for the discovery of the real cause of this phenomenon. He was the first to point out that the iridescence of Mother-of-Pearl does not reside in the shell, nor depend on the chemical nature of its substance, but is due to the delicate striations of its surface.

As far back as 1814, Brewster published the result of his researches on the structure of Mother-of-Pearl, in a letter addressed to Sir Joseph Banks, and presented to the Royal Society. His views on this subject were also set forth in his well-known "Treatise on Optics," contributed in 1831 to Lardner's *Cabinet Cyclopædia.*

The late Sir John Herschel also applied himself to the optical study of Mother-of-Pearl, and his results appeared in the *Edinburgh Philosophical Journal* in 1820.

An elaborate examination of the microscopic structure of shells was undertaken many years ago by the late Dr. W. B. Carpenter, and some valuable results obtained as to the nature of the nacreous varieties.

Microscopic examination of a thin section of nacre shows that the surface is traversed by numerous delicate lines ; in some cases almost straight, while in others they are crumpled and corrugated. These lines are produced by the outcrop of thin laminæ running more or less obliquely to the surface. It appears that Sir David Brewster regarded them as the edges of hard calcareous layers, alternating with softer membranous laminæ ; the latter being more readily worn away, would naturally form grooves, while the former being hard, would stand out as alternating ridges. Dr. Carpenter, however, regarded the lines on the nacre as the plaited edges of a single membranous layer.

Whatever be the exact nature of the lineation, it is certain that the iridescence is due to the interference of light reflected from the undulations of the delicately-grooved surface.

When a piece of Mother-of-Pearl is digested in

weak acid, the calcareous matter is removed ; yet the decalcified shell retains the iridescence as long as it remains undisturbed, but loses its lustre when pressed flat. It is, therefore, evidently the striated structure which gives rise to the nacreous lustre. A cast taken from a piece of Mother-of-Pearl in wax, mastic, or fusible metal, displays similar iridescence, in consequence of its having received the microscopic rippling on its surface. According to Brewster — "A solution of gum-arabic or of isinglass, when allowed to indurate upon a surface of Mother - of - Pearl, takes a most perfect impression from it, and exhibits all the communicable colours in the finest manner, when seen either by reflexion or transmission."

It is worth noting that the production of rainbow-like effects from delicately grooved surfaces produced artificially, is well illustrated by the ornaments called "Barton's Buttons." Many years ago the late Mr. John Barton, of the Royal Mint, succeeded in cutting grooves upon steel at a distance of from the 2,000th to the 10,000th of an inch apart. The metal surfaces thus treated displayed the most brilliant colours in consequence of the "interference" of the reflected undulations of light. His "iris ornaments" consisted of buttons and other objects wrought in brass and stamped

with hardened steel dies upon which the delicate
lines had been engraved. Nothing can better illustrate the nature of the optical phenomena presented
by nacre, or Mother-of-Pearl, than their artificial
reproduction by Barton's method.

It is therefore demonstrated that the iridescent
colours of nacre are produced by the light reflected
from the corrugated surface, resulting in that
beautiful appearance by which the very atoms
of the substance seem as if lit up by colour;
now at one end of the solar spectrum where violet,
blue and green rays predominate, and now at the
other end where red, orange and yellow unite in
such harmonious blending as to produce the most
pleasing offects.

This nacre then composes the whole interior
of the shell, and is the same secretion which in the
Pearl has assumed a more or less globular form:
between nacre and Pearls, therefore, there is virtually
only the difference of the form of deposition.

The Mother-of-Pearl shell lies on the sea bottom,
usually inclined at an angle of 20 degrees, with the
flat valve downwards, although it is frequently found
reversed. In young shells, more particularly the
black-edged variety, there is a *byssus* or bunch of
strong fibres which passes through the hinge or

heel of the shell, and attaches it to the bottom; in old shells however this *byssus* is completely wanting.

The oyster is usually open an inch or two at the lips, to admit the sea water and any organic substance that the tides and. currents may bring to serve as food. On being disturbed it immediately closes, and it is no uncommon occurrence when the water is thick for a young diver to come up with a shell fast on his fingers : in order to free him a knife must be used to cut the muscle of the oyster, and thus allow the shell to open. After being taken from its natural element, and exposed in a boat to the tropical sun the shell opens, but it shuts tightly again on being touched. The oysters do not generally live longer than twelve hours after being taken from the water, and a dry wind off shore hastens their death ; it is indeed a wonder, that, deriving their oxygen from the water, they can live so long in our atmosphere.

Mother-of-Pearl shells are taken as low down as 45 and 50 fathoms ; beyond this depth the divers have hitherto been unable to explore, and hence their extreme limit is unknown. One has, however, been brought up, when splicing a cable, from a depth of 150 fathoms. The zones of all sub-marine animal life are regulated by the pressure, temperature and composition of the sea water, and by the existence of a proper food supply.

There is one peculiarity with regard to these molluscs and, in fact, most inhabitants of the sea, which is not generally known, namely, the frequency of parasites, or as in many cases they are more aptly termed "messmates," since they live in the shell on apparently friendly terms with the oyster. Mother-of-Pearl shells almost invariable hold one or more, and on the Australian coast these inmates are generally crabs, lobsters, worms and shrimp-like creatures. One of the two former crustaceans is almost always present, and it may be truly termed a "messmate;" the latter are simply ordinary parasites, and are not by any means universal. In the shells found East of Cossack, on the West Australian grounds, the oyster is usually accompanied by one soft-shelled brown crab, of $\frac{3}{4}$ to $1\frac{1}{4}$ inches in width: this is said to be poisonous. Lower down the coast, the crab's place is taken by two soft transparent-looking lobsters, faintly spotted and tinged with red, the one three times as large as the other: probably they are male and female. These are delicious eating. The two principal claws or pincers are very small in proportion to the body of the lobster, especially in the larger of the two, and the body reminds one more of that of a drone

than of the segmental body of a crustacean. The
tail is either absent or rudimentary and the two
claws are modified into simple feelers, protection
from enemies being gained within the closed shell
of the host.

West of Cossack the lobsters are more common,
and in the Montebello Islands they are almost
universal. In Sooloo, the Mother-of-Pearl shells
may contain one, two, or three lobsters, but almost
invariably the number is two, while the crab is
very rarely met with. Occasionally a shell is
found without any other inhabitant than its owner.
When the shell is closed the messmate retires
within a hollow place, in the lower part of the
oyster itself, near to the hinge of the shell, and this
cavity is called by Sooloo men, the "lobster's home."

The idea that these messmates may play some
important part in the formation of Pearls seems to
be a groundless speculation, and their general formation as defenceless creatures, with great consuming
powers, would rather imply that they perform the
service of scavengers, clearing the shell of some of
the foreign substances which drift into it and annoy
the oyster. Even as it is, the *Meleagrinae* often
have to renovate their shells, and are in the habit
of burying such intruders as they cannot rid themselves of. Stones, mud, small shells, wood, and more

especially layers of weed are thus found embedded
in shells, forming unnatural excrescences on the
surface.

These "blisters" may be found apparently empty
and discoloured within, or full of water and half
decayed substances; in both cases an offensive
odour points out that the enclosed substance was
of animal or vegetable character. Pearls are also
frequently found in "blisters;" they escape from
the body of the oyster, and are then treated in
exactly the same manner as a stone or other
intruder, being covered over by each successive
layer of nacre. These unnatural protuberances on
the inner surface of the shell are gradually removed
by the oyster secreting thinner layers of nacre on
the top of them than at the base, until the surface
becomes again level. Slowly but steadily the exterior surface of the shell decays and disappears, until
the blister and its contents come within reach of
the advancing dissolution, and then these in turn
disappear. Any inorganic or insoluble matter in
the blister falls to the bottom; and thus the oyster
literally passes a stone or other intruder through its
shell.

This process is illustrated by Figs. 2, 3 and 4. (*See
opposite page*). In Fig. 2, a small Pearl, or other foreign
body fallen into the shell, has become cemented to the

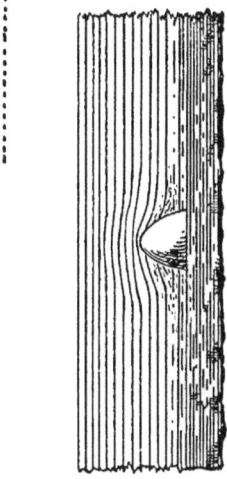

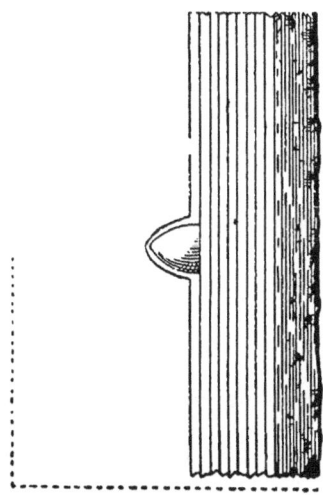

FIG. 4.

FIG. 3.

FIG. 2.

SECTIONS OF PEARL SHELL, SHEWING HOW A PEARL OR OTHER OBJECT MAY BE BURIED IN THE SUBSTANCE OF THE SHELL
AND ULTIMATELY DISAPPEAR.

internal surface of the valve by a single layer of nacre.
In Fig. 3, the obstruction has become buried in the
substance of the shell, and the inner surface is again
level, because the successive layers of nacre are
thinner on the top of the foreign body. At the
same time, the decay of the outer surface has been
advancing, until in Fig. 3, it has nearly reached the
Pearl or other intruder; and finally in Fig. 4, this
foreign body has entirely disappeared, together with
its encircling layers of nacre, having been set free
by the destruction of the external part of the
shell.

Besides the possession of this faculty, it is evident that the oyster is sensible to vibrations of
either sound or motion. When it is lying agape
in the boat, any slight concussion will cause it immediately to close tightly, like a vice. Many a
shell is discovered by bubbles of gas arising from
it, in the act of closing, on account of the near approach of a diver, and a consequent tremor of the
water. The most remarkable fact, however, is that
it is so far conscious of the point of attack of a
"borer" (Fig. 1, p. 85), eating its way through the
shell, that, in order to guard against the danger of
being pierced, the oyster secretes extra-thick layers of
nacre at that point, and thus, in course of time,
seriously disturbs the natural shape of its pearly

bed. This is seen in Figs. 5, 6 and 7. (*See next page*). The borer is represented in Fig. 5, attacking the exterior of the shell, and the oyster has secreted an unusually thick layer of nacre opposite the point of attack. In Fig. 6, the borer has penetrated into the substance of the shell, but successive deposits of nacre have been formed to resist the intrusion. In Fig. 7, the decay of the external part of the shell has removed the borer, while the internal surface has resumed its natural form. The three figures are placed at different levels in order to shew that as external decay proceeds, the oyster adds to the internal surface. All these figures are taken from photographs of the Pearl shell.

The oyster's sole means of protection against crabs and other enemies, is that of closing its shell; if, however, this shell is pierced completely through by a " borer," (Fig. 1, p. 85), a breach of its walls is effected, and the defenceless citadel is open to attack. Thus dead shells generally exhibit the cause of their late owner's disappearance. A large species of *Murex*, a Univalve, is also an inveterate enemy of the Mother-of-Pearl oyster, attaching itself to the shell, and boring through it. When, therefore, a shell is found with any unnatural protuberance on its interior surface, the pearler scrapes away a little of the decaying shell at the back of this spot, and if

G

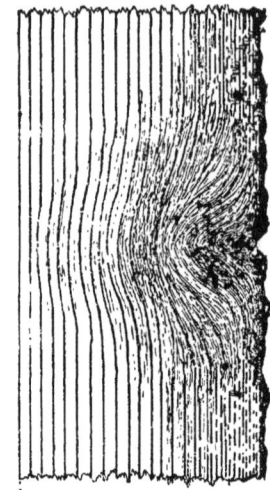

FIG. 7.

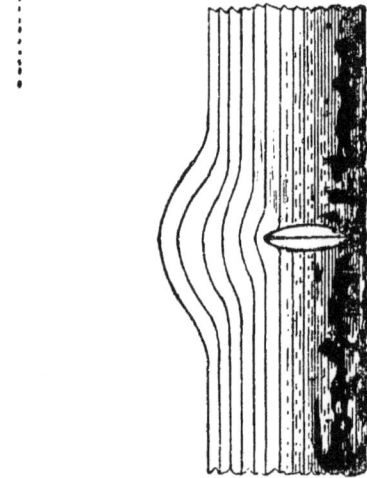

FIG. 6.

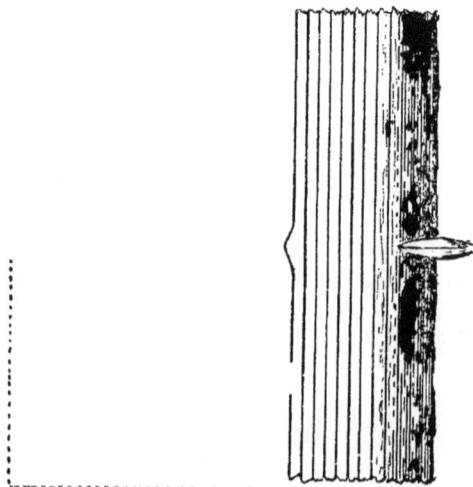

FIG. 5.

SECTIONS OF PEARL SHELL SHEWING THE THICKENING OF THE INTERNAL SURFACE, OPPOSITE THE POINT OF ATTACK OF A BORING MOLLUSC, WHICH IS PIERCING THE SHELL FROM WITHOUT.

the hole of a borer is disclosed, the shell is passed aside, if, however, the shell is solid at that spot, the blister is cut out with a hammer and punch, and split open, in the hope of finding a Pearl within.

The *Meleagrinæ*, in common with all oysters and mussels, produce an enormous quantity of ova, a very small proportion of which ever escape their numerous enemies, and succeed in establishing themselves in their sub-marine world. The "spat" is carried here and there by the currents until it succeeds in attaching itself to some obstacle that may have arrested its onward course, and here it probably remains for life, unless some accident happens to detach it again, such as the heavy seas caused by hurricanes. Several thousands of Pearl shells have been washed up on the Australian coast after a "blow." Turtle also may disturb shells; they are very fond of the luscious morsel within, and full-grown shells may be found bitten to pieces by their powerful mandibles. There was found by our fleet in 1884, a shell that at a certain period of its growth had been broken, probably by a turtle, but the oyster had succeeded in secreting fresh layers of nacre within, before harm came to it, and the old accident was only detected by the fracture at the back of the shell. This case again furnishes

an absolute proof that the shells grow from within
and not from the outside, as has sometimes been
maintained.

It is difficult to state anything definite as to
the rate of growth of the Mother-of-Pearl shell, but
a case that occured in 1883 may be worth mentioning as it excited considerable interest in the
West Australian fleet.

In February 1883, the "Louisa," a cutter of
28 tons, was beached on the Lacepede islands and
her copper was thoroughly scrubbed and cleaned.
After remaining pearling during March, she was taken
into a creek in Roebuck Bay to clean and paint
up for returning to Cossack, the season being over.
When the ebb tide left her high and dry, it was
found that her bottom was covered in many places
with small Mother-of-Pearl oysters, from $1\frac{1}{2}$ to 3
inches wide ; one solitary shell however measuring
$5\frac{1}{2}$ inches across. The only feasible explanation
of this seems to be that these small shells were
originally in the dirt and scrapings of the shells
which were thrown overboard the evening after
the copper was cleaned in February : this was
before the vessel was floated. The tide must
then have washed them against the bottom, to
which they adhered. Considering, therefore, that
they were found only six weeks after the cutter's

bottom was thoroughly cleaned, this fact, if the above explanation be correct, would point to a far more rapid growth of oyster shell than pearlers have hitherto thought possible.

It is often maintained in Australia, that as certain spots are left at the end of one season, rich in shell, and six months afterwards the identical spots are found bare, the oysters must possess the power of migrating at will. There is, however, no evidence of value to lead to such a conclusion, and the inference from the disappearance of shells is, that some change has taken place at the bottom of the sea, the shells having been probably buried by sand or mud, which doubtless is continually shifting, especially where the tides are strong and the sea shallow.

The geographical distribution of the true Mother-of-Pearl shell is confined to the Pacific and Indian Oceans and their connecting seas. Cape Horn, and the Cape of Good Hope stretching away down into cold latitudes, appear effectually to have prevented their successful migration in the present age, by any favouring current to the Atlantic.

The ancient history of the Mollusca, as told by Geology, is well worth studying. The Lamelli-branchiata or Conchifera, existed as far back as the

Lower Silurian period, if not earlier, and they have
not only held their own, but have gradually increased in number and variety of type, up to the
present day. The family of *Aviculidæ* flourished in the
Carboniferous period, and beds containing immense
numbers of *Avicula Contorta* occur in the Triassic
or Rhoetic series, in the Austrian Alps. The more
interesting Gasteropods and Cephalopods also have
their histories clearly marked out from a very early
date. Bivalves have undoubtedly been most successful in the struggle for existence, and this power
may be partly attributed to their ability of closing
their shells when attacked, and presenting an im-
penetrable front of "masterly inactivity."

It is needless to enumerate the articles for the
manufacture of which Pearl shell is sought after.
For buttons and studs, for knife-handles, card-cases,
and for ornamental work generally, Mother-of-Pearl
has no rival. Its adoption is of no modern date,
articles of this substance having been discovered
in the excavations at Nineveh and Babylon.

One important application of Mother-of-Pearl
is that of hafting cutlery, especially fruit knives
and pocket knives. The two flat plates of shell,
which are rivetted to the central part of the handle,
are technically termed "scales," and these require to
be tediously ground down and polished by hand.

At one time about 100 tons of Mother-of-Pearl were consumed annually by the Sheffield cutlers.

Visitors to the Holy Land usually bring away as mementoes, specimens of Mother-of-Pearl, ornamented with religious subjects, elaborately carved in low relief. These are frequently preserved in collections of curiosities under the name of "Pilgrims' shells."

Mother-of-Pearl is often ornamented by a process of engraving, especially in China. Among the objects commonly made of this material, are the Chinese card-counters, frequently shaped like fish. Such objects are ornamented by elegant patterns incised in the shell; but in some cases the design is etched by means of an acid, which attacks the shell in the same way that nitric acid bites into a copperplate, in the ordinary process of etching.

Mother-of-Pearl plays an important part in the manufacture of papier-mâché. Mr. W. C. Aitken, of Birmingham, in an interesting paper on this manufacture, informs us that "Pearl-shell inlaying, which contrasts so well with the brilliant black of English papier-mâché, a process suggested by foreign lac-work—was introduced by George Souter, a decorator in the employ of Messrs. Jennens and Betteridge, who patented the invention in 1825.

The Pearl ornaments were made from thin laminæ
of shell, from one-hundredth to one-fortieth part of
an inch in thickness. The ornament was painted
on the Pearl with varnish or 'stopping-out' material;
acid was then applied, and the portions of Pearl
not protected eaten away. By this method the
most delicate ornaments were produced."

It should be remarked that for the manufacture
of papier-mâché, and for buttons and various trivial
ornaments, much use is made of certain iridescent
shells, distinct from Mother-of-Pearl, yet often
confounded therewith : these are principally the
brilliantly prismatic shells of the *Haliotis*, sometimes
termed, from their shape, " ear-shells," and from
their iridescent colours "aurora-shells;" together with
certain species of *Turbo*, such as *T. margaritaceus*,
known also as " Maara shell."

A few years ago, when "Smoked Pearl," derived from the black-edged shells, came into use
in this country for the manufacture of the large dark
buttons, then so fashionable, it was remembered that
about thirty or forty years previously, some dark
shells had been imported, but being then regarded as
almost useless, were buried in piles in Birmingham.
Attention was now naturally directed to their exhu-
mation. "An anecdote was recently told me," said

Mr. P. L. Simmonds, writing in 1879, "by a large wholesale shell merchant in London, of a workman in Birmingham having volunteered to dig up his neighbour's yard or garden free. The offer being declined, the man persisted, agreeing to give £5 if he might be allowed to do it, and cart away the rubbish. Consent was at last obtained, and the digger cleared £20 by the Pearl-shells he thus obtained, and sold. My informant also told me that the Town Hall of Birmingham is built on such mounds of these shells that it would almost pay, at present prices, to pull it down and rebuild it, for the sake of the shells that could be thus obtained."

In a valuable paper by Mr. J. S. Wright, on the Jewellery trade of Birmingham, we are told that the workers in the Mother-of-Pearl shells occasionally find real Pearls embedded in the shell. "A few years since (this was written in 1866) a small lot of shells was brought to Birmingham, which either from ignorance or mistake had not been cleared of the Pearls at the fishery. A considerable number were found and sold; and one especially was sold, by the man who had bought the shell for working into buttons, for £40. The purchaser, we believe, re-sold the same for a profit of £160; and we have heard it was afterwards held in Paris for sale at £800."

In countries where Mother-of-Pearl is abundant,

it is occasionally employed as a decorative material in architecture. Thus, in Manila, the verandahs of the houses are ornamented with Pearl-shells, while in Panama the cathedral and some of the churches are similarly adorned. Even in our own Channel Islands, where the lustrous ear-shells or "ormers" (*Haliotis tuberculata*) are abundant, the shells are utilized by being let into the walls of some of the houses and disposed in symmetrical patterns. The brilliant effect of nacreous shells when massed together on a large scale, was well illustrated by the column of Mother-of-Pearl shells, which formed so conspicuous a trophy in the Western Australian Court of the Colonial Exhibition of 1886.

The present value of Mother-of-Pearl varies from £60 to £200 per ton, and the Australian fisheries of Torres Straits and the North West Coast and those of the Sooloo seas, contribute about one half of the total supply.

CHAPTER VI.

THE ORIGIN AND FORMATION OF PEARLS.

" Some asked how *Pearls* did grow and where?
　　Then spoke I to my girl:
　To part her lips, and showed them there—
　　The quarelets of Pearl."
　　　　　　　—Robert Herrick.

O many difficulties surround the study of the Formation of Pearls, that it is by no means surprising that a host of conjectures, often of a very fanciful and even wild character, have from time to time been promulgated with the view of explaining the origin of these enigmatical little bodies. Many of the ancient ideas respecting Pearls have been set forth in an earlier chapter ; but with the advance of science these crude fancies and curious fables have gradually passed away. It is the object of the present chapter to present a rational explanation of the origin, and formation of Pearls, so far as the lights of our present knowledge can guide us in solving these difficult problems.

For a long time it was currently believed that Pearls were found only in diseased shell-fish, and to this day in some parts of Great Britain, when a Pearl is discovered in a mussel or oyster, the edible part is thrown away as unfit for use, while the Pearl, however valueless, is carefully preserved. Hence we often find, even at the present day, that Pearls are alluded to as " morbid secretions."

On this subject, Professor Coutance, of the Medical School of Brest, has some remarks which are at once sensible and amusing :—" Au point de vue physiologique, l'huître ne fait, en produisant la Perle rien d'anormal, puisque la nacre de la coquille est formée de la même substance. Elle ne tire de son fond aucune matière nouvelle poure faire la Perle : elle y emploie seulement, peut-être au préjudice de sa coquille, une part de l'élément carbonaté qui constitue celle-ci, ou sert même à la réparer. La maladie de l'huître n'est donc qu' une hypersécrétion ; c'est sans doute beaucoup, et nous continuons à la plaindre, comme nous plaignons un homme enrhumé du cerveau. Une autre observation à faire, c'est que rien n'est changé dans l'animal qui sécrète ou qui à sécrèté la Perle. Aucune modification dans la conformation ou dans la nature histologique de ses tissus n' indique une maladie, un trouble organique ; la présence seule de la Perle est l'indice de quelque chose d'anormal."

And after a few more pages in a similar strain, he proceeds to say of the Pearl-oysters, in reference to their secretions :—" Au lieu de les en plaindre il faut les en féliciter. Et si nous voulions à toute force conserver à la sécrétion calcaire ce nom d' affection morbide, il faudrait dire alors ; ' combien ces huîtres seraient mal portantes si elles n' avaient pas cette maladie ! En considérant désormais de riches pendeloques ornées de Perles aux oreilles fines et délicates d'une aristocratique beauté, nous penserons non plus à une huître malade, mais à une huître sauvée. *C'est plus gai.*"

The prevailing idea among scientific men, at present, is that the formation of Pearls is caused by an effort of the oyster to rid itself of irritation, caused by the presence of some foreign body which has found entrance from without.

Year by year some thousands of Pearls are cut in half by working jewellers, and their universal experience is, that a nucleus is always to be found. On the other hand the pearlers in the North West of Australia, state, that most of the Pearls broken there have presented a small golden-coloured cavity capable of holding a No. 8 shot. The experience of these pearlers on the general subject, however, is much inferior to that of the jeweller.

The nucleus of the Pearl may be either a grain of sand, or the frustule of one of those minute siliceous vegetables known as *diatoms*, or a minute parasite, or even one of the ova of the Pearl oyster itself. Around this foreign body thin layers of nacre are deposited, one after another, like the successive skins of an onion, until the object is completely encysted. The Pearl is formed of concentric layers of carbonate of lime, of extreme tenuity, but of the same general character as those composing the shell.

Sir Everard Home, a distinguished surgeon in the early part of this century, having been led to study the structure of Pearls, came to the following conclusion : " A Pearl is formed upon the external surface of an ovum, which having been blighted, does not pass with the others into the oviduct, but remains attached to its pedicle in the ovarium, and in the following season, receives a coat of nacre at the same time that the internal surface of the shell receives its annual supply." While admitting that an ovum may occasionally form the nucleus of a nacreous concretion, we cannot admit the general application of Sir Everard's explanation.

The finest Pearls are found within the mantle of the mollusc, close to the lips of the shell, or in the soft part of the oyster near the hinge of the shell; the worst Pearls are those found within the close, coarse fibres of the adductor muscle. At very rare intervals they are found loose in the shell outside the body of the oyster; and may, when large, get washed out of the shell and thus be lost. Lastly, Pearls are often found imbedded more or less deeply in the shell, having in some cases escaped from the soft tissues. It is notable that the adherent Pearls occur almost invariably in the flat or lower valve: occasionally, it is true, they are found imbedded in the rounded or upper valve, but in such cases it is observed that the shell has been lying at the bottom, in the reverse position, thus making the rounded valve the lower one. This is by no means an uncommon occurrence.

The Pearls found imbedded in or under the " muscular impression " are always small, irregular, and worthless, similar to those found imbedded in the adductor muscle itself.

Pearls are found in infinite variety of form,

and the consecutive layers vary in brightness, colour and perfection. The most highly prized Pearls are quite spherical, and it is evident from their shape that these must have been formed free in the mantle or in the soft tissues of the mollusc, and not cemented to the shell. Some Pearls shew defects, caused apparently by the contact of new foreign substances, organic or inorganic, such as grit or a film of weed ; and in some cases it requires a number of layers to completely hide these defects. Thus, every new layer secreted, changes the value of the Pearl.

When a Pearl that has been cut from the shell presents a hemispherical surface, it is sometimes called a *perle bouton;* such a Pearl is flat on one side, and rounded or convex on the other. If a solid Pearl has an irregular shape, having grown over a rough object, it is known to jewellers as *baroque pearl.* Sometimes the warty Pearls are hollow, and pass under the name of *coq de perle.*

An attempt has been already made in a former chapter to explain how the Pearl-oyster rids itself of any foreign substance that may get into its shell, such as a stone or piece of wood : and in now dealing with the subject of real Pearls, the same explanation of the formation of "blisters" must be borne in mind. Blister Pearls are generally hollow nacreous bodies, of irregular shape, and are often due to the deposition of nacre at some point where the shell has been attacked by a parasite from without.

That the oyster does not work magic may be taken for granted, and the following explanation of the vexed question of the formation of Pearls is now submitted to practical pearlers and conchologists. The principle involved is applicable to all molluscs, but due consideration in each case must be given to the natural position of the shell, and its owner's habits.

The oyster lies at the bottom of the sea at an angle more or less considerable, but is generally inclined to the sea bottom at about 20° to 25°. The shell is usually open about 1½ inches, to admit the entrance of water, its owner's natural sustenance, and the mantle is spread out over the horny outside lips of the shell. Respiration is carried on by means of the gills, and any organic particles in the water which bathes these vascular organs are transferred to the mouth. Scientists have taught us that "hæmoglobin," or the colouring matter of the blood in the animal kingdom, is the agent, that owing to its great affinity for oxygen, extracts that supporter of life from the air inhaled. Of the agent that

H

extracts the oxygen from water, either salt or fresh, we are, however, still untaught. The water is admitted between the " mantle lobes " into the " pallial chambers," where it is oxygenated : the oyster evidently retains a considerable quantity of gas within itself, many shells being discovered by the divers, simply by the betraying bubbles of gas emitted by the oyster, in the act of closing its shell. The effete water is renewed by diffusion, as there is no regular pulsating movement to eject it.

In most fishes there is a special arrangement to guard against the admission of foreign substances to the respiratory organs, the branchial arches being developed into a kind of fringe. In the invertebrates however, there is no special apparatus for that purpose, and when, after storms or other disturbing causes, the water becomes thickly charged with sand, mud, and other substances in suspension, it is evident that the water admitted within the pallial chamber of the oyster must be equally thick, and it can hardly be doubted but that some particles of this suspended matter are accidentally retained entangled in the tissues of the oyster, especially if the latter happen to be weakened by disease.

The healthier the appearance of the oyster, and the greater the amount of water emitted when opened by the knife, the less probability will there be of finding any Pearl. As previously stated, it is within the mantle that many of the Pearls are found, and the inference is, that the interior surfaces of this integument secrete the fine pearly layers around the nucleus of what is to become a Pearl ; whilst the layers of the shell are secreted mainly by the exterior surfaces of the mantle. With the first layer deposited around it, the intruder becomes a Pearl, and if this nucleus is of animal or vegetable matter, decomposition, or probably absorption, will in time leave an apparently empty space, the cavity being lined and discoloured by the residue ; a hollow Pearl is thus formed, just as the hollow "blister" is formed in the shell as already described.

The oyster is not entirely dormant, and its movements, together with the varying position of the Pearl within its tissues, probably regulate the shape assumed by the constantly accumulating layers ; owing, however, to the inclined position of the oyster, the tendency of the Pearl is always to work downwards through the tissues, towards the hinge of the shell. Small Pearls often work their way into the adductor muscle, and, owing to the fibres of this part being coarse and close, it is almost impossible for a large Pearl to penetrate them, but numbers of small ones are frequently found here, bound together like a cluster of grapes, showing that even within this muscle these Pearls receive further accretions. In course of time such Pearls as avoid passing into this muscle find their way downwards to the lowest part of the oyster, and according to their position therein, may or may not find their way out of the tissues of the oyster into the shell.

Up to this time the Pearl has received regular layers all over its surface, but rings, and other marks of lesser brightness frequently occur, the result probably, of contact with the coarser tissues of the oyster. For a short time the Pearl is loose in the shell, and it falls into the same category as a stone, or any other intruder. It is encircled by the growing layer of shell, and proceeds on its downward course through the shell, like an ordinary " blister," the upper portion receiving further layers, until it is hidden beneath the shell which by degrees, resumes its natural shape. This process is well illustrated by Figs. 2 and 3, p. 95.

The shell, as stated in the last chapter, is worn away from the outside at the same rate that it is renewed within, so that in time, the Pearl with its surrounding tomb yields to the general dissolution, and the nucleus of the Pearl, if of inorganic matter, after having been the cause of infinite annoyance to its unfortunate captor, is returned to the place from whence it came. In Fig. 4, p. 95, we have a representation of the oyster shell after the Pearl has been passed through the substance.

It may be urged that the layers of shell enveloping the Pearl or blister, are laid equally upon the top of it and at the sides ; and that an unnatural excrescence would still remain on the inner surface of the shell long after the original cause of it has passed away ; but this is not so. It must be remembered that the laws of development by which creatures are adapted to cope with the surrounding conditions and difficulties of their existence, are as applicable to an oyster as to any other form of life, and the same power that taught the oyster to protect itself against the inveterate attacks of its enemy, the " borer," by increasing the thickness of its shell at the point of danger, might also teach it to rid itself of an uncomfortable tenant in its bed, by exactly the reverse process.

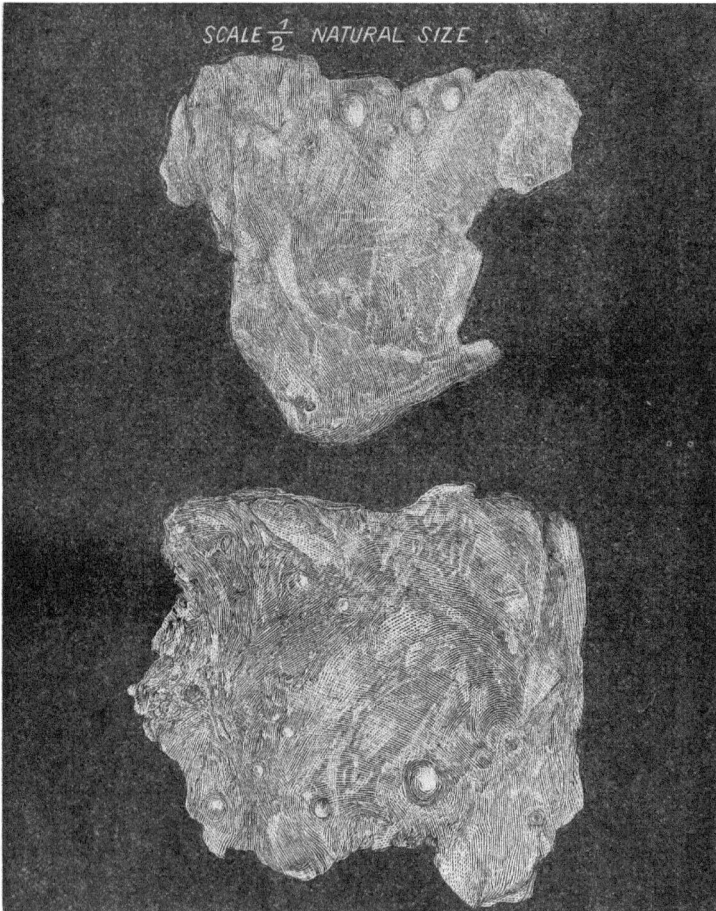

FIG. 8—SPLIT SHELL DISCLOSING EMBEDDED PEARLS.

Pearls embedded in the shell are generally found in close proximity to the hinge, and in splitting shells open to examine a "blister," an embedded Pearl has often been found (see Fig. 8.), at a place where the surface of the shell gave no indication of its presence.

In the British Museum (Natural History), at

South Kensington, and in the Museum of Practical Geology in Jermyn-street, there are specimens which clearly illustrate the processes of re-lining the shell, and of burying foreign substances. They are flat shells (the lower valves), with a number of figures of Buddha lying embedded at equal distances apart, on the upper portion of the shell near the lips, but not so deeply buried as to be hidden. These are not uncommonly produced artificially in China, in order to make a profit out of the unquestioning religious faith of the people who, upon seeing the apparently supernatural work of a senseless mollusc, would lift their hands in awe, and utter an exclamation which would be an equivalent of the Moslem "Allah is great!" The little figures are slipped carefully below the mantle of the oyster, and the process of deposition described before covers them with nacre. The whole subject of the artificial production of such pearly bodies will be discussed in a subsequent chapter.

If this system of burying Pearls be understood, the art of "peeling Pearls" in order to get rid of the incomplete layers of shell, or to deprive the Pearl of one of its own delicate layers, in the hope of finding the subjacent layer more perfect, may readily be understood. Both Chinamen and Sooloo men resort to it frequently, and become great adepts in the art. In Europe too, it is successfully carried on, and Western Australia can boast of some skilful workers. The term by which this delicate operation is known in that colony, has probably been derived from the convicts. This process of "faking" a Pearl however, is an art possessed only by a few individuals, combining great skill with patience. The best "faker" in the fleet is Duncan McRae, the owner of the "Dawn," a man of splendid physique, the boldest and most successful pearler, and the fortunate discoverer of the wealth of Roebuck Bay. At this delicate work the leisure hours of this horny-handed son of toil are passed—a very sharp knife, various sorts of files, some pearl powder, and a piece of leather being the only articles employed. Chinamen, however, use a certain kind of leaf to obtain the final polish. The shelly coatings over a buried Pearl are very hard, and must be cut off piece by piece, except at the lowest point, where the loose Pearl originally made contact with the shell after its escape from the oyster: at this point the layer of shell below comes away quite freely. The sense of touch conveyed by the blade of the knife is of equal, if not greater service to the operator, than his sense of sight.

The value of a Pearl depends upon its size, shape, colour, brightness, and freedom from defects,

The most valuable Pearls are those which are perfectly round ; the *bouton* or button-shaped Pearl
ranks next, and then comes the drop or pear-shaped
Pearl. Perfectly round Pearls over 25 grains in
weight, are extremely scarce, and secure high prices.
They are greatly sought after to form the centre of
necklaces, and large Pearls of this character are
safe, and very profitable investments. New discoveries of diamond-fields have before now so
largely increased the supply of diamonds, that
these gems are by no means steady in price. Other
discoveries may again cause a fall in value ; but the
source of supply of Pearls is far more closely sealed,
and the difficulties attendant upon the prosecution
of Pearl-fishing are as great as its disappointments,
risks, and uncertain character, are deterrent to the
would-be explorer. There is, indeed, no prospect of
Pearl-fishing being increased to any great extent,
nor are the habits of the Mother-of-Pearl oysters
likely to alter and render the formation of fine
Pearls a less rare occurrence.

The finest Pearl that has been seen for years
in England, was taken by Mr. Streeter's fleet, having
been found by the late Capt. Chippindall, of the
Schooner "Sree Pas Sair," on December 26th,
1884, off the North West coast of Australia. It
weighed 40 grains, was absolutely round, and was

perfect in quality. The shell in which it was found was only knee deep in water, and the Pearl is probably the finest which the Australian fisheries have hitherto produced.

The following instances of the development of blisters, will assist the reader in the study of the growth of shell and Pearls. In 1883, a young shell not one third the average weight and size, was found with two blisters within. In each of these a small stone was seen uncovered in part, and the rest thinly covered over with a pearly film, the stones being plainly discernible on all sides.

In another shell a blister was found more than one inch in height from the plane of the shell. This blister was full of black mud, and the pearly covering was not more than $\frac{1}{30}$th part of an inch in thickness.

In 1882, on board the "Dawn," a small protuberance was noticed in a shell on the point of the inside part of the hinge. A little of the outside surface of the shell was scraped away, and the round surface of a large shell was discovered; the hinge of the shell was then cracked with a hammer and chisel, and eventually a very fine coloured and fairly-shaped Pearl weighing 80 grains was extracted.

In 1883, on board the same ship, another

similar protuberance in the same position was noticed. Again the cold chisel was resorted to, and again a large Pearl was found. This time, however, although perfectly round and the size of a large solitaire marble, it had come within reach of the advancing decay of the shell ; one third of an inch was rotten, and after its weight was reduced from 84 to 45 grains, a round slate coloured Pearl was obtained, but of little value. A year previously this Pearl might probably have been found perfect, and have been worth say from £2000 to £3000. It is worthy of remark that when decay reaches the lower point of an embedded Pearl, it spreads upwards around the Pearl, aided apparently by the upward tendency of the layers of the blister, and eats into it, at an almost equal rate all round.

In 1882 the "Harriet" was fortunate enough to find a Pearl, weighing 103 grains, within an enormous blister. It was a beautiful bouton, of fine colour on the top, but somewhat chalky beneath, owing to the contact of salt water admitted by a "borer," that had chanced to pierce the shell just at this spot, and had penetrated nearly $\frac{1}{4}$ of an inch into the Pearl.

In 1885, the "Ivy" found a Pearl in the lips of a small-sized shell, whilst fishing in Exmouth Gulf.

This Pearl was faultless in colour and weighed 104
grains, but its shape was that of an equilateral
triangle ; each point being beautifully rounded off.
Although its value was comparatively small, yet
it was a great curiosity to the student of Pearl-growth.
The symmetry was in every way perfect, but unfortunately it was badly damaged by the knife used in
opening the shell. This remarkable Pearl was exhibited at the Colonial Exhibition of 1886.

The varying tints and colours of Pearls are less
difficult to understand than some of their eccentri-
cities of growth. The changing condition of the
sea, both as regards purity and temperature, the
health of the oyster, accidents such as the discharge
of the inky fluid of the cuttle fish in the neighbourhood of the oyster, all will probably affect the
colours of the successive growth periods of the Pearl.

Pearls when of extraordinary beauty, size, or
brilliancy will sell for sums which appear extravagant
in proportion to what is given for ordinary specimens.
The reason for this is obvious, for no sooner is one
of surpassing beauty in the market than it is removed from the common category, and the price
will depend more upon the fancy of the purchaser
than any system of valuation.

It appears that the various forms presented

by Pearls had attracted the notice of the ancient Romans and led to a systematic nomenclature. The *Unio* was the name of the globular Pearl; the *tympania* of the hemi-spherical; the *elenchus* of the pear-shaped ; and the *margaritum* of the irregular or baroque Pearl.

The baroque Pearls often assume very whimsical forms, and advantage has sometimes been taken of this fact by mounting the warty Pearls as grotesque ornaments. Dinglinger, the court jeweller at Dresden in the latter part of the seventeenth century, was famous for his ingenuity in this direction, and some beautiful specimens of Pearl mounted in gold and enamel may be seen in the Jewel Room of the Green Vaults at Dresden.

The chemical composition of the Pearl as previously stated is carbonate of lime associated with a small proportion of organic matter: it is easily affected. by acids and fœtid gases, and may be calcined on exposure to heat. It possesses a lustre peculiar to itself which is known as the "orient." Its specific gravity is 2.5 to 2.7, those found on the coast of South America, termed Panama Pearls, being somewhat denser than the Oriental Pearls.

The beauty and value of Pearls depend on their

form, colour, texture (technically called "skin") and lustre. A Pearl to be perfect must possess the following qualifications :—

    I. It must be perfectly spherical, seeming as if it had been artificially fashioned or turned into shape.

    II. It must have a perfectly pure white colour ; (but in India and China the bright yellow colour is preferred).

    III. It must be slightly transparent.

    IV. It must be free from specks, spots, or blemish.

    V. It must possess the peculiar lustre, or "orient," characteristic of the gem.

CHAPTER VII.

THE SOOLOO ARCHIPELAGO.

" Pearls and gems of lustre bright,
All sleep beneath the wave."
Barton.

THE islands constituting the "Sooloo
Archipelago," whence the greater number of the finest round Pearls are
derived, lie on the north side of Borneo, between
the parallels of 4° 40' and 6 50' north latitude ; and
the meridians of 119° 20' and 122° 20' east longitude.
The group consists of nearly 150 islands, extending
to within 40 miles of the Bornean coast; but
geographically and geologically they belong to the
fertile chain of the Philippines, rather than to the
dismal forest-clad island of Borneo.

The appearance of the Sooloo Islands from sea-
wards is extremely beautiful; there are several

extinct volcanoes of considerable height, and the
very extensive clearings which have been made for
the cultivation of hill-paddy (rice), give a charming
park-like appearance to the landscape.

The soil is of the richest volcanic nature, and
here the delicate cacao tree (*Theobroma Cacao*)
flourishes, undisturbed by the devastating hurricanes
and volcanic eruptions, that from time to time
spread such disaster in the Phillipines and in
Java.

At Maimbung, the native capital, the Sultan
of Sooloo resides, but his authority over the people
is very slight. He claims sovereignty over and
receives tribute from, the islands of Palawan and
Balabac ; but his rights over Sabah, a large territory
in North Borneo, have been ceded to the British
North Borneo Company for the trivial sum of
5,000 dollars per annum, including his share in the
birds'-nest caves. This is considerably less than his
original income from the territory, and there is but
little doubt that when this concession was granted
the Sultan fully expected to receive help from the
English nation to rid himself of his enemies, the
Spaniards. The presence of the Governor of the
British Colony of Labuan at Maimbung during the
negociation of the concession, would naturally

heighten this impression, but the expectation was doomed to disappointment.

For many years a weary diplomatic correspondence has been going on upon the subject of the Sooloo Archipelago. Spain has expended much money, and lost many of her sons in attempting to reduce the Sooloo Sultan to a state of vassalage, and for years a desultory kind of warfare has been prosecuted. This was originally occasioned by the necessity of putting an end to the frequent piratical attacks of the Sooloo slave-praus upon the comparatively defenceless natives of islands under the Spanish rule. England, however, persistently refused to recognise the Spanish claim of sovereignty over the group, and certain high-handed measures on the part of the Spanish authorities against various English and German merchant vessels brought about the Protocol of 1877, by which Germany and England secured freedom of trade in Sooloo; and on this point Spain has more than fulfilled her obligations. In 1878, Spain at length forced the Sultan to sign the "Capitulation," constituting himself a subject of Spain. For this he receives an annual pension of 2,400 dollars, and by virtue of this treaty, Spain not only reiterated her claim of sovereignty over the Sooloo Archipelago, but also over the Sabah territory, ceded to the British North

I

Borneo Company. It is only within the last year or two that Spain has renounced this latter claim, and England and Germany have formally recognised the sovereign rights of Spain in Sooloo, a certain freedom of trade being, however, provided for.

The Spaniards have a walled settlement on the north side of the island of Sooloo, called Jolo or Tiangi. It is situated on a swamp, that causes great mortality in the town. There is a garrison of 800 soldiers, besides a large number of convicts from the Philippines, and the Spanish officers serving there receive extra pay, as if on active service. There are three other Spanish occupations in the Archipelago, all of the very smallest dimensions, but sufficient for the purpose. Several gun-boats are also kept there.

Up to the present time, but little or no intercourse has taken place between the natives and the alien race. The few opportunities of conciliation, such as the famine of 1879, and the outbreak of cholera in 1882, have been allowed by the Spaniards to slip by neglected, and a bitter hatred now exists against them, which will probably never be thoroughly overcome. This is exhibited occasionally in savage, bloodthirsty outrages, which — however they may be condemned by Europeans — will always be regarded by this fanatical Sooloo race as noble acts of patriotism.

Physically the natives are far superior to the ordinary Malay type, and the national character is a strange mixture of villainy and nobility; but the people must be long studied before the latter will become sufficiently evident to be appreciated. Even in these modern days, when the Malay Archipelago is traversed by innumerable merchant steamers, and real piracy may be said to have well-nigh disappeared, the Sooloo name is still regarded in the other islands as the synonym for cruelty, treachery and ferocity. In the days of the late Sir James Brooke, fleets of piratical praus were fitted out in Sooloo, and carried their depredations as far as Singapore and Bangkok on the one side, and New Guinea on the other. They spread devastation and misery wherever they went, and there is reason to believe they penetrated as far as Polynesia. Even at the present day every Sooloo man is a pirate at heart, and although steam and breech-loaders have compelled the adoption of a less violent means of livelihood, yet the character of the race is still unaltered. Murder, theft and violence are in Sooloo acts of everyday occurrence, whilst prevarication, and even a total disregard for truth are found in company with a grave, polite and dignified demeanour. The people are intelligent, independent, daring, and fairly moral in their lives. The means of livelihood are not hard to attain, and the struggle for existence being thus light, the Sooloos live a free and happy life ; indeed, the dull understanding and the mental vacancy of our Western peasant are conspicuous by their absence.

The Sooloo nation presents the interesting picture of an old civilization, the product of the Mussulman faith, struggling against the inroad of the innovations of Western civilization. Doubtless the influx of strangers would enrich the Sultan and the Sooloo aristocracy ; but the people generally would not be benefited by it, but rather the reverse ; they are wise enough to see this, and to be contented to live the life of their fathers.

Famines and epidemics might be averted or mitigated by Europeans, but these are only temporary misfortunes, and tend to keep up the standard of the race, by weeding out the weaker individuals. On the other hand, the vices of the West would take root, and multiply rapidly on what is, to our minds, very rank soil, and the evil would far outweigh any benefits. At present the chiefs take good care to relieve a man of any superabundant wealth, and the consequence is, there is no great ambition to amass it. Polygamy and slavery, the accompaniments of the Mohammedan faith, flourish in Sooloo.

In Sooloo a man hardly understands what it is to work for wages; he is somewhat ashamed to let himself out. There must, however, be hewers of wood and carriers of water, whether they be slaves who are a part of a man's establishment, and who identify his interests with their own, or servants earning a poor pittance, with far harder work, and liable to be cast adrift on a pitiless world. There are exceptional cases in which a slave meets with a hard master, but generally speaking, the slaves are fairly happy, well treated, and not over-worked. They live on the same food as their masters, and the wife they wish for is generally obtained for them, but their children are also slaves. Some men are born slaves, others are stolen into captivity, others are slaves from debt, and lastly there are certain men who admit their liability to servitude under the sons of their father's masters, but they are never called upon to render service, and are practically free agents.

Divers will occasionally sell for as much as

100 dollars, but ordinary lads and men are worth 40 to 60 dollars, whilst girls vary from 50 to 100 dollars, according to age and beauty.

The Sooloo language is a difficult one, and there are not a dozen Europeans who can speak it. Mr. Haynes, who has lived for several years in the group, has framed an extensive dictionary, and he finds a far greater resemblance between the Sooloo and Fijian tongues, than between the Fijian and the other Malay languages. Whether the migration has in former ages flowed from Polynesia westwards or whether the current took an easterly direction from Malayan countries, will probably never be known ; but there is a very close resemblance to be found in the words expressing the numerals, and those elements and natural phenomena which are everywhere the earliest and simplest forms of speech.

In the formation of verbs also there is a remarkable similarity, the Fijian prefix *vaka* being closely akin to the invariable Sooloo prefix *mak.*

The Fijian language may be said to abound in dental consonants and final vowels, whereas the Sooloo native, with his mouth full of betel nut and sirih, delights in labial and guttural consonants, eschewing dental sounds to a great extent.

It is notable that the Sooloo people have preserved the tradition of Sarah and Abraham, as recorded on pp. 32, 33.

The commerce of the group of Sooloo Islands is carried on through the medium of Chinese traders who exchange Manchester goods, opium, tobacco and other articles for Pearls and Pearl-shell, sharks' fins, bêche-de-mer and native-manufactured cordage. Of these articles Pearl-shell forms by far the largest proportion of the trade, and is sold in London as "Manila" shell.

Pearls also find their way out of the country, but to a great extent by stealth, as it is as much as a man's head is worth to sell any Pearl over a certain size, these being the Sultan's perquisites. The Pearls from Sooloo have ever been renowned as being the finest in the world, and may be said to be found in very "high bred" shells, in deep, clear and rapid tide-ways.

When the father of the present Sultan died in 1879, he left a box full of Pearls of large size and fine quality. At his death the contents of this box met with foul play; a portion of these

Pearls remained in the possession of his son and successor the late Sultan Buderoodin, who died in March, 1884, and these were sold by him in 1882, to defray expenses on his trip to Mecca. His mother, who is still living (1886) and is the most influential personage in the country, retains a number of these Pearls, and can with difficulty be persuaded to show any of them.

Whenever she is induced to offer a Pearl for sale—a most unusual event—she sets a higher price on it than it would be worth in London, and she abates but very little from it. She does not wish to sell at all and always remarks "Why should I sell my Pearls? if the Spaniards come to attack us I can put my Pearls into my handkerchief and go into the hills, but if I have dollars I should need a number of men to carry them." Where the stolen portion of the box went, still remains a mystery.

The native population of Sooloo may be divided into two classes—the hillmen (*tan gimba*) the tillers of the soil, and the coast people (*tan Bajan*) the toilers of the sea. The former cultivate rice, tapioca and other food plants, and breed horses, cattle and water-buffaloes. There are twenty varieties of rice from the island of Sooloo now at the Royal Botanic

Gardens, Kew, including black, red and green rice
and bearded paddy ; yet these do not exhaust the
varieties existing in Sooloo.

But it is with the Bajans who reap the harvest
of the sea that our subject lies. During the months
of January, February, and March, when the North-
east monsoon is at its strongest, there is but little
done by these people, except perhaps shark-fishing
under the lee of the southern islands of the group,
But from April to December, Pearl-shell fishing
goes on more or less uninterruptedly.

The boats used for this purpose are handsome
well-built little canoes with fine lines, and they are
capable of standing considerable weather. A double
outrigger of bamboo is used, and the usual Malay
triangle mast, so admirably adapted for small boats.
The sail is of grass matting, and the ropes are made
from the true Manila hemp grown in Sooloo. Mats
are spread over the canoe during the heat of the
day, and under these the occupants rest at their
ease. In such boats the Bajans or "sea-gipsies"
live with wife and children for months at a time,
wandering about and living on the produce of the
sea.

Pearl shell is obtained in three different ways,
the natives of various places working according to

local custom. The Sooloo and Tawi-Tawi men are
principally divers, those from the town of Parang
and the little island of Secubun, especially attaining
great depths. By dint of practice from childhood,
by hereditary gift, and by means of a naturally
fine physique, the Sooloo natives can show as fine
divers as any in the world. They dive head first,
invariably without any artificial assistance whatever;
and the average time they remain below the surface
is from a minute to eighty seconds; but there is
European evidence that on one occasion a dive lasted
as long as 180 beats of the pulse, which may roughly
be called two and a half minutes. The greatest
depths that Mr. Haynes has seen accomplished is
seventeen and a half fathoms (105 feet) and the
same man did fifteen and a half fathoms in the
presence of the captain and officers of H.M.S.
" *Champion.*" On that day he failed to reach
bottom at nineteen fathoms, but he was considerably
past his prime in years, and was alone. In descending
these great depths the men are afraid of sharks,
unless four or five divers go down together. But
there is little doubt that there are divers in Sooloo
who can do their twenty fathoms and even more.
A report has been published lately by the French
Government on the Tahitian Pearl fishing, in which
it is stated that the natives there can accomplish
thirty fathoms. This is probably an exaggeration

on their part; in the same way a Sooloo man will
say he can do thirty fathoms; and when challenged
as to the possibility of such a statement, replies
" Well, I can do fifteen fathoms down and fifteen
up again. Is not that thirty ? "

The Sooloo Pearl-shell banks are worked by
natives of Sooloo only, and there is no European
engaged or even interested in the industry. There
is very litttle shell in Sooloo waters under nine
fathoms, but this is not of much consequence to
the divers, as they seldom make more than fifteen
dives in the course of a morning. On good ground
a fair diver can obtain enough shell in five or six
dives to support himself and his family for a month,
and for the rest of the month he generally leads an
idle life. Slaves have to go out more frequently and
dive oftener, but even their day's work is far less
than what a white man would expect from a man
to whom he paid wages.

Every shell is opened on being brought to the
surface, and the oyster, after being carefully searched
for Pearls, is placed in the sun to dry for food ;
a thin piece of bamboo, and not a knife, is used to
open the shell.

The loss of life from sharks is not great,

considering the large number of people who earn their living by diving. Nevertheless, accidents do occur every now and then.

A Pearl shell diver is called "*tan maksab*"; the act of diving being expressed by the word "*maklurop.*" A Pearl shell is called "*tipei*" and a Pearl "*muchia.*"

The second method of obtaining shell is by dredging for it (*makbajak*) as low as fifty fathoms. This dredge (*bajak*) of which a sketch is here given

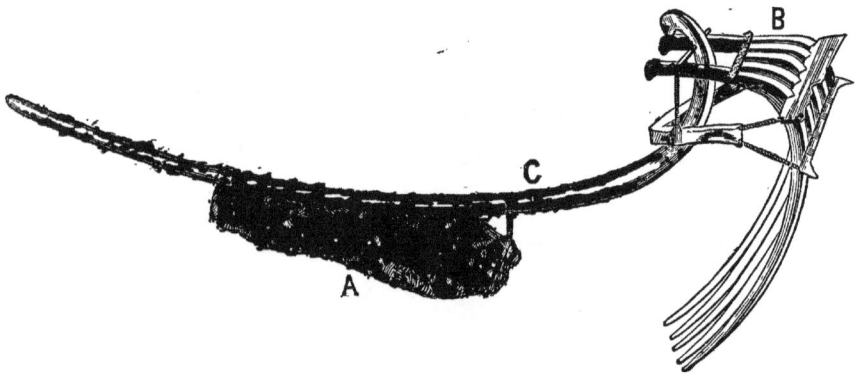

FIG. 9.—DREDGE FOR PEARL OYSTERS.

(Fig. 9.) is beautifully constructed of heavy sinking wood, the parts being bound together with rattan; and two heavy stones are used for sinkers. It is admirably designed and adapted to its purpose. It consists of five curved teeth spreading outwards, the extreme width covered by the points being about 1 foot, 8 inches; a rattan rope is used to drag the dredge along, and is attached to what may be termed the handle at each end of the stone A, (*See Fig.* 9) a second line being made fast to the upper part of the rake, where another but smaller stone is attached, and by the second line the "*bajak*" is carefully lowered to the bottom. This line is left adrift and is used to detach the rake from any impediment that it may foul in its course. The long rattan rope is made fast with a bridle to each end of the canoe, which, drifting 'thwartships in the strong tideway, drags the dredge slowly along, resting not on the points of the teeth, but on the curve of the rake, so that the points are free in an almost horizontal position. On their entering the gaping shell, the oyster instantly closes tightly on the intruder, and effects its own capture.

The inhabitants of Siassi, Tapul and Lamenusa adopt this plan of deep dredging.

The third method is expressed by the word "*tong tong*" and consists of peering down into the clear water under the shadow of the universal broad brimmed leaf hat. The shell when distinguished is carefully scooped up by the "*bajak*." Certain men in each town are particularly proficient in this test of the eyes, and the bottom can often be seen at a depth of thirteen fathoms.

Throughout the Sooloo Archipelago the tides

are very strong, and at spring tides the tide rips in certain places must be carefully avoided. The flood flows for two hours after it is high water and the ebb continues to run a similar length of time after the water commences rising again. It is the sweeping tides and the vast amount of living reef that make the Sooloo waters so favourable for the growth of the Mother-of-Pearl oyster; and the prosecution of the fishing amongst the turbulent waters of their island homes, developes the Sooloo lads into bold and enterprising sailors.

The plate opposite represents the head-quarters of the author's exploring party at Lamenusa. It was built on the edge of a reef about 200 yards from the shore, beautifully sheltered by neighbouring reefs from the swells of the ocean. At high tide there was six feet of water under the house, so that boats and a steam launch could come alongside. This house was wantonly pillaged and wrecked during its owner's absence in March, 1884, at the time of the civil war which broke out after the death of the late Sultan. The town of Lamenusa, which contained fully 2000 inhabitants, has been entirely destroyed, the people being killed, dispersed, and many of them sold into slavery. No roof has been left, and where the merry voices of scores of Bajan children at play used to echo from

MR. STREETER'S HOUSES IN LAMENUSA HARBOUR. ISLAND OF SIASSI SOOLOO ARCHIPELAGO.

DESTROYED BY THE SPANIARDS IN 1884

morning to night, silence and desolation now reign supreme.

Twice a month small steamers belonging, to Chinese merchants at. Singapore, call at Jolo and Maimbung to deliver goods, and take away the shell and other produce to Singapore. These steamers fly the English ensign, and are officered by Englishmen; but the business of the ship and cargo is managed entirely by Chinamen.

There is one other European living in Sooloo outside the Spanish walls, Captain H. Schück, a German, who has traded for many years there, and now devotes his energies to planting cacao. Twice a year a German man-of-war visits Sooloo on his behalf, and many English officers and other visitors still retain a lively recollection of the hospitality of this patriarchal establishment..

CHAPTER VIII.

NORTH-WEST AUSTRALIAN FISHERY.

" What hids't thou in thy treasure-caves and cells,
    Thou hollow-sounding and mysterious Main ?
 Pale glistening *Pearls*, and rainbow-coloured shells,
    Bright things that gleam unrecked of and in vain."
                                    —*Hemans.*

PEARL-SHELLING was commenced on this coast in 1868, and in spite of its natural difficulties and the great fall in the price of Pearl-shells, the industry has, up to the present time, been actively and prosperously maintained. It commenced in a modest way; the shells being simply picked up at low water on reefs almost dry for two hours in the day, but covered by from three to five fathoms of water at high tide. As these "dry shells" became exhausted, small boats and dingies were introduced, each boat with a white man and six to eight natives, diving in one or two fathoms of water, wherever they could see the shells. These shallow waters in turn became exhausted, and the boats were increased in size to five or six tons; such boats were capable of shifting from one ground to another, but always kept within a short distance of the shore. At the present day there is a large fleet of cutters and schooners, varying between 25 and 80 tons, with three to six dingies each, working almost out of sight of land, and several hundred miles away from any settlement.

The whole northern coast of Australia, from Cape York to the North-west Cape, a distance of 2000 miles, is the habitat of the Mother-of-Pearl oyster. Immense quantities of shell have, it is true, been taken in Torres Straits, but there the conditions of working are far easier than in the North-west, where hurricanes and six months cold weather, deter any but men of a very adventurous and hardy character from embarking in the industry.

The West Australian grounds extend from Exmouth Gulf eastwards as far as King's Sound; beyond these limits the boats have seldom gone. Roebuck Bay alone has in two seasons yielded as much as 440 tons of shell. The head-quarters of the pearling fleet are at Cossack, a township

K

which, until lately, consisted of about twenty wooden buildings on the bank of a creek; but the recent discovery of the Kimberley gold fields has led to its rapid development. Cossack, otherwise known as Tien Sin, and Port Walcot, is situated in 21° 41′ S. lat., and 117° 08′ E. long. It is the port for Roebourne, ·eight miles inland, and the capital of the North-west, with which it is now connected by a tram line.

The immediate surroundings of both Cossack and Roebourne were, until this year, most dismal. With the exception of a few scanty, hurricane-torn mangroves ·in the creek, neither tree nor blade of grass is to been seen. There are, however, a number of thriving sheep stations not many miles distant.

The coast is regularly visited by severe hurricanes — revolving storms, known elsewhere as cyclones or typhoons. In March, 1882, both Cossack and Roebourne were literally levelled to the ground in the course of a few hours. The hurricane months are from December to March inclusive, and every year several Pearling craft are damaged, if not totally lost. The rise and fall of tide varies on this coast from 18 to 40 feet.

Cossack Creek, which is almost dry at low

water, affords a suitable place for the repair of boats, and most of the Pearling-fleet are laid up here from April to October. During these months the temperature of the water and atmosphere is so low, that naked diving cannot be carried on, and thus these fine calm months of easterly weather are lost to all but a few, who are now beginning to use European diving apparatus, the author having been the first to use them on a large scale.

The "Pearlers" or "Nor-Westers" as they are usually styled, generally combine sheep farming with Pearling, thus employing the divers on the station during the cold season. A finer but rougher set of men it would be hard to find. They are the product of a hard and dangerous but healthy life; and there is amongst them an unwritten code of honour that is seldom broken, and is indeed, more strictly observed than the rules which receive tacit consent but sparse observance, in more refined circles. Removed from the amenities and restraints of more civilised life, it is not to be wondered at that drinking, gambling and fighting are favourite recreations of this bronzed and stalwart class, but their fighting is carried on in true English fashion, and the effects are transient and harmless.

These men are clannish to a degree, and a new arrival is not unfrequently made the subject of rough practical jokes, and horse-play, if he adopts a more civilised garb and demeanour than his new companions.

Let us here narrate the most favourable introduction a new-comer could receive. As soon as the anchor is let go, several of the pearlers come up the side of the vessel and introduce themselves; this is the signal for imbibing refreshment, and as soon as the meagre scraps of Fremantle news have been exchanged, all repair to the wooden drinking shanty or inn on shore. " Let me introduce you," said one of them (a man of fine powerful figure and healthy face) " to the White Hart Hotel of Cossack : this is Frank Craig, our landlord, and here" (pointing to various slumbering forms lying about the house) " are the pearlers in their usual state."

The Government regulations for the prosecution of the industry, are superintended by a magistrate residing at Roebourne; he issues licenses to the vessels, and every Australian diver employed in the fleet has to be passed by him. There is also an inspector of " Pearl-shell fisheries " who besides being a professional sailor, is in the commission of the peace. He has a small schooner, and visits the fleet at work, in order to see that the regulations are complied with, and he adjudicates on the spot. This post requires great tact and ability, and the Western Australian Government may be congratulated upon the selections they have made to fill it. The cost of a pearling licence is nominal, but the colony derives considerable revenue from an export duty of £4 per ton on the shell raised. This system works satisfactorily on both sides, except in one respect. When the licence is issued, the magistrate retains the ship's papers until the end of the season, and the return of the ship, as security for the due payment of the duty on the shells. In the case of vessels working Australian aborigines for divers this is reasonable, but in the case of those who, like ourselves, employ Malay divers from the Dutch islands, it works badly, especially if, as is often the case, "beri-beri" breaks out amongst the divers: should the ship for instance, be working in Roebuck Bay, instead of being able to sail at once for Kœpang to return the men to their homes, she must first go to Cossack to pay the duty, and obtain possession of her papers before she can sail for a foreign port. This involves an extra distance of about 700 miles, besides the delay in Cossack, and if, as is often the case, baffling winds or calms are met with, many valuable lives are lost, and the employer has to pay wages and keep the men during the extra time. He is already under a heavy guarantee to

the Dutch government to return the divers, and
pay their wages punctually. A banker's guarantee
has been offered to the Australian government for
the due payment of the duty in order to retain
possession of the ship's papers, but the dispensation
has been denied.

The crews of all the vessels, except in the case
of the "Sree Pas Sair," and her fleet, consist of the
owners and other white men who work as dingy
hands, each dingy carrying six to eight divers,
either Australian aborigines, or Malays. The vessels
anchor near together, often ten or fifteen miles
from the land, and are left during the day with
only the cook on board, or sometimes entirely
deserted, dipping bows under in the rough sea.

At dawn the men are astir, and by 6. a.m., the
shells that were obtained the previous day are all
scraped, opened, and stowed away. Then comes
breakfast, which consists of salt beef and bread,
varied occasionally by fish, dugong, or turtle ;
perhaps the gristly part of the oyster is discussed.
Eight hours' diving is allowed ; and these hours vary
between 7. a.m. and 6. p.m., according to the state
of the tide. On their return to the vessel, the shell
is taken out of the dingies, and each man's "tally"
being taken down in a book, the dingies are cleaned
out and made fast for the night. Dinner of the

same character as the breakfast is then served, and all hands lie down to sleep until dawn. Diving on Sunday is strictly prohibited, and indeed the seventh day's rest is amply earned and needed.

The method of working the dingies is as follows: the white man stands on the after 'thwart with an oar over the stern, and sculls the dingy against the tide; the divers all go down together, partly for the sake of frightening any sharks that may chance to be below, and partly that the bottom may be more systematically examined. During the time the men are below, the white man must scull against the wind, so that his men may come up near to the boat, and his task is regulated by the force of the wind. The divers swim to the boat and clamber into it to rest, each man's shells being stowed separately. The white man continues sculling against the tide to prevent his drifting away from the ship too rapidly. If a dive is unusually productive a buoy is thrown out and the dingy is sculled up to the same spot again. This soon attracts the other boats, and as soon as shells get scarce, the buoy is taken in and the dingy allowed to drift slowly over the ground. At times these little boats are more than six miles away from their vessels, and then the oars or paddles are got out, and in case of a sudden squall coming on, the divers pull the boat back to the vessel. These squalls are known

locally as "cock-eyed bobs;" they come off the
shore and last from half an hour to four hours. The
wind, heated by passing over the scorched plains, is
very trying, parching the skin and burning the
nostrils; this wind is very furious, and the vessels
at anchor, even with top masts on deck, heel over
as far as scuppers under before they can swing to
it. In one squall in Roebuck Bay nine anchors
were lost, and various quantities of chain, most of
the dingies being miles away from their ships at
the time; whilst two vessels were cruising about
close reefed, having lost both anchors, and waiting
for the squall to pass to borrow others.

On average ground, a diver does a fair day's
work if he finds one "pair" of shells in eight dives,
but two or three pairs are frequently brought up
at once, and even five, the man carrying two in
each hand and one under his arm. His daily "take"
averages from ten to twenty five pairs, but a diver
has been known to get one hundred in a single
day. In the "Dawn" in 1882, the best day's take
was 2,320 pairs to 37 men; and in 1883, the highest
tally was 840 pairs to 42 men on the same ground;
350 pairs being the lowest. This plainly shows the
exhausting effect of a season's fishing.

From December to March the sea is rough,
and the white man's task of sculling the dingy all

day under a tropical sun, wet with salt water and occasional rain, is no light one. When the weather is exceptionally bad and the barometer lower than usual, the anchors are hove up and the fleet scatters for shelter within the numerous mangrove creeks on the coast. There the vessels lie, two or three in company for weeks together, dry at low water, and swarming with flies and mosquitoes; the white men meantime, having nothing to do until the weather moderates, but to gamble and compare Pearls. It is particularly noticeable, how even the yield of shell continues on this coast; the only bad bottom is mud or sand. The state of the tides and weather, and consequent thickness or clearness of the water, affects the yield as much as the locality.

In the evening the men who have worked badly, have to scrape the dirt, coral cups, and other submarine growth off the shells and wash them, stacking them in heaps on the deck. In the morning the white men open them with a knife, holding the shell with the hinge on the deck and taking care not to scratch any Pearl that may be within. Immediately the muscle of the oyster is severed, the shells spontaneously spring open, and the oyster is cut away from the shell as cleanly as possible. Any good Pearl is usually seen at once, but a smart little boy generally sits alongside each opener

whose duty it is to take the oyster in his fingers
and carefully feel all over it for the small Pearls.
These he places in a small shell, and very few
ever escape these sharp little fellows.

When all are opened, the empty shells are
stacked so that the sun and wind may dry the
hinges, which after seven or eight hours are brittle
enough to be broken without injuring the shells.
The shell is then stacked in bulk in the hold, or
packed away in hogsheads for export. This operation is one in which the pearler takes considerable
pride. A well-packed hogshead weighs between
5 and 6 cwt. The Pearls are handed over to the
"boss" of the vessel, who washes them clean, and
puts them away—the good ones into his cash-box,
and the common ones into a pickle bottle. Every
day a few Pearls are found, but it is rarely that
anything of much value is discovered. Men have
opened over 5,000 pairs, and never found a Pearl
worth £5. The yield of Pearls in shells taken west
of Cossack, is far larger than in those from the
Eastern grounds; the usual proportion in value of
shells and Pearls taken West being 3 to 1, whereas
East it is only 5 to 1: that is to say the Pearls
found in £5,000 worth of shell will average about
£1000.

West of Cossack shells are scarcer than to the

eastward, and hurricanes are more frequent, but there is better shelter, and fresh water is more easily obtained.

The loss of life and material from hurricanes has been very great. When a vessel has succeeded in entering a creek, she is beached as high up as possible, and moored as securely as can be in the most sheltered spot. If the hurricane actually comes on, it is best to leave the ship and get up on the sand hills, as the tide rises considerably above high-water mark, and the low land is flooded : on these sand hills both white and black men are huddled together, but the exposure is very severe. The vessel will probably be driven inland some distance or lodged amongst the mangroves.

Sharks and porpoises are driven on shore and killed, and vessels that have not succeeded in entering a creek, are either totally lost, driven in shore, or scuttled in shallow water.

The greatest difficulty attending the successful prosecution of the West Australian fisheries is, as on all other grounds, the supply of divers. The usual plan in the North-west is to take up a tract of land for a sheep or a cattle station ; thus most of the Nor' Westers are styled in the official directory, " Pearlers and Graziers."

It may be of interest in this place to say

something about the natives of this part of Australia. These aborigines do not form distinct tribes, but are dispersed in families scattered over the face of the land, and they gain a precarious living by hunting. When, however, a white man takes up his hunting grounds, erects a house, digs wells and introduces stock, these people come in, and in return for a regular supply of flour and tobacco they undertake shepherding, and other light work, looking at the new arrival as their natural superior. The old men however are equally jealous of the exclusive possession of the women as of the flour, and they are only too glad to see the lads and young men go to dive for the white man ; the junior members of the community invariably obey the wishes of their seniors. Thus for six months the young men work as divers, and during the remainder of the year, they are taken care of on their stations, and become useful as shearers, etc., returning to diving at each successive season.

Although many of these aborigines, when first set to work, can neither swim nor dive, they soon become adepts in these arts, and after two seasons an Australian becomes a first-class diver. They enter the water feet first, turning so as to swim downwards; they do not attain such excessive depths as some other races, owing to the nature of the ground worked ; but for finding shell they cannot be beaten, whilst for powers of endurance an Australian native is unequalled in the world. Their struggle in endeavouring to gain a bare subsistence in this thirsty land, is most severe, and their endurance of thirst, their patience, and their tenacity of purpose are marvellous.

They are all passed before the magistrate at Roebourne every season, and he sees that each man is willing and physically fit for the work, and that at the end of the season he is returned to his home. The regulations providing for their food, clothes, and remuneration, are carried out fairly, although the latter is of far less importance to these men than the former. " Damper," or unleavened bread, forms the staple food of Australian divers, and they consume great quantities of it ; it is good food to work on—far better than rice—and fish, dugong, and turtle, serve as welcome additions. Their powers of sight are very keen ; when walking on a dry reef, they will follow a white man and pick up numbers of shells that he has passed over. It is a curious fact that a man who by some mischance has lost an eye, is always the sharpest in finding shell.

On some days the men are in good spirits, laughing and joking continually ; but at other times they are inclined to be sullen and morose and dive for hours without speaking a word ; indeed, the quantity of shell brought up varies greatly with the disposition prevailing among the men, the happy mood generally producing the best results. A kind of freemasonry exists between the men, and at times they agree amongst themselves not to bring up shell, although they are well aware that failure to do so, will not lesson the necessity of their pretending at least to seek for it, and at the same time will entail a loss of the small benefits that they receive for a successful day's work.

A notable instance of this fact occurred with the divers of four vessels. These men, although on what afterwards proved to be good ground, persisted for days in declaring they could find no shell. At length, the vessels left for other ground, and shortly after another craft with Malay divers came upon the vacated ground, and secured a large quantity of shell, that was found stacked in heaps at the bottom by the divers of the other vessels.

These aborigines possess fine constitutions, and contrasted with the natives to be seen in the southern parts of Australia, are of high physical development. There is but little sickness amongst them, but they are unrivalled adepts in simulating

illness, especially "fits" in the water. Fits do undoubtedly occur occasionally, but the vast majority
of the cases are feigned, probably not more than
two or three real ones occurring in the whole fleet
in the course of a season; and even in these cases,
the results do not appear to call for the alarm
which their occurrence causes. The power of imitation however, is so great, that the most experienced
pearler can never be absolutely sure of his judgment of a case.

Although sharks are very numerous, accidents
attributable to them are fortunately rare. The loss
of life from this cause is only from a half to one per
cent. in the season. Alligators are much more
dangerous, but they do not go far out to sea, and
are never found south of King's Sound.

The wholesome regulation against the supply
of spirits to the aborigines is doubtless of advantage
in keeping up the standard of the race, but nowhere
in the world is the "native policy" a more vexed
question than in Australia. In that Continent the
gradual extinction of the natives before the usurping
white race appears to be inevitable.

There is little to be said about the Malays that
are employed in the fishery; they are a tractable

set of men, quick to learn from a white man, and
pleasant to teach ; in diving, however, they are not
equal to the Australians, their powers of endurance
being far inferior.

In 1872, the " Australian Fishery Company "
was floated in London, and two fine yachts were
fitted out in England—the "Enchantress" and the
" Flower of Yarrow "—for the purpose of prosecuting
this industry on the North-west Coast. Ample
capital was available, but the venture proved disastrous. The promoter actually estimated in his
prospectus, that each diver could bring up a hundred
shells in an hour! and based his reduced estimate
upon a yield of eight tons of shell from each diver
in the season; as a matter of fact, 1¼ tons is the
highest that has ever been obtained, and that only
under extraordinarily favourable circumstances. The
whole proceeding was a fiasco, and ludicrous to
all, except the shareholders. The working expenses
alone would have eaten up all the profits, even if
a reasonable quantity had been obtained. The
" Enchantress" was lost and the "Flower of Yarrow"
was sold. She traded in the Malay Archipelago
for a number of years, running the Spanish blockade
in Sooloo several times, and up to the date of her
recent wreck was known as the handsomest and
fastest craft in the East. The promoters of the

scheme came to an untimely end in the wreck of the "Gothenburg."

Pearl fishing has perhaps about it a glamour of romance, but in order to bring about successful results, it requires, as much as any other industry, economy and experience. If ever there was an expedition fated to end in disaster it was this: roomy, even-keeled vessels are required, not beautiful yachts, and the failure may be said to have occurred in consequence of the expedition having been carried out in "white-kid-glove" fashion.

To the southward of the North-West Cape, the smaller Pearl-oyster (*Avicula* or *Meleagrina fucata*) is found in Shark's Bay. Here dredging is carried on, and the oysters are allowed to decompose, in order that the Pearls may be more easily secured. It is, however, an industry conducted only on a small scale; it is not very remunerative, and it presents no features of interest to the general reader.

From the following statistics of exports, which unfortunately are of necessity incomplete, we may trace the history of the Pearl-shell fishery in Western Australia so far as our data permit:

YEAR.	SHELLS, VALUE.	PEARLS, VALUE.
1862 ...	... £250 ...	... —
1869 ...	... 6,490 ...	... —
1872 ...	... £25,890 ...	... —
1873 ...	... 28,388 ...	... £6,000

L

Year.	Shells, Value.	Pearls, Value.
1874 ...	... 62,162 ...	... 12,000
1875 ...	... 64,642 ...	... 12,000
1876 ...	... 75,292 ...	... 8,000
1882 ...	... 28,440 ...	... 9,000
1883 ...	... 30,300 ...	... 6,000

In the season 1882—1883 there were employed in the Western-Australian fishery nineteen vessels, manned by 539 divers, who raised 250 tons of shell, showing an average of under half-a-ton per man.

In 1882, the Union Bank of Australia opened a branch at Cossack and Roebourne. Previously to this, the wants of the community were aided by the issue of rough promissory notes, by a store-keeper, for any sum between 6d. and £5, and the general acceptance of Dutch guilders as two shilling pieces. The manager of the bank and his assistant were brutally murdered at Roebourne in January, 1885. In 1884, a steamer began to ply regularly between Fremantle and Singapore, touching at Cossack, and in 1885 the telegraph line was extended 700 miles from Geraldston to Cossack, thus placing this lonely station within a few hours' communication with Europe. The recent development of Cossack, consequent on the discovery of gold in the Kimberley district, in the north of Western Australia, has already been mentioned.

It may not be out of place to remark that

Mr. E. T. Hardman, in his geological exploration of the Kimberley country, a year or two ago, detected gold for a distance of about 140 miles along the course of the Ord and Elvire rivers; this discovery led to the systematic working of the alluvial deposits, and several nuggets of considerable size, one weighing as much as 28 ozs., have been brought to light. Mr. Haynes, in a letter to the author, dated July 26, 1886, states that 3,000 people have already arrived at these gold-fields. On the 20th of August, the " Assam " left London, carrying on board an enterprising gentleman, who has gone out with the intention of building several towns on the north-west coast, to be connected by railways. The rapid influx of immigrants in the northern part of Western Australia, has caused Cossack to acquire an importance, which, a short time ago, would never have been anticipated.

CHAPTER IX.

TORRES STRAITS.

"The Diamond sleeps within the mine,
The Pearl beneath the water."

LTHOUGH this fishery has been of more importance than that of Western Australia, and has produced considerably more than double the quantity of shell, it is needless to describe it at great length, inasmuch as the Pearls which it yields are of very little value. Torres Straits are situated at the extreme North-Eastern corner of Australia, separating Cape York from New Guinea. This passage of water was discovered in 1605, by the Spanish navigator Torres, after whom it was named. It measures about eighty miles across, and is crowded with islands, shoals and reefs. At Thursday Island a Police Magistrate is stationed, and his main duty is to regulate the Pearl fishing and to collect the revenue therefrom.

The British India Mail Steamers from London to Brisbane call here fortnightly, besides other lines. Upon the islands, dotted about in the Straits, the various shelling stations are established. These consist of the manager's house, "shell" house, and other buildings devoted to the repair of boats, diving dresses and pumps.

The diving boats are fine little craft, of nine or ten tons, rigged with two standing lugs, and they carry six hands—the diver, the tender, and four pumpers. There are no Europeans in the boats, but coloured men of all sorts and conditions are to be found there.

The boats are provisioned for a fortnight, and go wherever the diver chooses. At the end of the fortnight the boats rendezvous at some spot agreed upon, to meet the tender from the station—either a cutter or small schooner—which takes over the shells and issues another fortnight's provisions. After a year's work the diver proceeds to Sydney

with often as much as £300, and usually spends
this large sum, and the proceeds of his bottle of
Pearls, in a few weeks of riotous living.

The owners of boats unfortunately have not
pulled together; they have bid one against another
for the services of the men who are able to use
the diving dress, and have now to pay them £10
per month wages, and as much as £40 bonus for
every ton of shell raised. The consequence is the
men are very independent, and the owners submit
to all their whims and vagaries. They refuse to have
a white man in their boats, so that they may secure
all the Pearls for themselves. The Pearls from
here are mostly *Baroque,* very few fine spherical
Pearls having been produced in the Torres Straits
fishery.

During the year 1883, 206 vessels were licensed,
employing about 1,500 men ; and 33 licenses were
granted for fishing stations. The yield of Pearl-
shell for that year, was 621 tons, being 207 tons
less than that of the previous year ; besides this,
118 tons of bêche-de-mer were exported. The total
revenue collected at Thursday Island for the year
was £10,412. The export from West Australia
seldom exceeds 250 tons for the six months' diving
season. The amount of capital in this industry is

less than in Torres Straits, but more white men find employment in the West.

The Torres Straits fishery dates back only to 1874. The boats work all the year round, and large profits have been made, but the ground is far more limited in extent than in the North-west Australian waters, and in the future the latter will be of far greater value. Indeed, this year (1886) all the boats have left Torres Straits to work on the north-western coast.

CHAPTER X.

PEARLING LIFE AT THE PRESENT DAY.

> " Ocean's gem the purest
> Of Nature's works! What days of weary journeyings,
> What sleepless nights, what toils on land and sea,
> Are borne by men to gain thee!"

THIS chapter is written in order to give our readers some little idea of an industry which is carried on in remote places, until recently out of the track of ordinary shipping, away from all centres of civilization, and under circumstances of no ordinary danger.

The finest and most complete pearling vessel afloat is the "Sree Pas-Sair," (" The Belle of Pas-Sair," a district in Borneo), a brigantine of 112 tons, bought and equipped by the late Mr. E. C. Chippindall, R.N., at the expense of the author

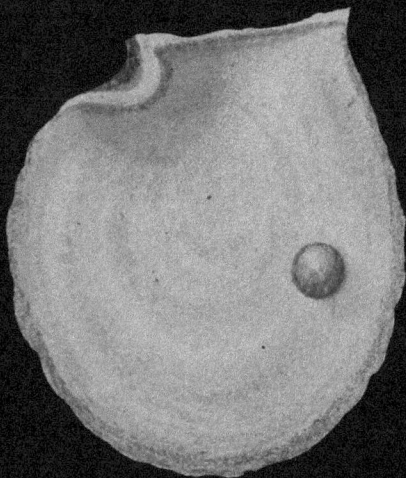

VALVE OF PEARL OYSTER *(Meleagrina Margaritifera)* WITH A PEARL.

of this work. She has large and comfortable accommodation, having a high poop. She carries eight dingies, each 14 ft. 6 in. in length, six being carried on davits, and two on deck ; and she draws 7 ft. 6 in. aft, and carries sufficient fresh water to last 80 men for three months.

We will first describe a prospecting cruise, and then return to an ordinary pearling cruise on old grounds.

In September, 1883, the " Sree Pas-Sair " left Singapore in charge of Mr. Chippindall, with a crew of Malay sailors, a Chinese carpenter, cook and " boy." In Sooloo seven men only were shipped, although sixty were required ; but these natives had never served a white man before, and were afraid to leave their country. The vessel then proceeded to the island of Solor, not far from Timor, and having recruited sixty-one Solorese divers, and signed them on before the Dutch Governor at Koepang, Mr. Chippindall sailed for the Australian coast, being accompanied by the late Mr. Harry E. Streeter, a son of the author. There was thus a total of seventy-eight men on board. Admiralty Gulf was visited, and thoroughly searched, but to no purpose ; and the vessel continued her course eastwards along the coast, prospecting all the way. At one place seven days were employed in collecting and curing the Chinese dainty, "bêche-de-mer" (*Holothuria*), this creature being discovered there in profusion. No natives were seen for the first two days, and drying sheds were erected on the beach. Suddenly, however, a body of natives appeared on the scene, and attacked the party in the open. The Solorese jumped into the sea, and swam off to the ship, leaving the white men and the dingy on the shore. As the spears were flying thickly, and sticking quivering in the sides of the dingy, the white men were forced to fire for their own protection. The natives soon made off, fortunately without loss of life on either side. Twice again that week attacks were made, and then to avoid bloodshed, the ship left. The remains of a Malay prau were seen here, the crew having been probably murdered by the natives.

The pearling vessel proceeding eastwards, prospecting all the unsurveyed coast up to Port Darwin, but found nothing until that port was reached. On the first day at Port Darwin, "shell" was struck close to the town, to the great excitement of all the inhabitants, the good news being telegraphed all over Australia. As soon as shell began to get scarce in the shallow water, Mr. Chippindall decided to prospect outside; but the easterly monsoon setting in, he stretched across to the Aru Islands,

on his way to New Guinea. Seven days were
spent at Dobbo, in Aru, and here a strange incident happened, worth mentioning. On attempting
to heave up the anchor, it was found to be foul;
on sending a man down to report (in 12½ fathoms),
it was discovered that the anchor had dropped into
a small hole in a rock, standing solitary on a smooth
bottom, and that the flukes were firmly fixed below
the overhanging edges. The following device was
resorted to in order to clear the anchor : a man
having gone down, and made fast a small line to
the fluke of the anchor in the hole, all chain was
veered out to ensure the safety of the ship ; four
candles of dynamite were bound together with a
fuse inserted, and attached to a thimble on the line.
The line was then held quite taut and vertical, the
fuse lit and the charge dropped, the line being
held until the charge was felt to have reached the
bottom. The dingy then paddled away from the
spot and the charge was exploded. The result was
that the anchor came up with a broken fluke, and
the rock was shattered to pieces.

On April 4th, when the New Guinea coast was
sighted, a Solorese diver was suddenly taken ill.
His pulse being very weak indeed, it was thought
that a spoonful of brandy might revive him, but on
its being given, the man died in less than a minute.

At New Guinea some chiefs came on board, and were entertained by the mate, whilst Mr. Chippindall pulled ashore some five miles off. Here his dingy was surrounded by hundreds of canoes with armed savages, but everything passed off well, probably owing to the fact that their own chiefs were on board, and might be looked upon as hostages.

On the 10th of April another diver died. On the following day very rich ground was found, and some enormous shells were raised. On the 12th of April the third man died, and Mr. Chippindall, judging from previous experience that more deaths would occur, determined to immediately send the men back to their homes. He therefore sailed that day. By the end of a fortnight the total number of deaths amounted to nine, and while in Port Darwin harbour, in four days five more died. Every effort was made to rouse the men and distract their attention, but it was useless; the ship was like a charnel house. Meanwhile the seven Sooloo men were looking on, and ridiculing the Solorese as cowards.

During the vessel's absence from Port Darwin, large numbers of boats had arrived from Torres Straits with diving dresses, and the harbour presented a most lively appearance. They did very well for a short time, but the South-Australian Government besides enforcing heavy license fees, offered no inducement to get the coast prospected, and at the present time there is not a single pearling boat left in the waters of the northern territory. The dream of wealth has vanished, and the golden goose is asleep, if not dead.

The fifteenth death occured on May 6th, on arrival at Koepang, where the Solor men were paid off. The last death happened very suddenly in the street, two hours after paying off. The loss in one month was thus sixteen out of the sixty-one men originally shipped from Solor.

The disease from which these men died is called *Beri-beri,* and it appears to be allied closely to dropsy; large numbers of sailors die of it yearly, and in the tin-mining districts of Perak, there are sometimes as many as 950 Chinamen in hospital at one time. Even the best qualified doctors are at a loss to determine its cause or its cure. Our own experience tends to point to the long-continued rice-diet as the cause, and the natives themselves are beginning to believe this.

In the " Sree Pas-Sair " the Solorese attributed the deaths to the coast of New Guinea " being unlucky," but the ship herself remains as popular as ever. The " Flowerdale," another pearling schooner,

has, however, not escaped so well. She lost 19 out of
72 Solorese during the same season, and the men assert
that she has a ghost on board, in the form of an old
sailor, with a white beard and a long knife,. This
ghost was supposed to live in the hold in the day
and go up aloft at night; and so great was the
fear produced, that men would only enter the hold
during the day in company with seven or eight
others, all joining hands. On suddenly waking at
night, the men would declare they saw the ghost
touching them with his knife; and screaming with
terror they would fall ill and die in a few hours.
The survivors were all in Koepang when the
"Sree Pas-Sair" returned; they had refused to
put a foot on board the haunted ship again, even
for the few hours' run across to their own homes,
and the "Sree Pas-Sair" therefore gave them all
a passage, eventually arriving in Singapore on the
20th June, and dropping anchor for the 152nd time
since she left in the previous September.

On the 1st of August, we again find the vessel
fitted out for a two years' voyage, and leaving
in charge of Mr. Haynes, bound for the Sooloo
Archipelago.

On the way up a dangerous shoal, with only
3½ fathoms of water, was found, in the Koti Passage of the Natuna group. This shoal has been

inserted in the latest Admiralty charts, under the name of " Haynes' Shoal." Another but less important reef was discovered the same week, to the southward of the North Luconia Shoals.

At Sooloo, the seven Sooloo men were gladly welcomed by their friends as returning heroes ; and after relating all the experiences of the late voyage, crowds of divers came forward eager to join. Fifty three men were engaged, including three of the old hands, and the ship sailed for Macassar and Australia.

It was interesting to observe the demeanour of these new men. They were proceeding to unknown lands, under the control of a white man, for the first time in their lives ; the ship was equally strange to them, and a superstitious feeling of approaching awe was aroused. In the Straits of Macassar, at night, the ship passed slowly close to a great mass of floating wood, probably some tree brought down by a river in Borneo. This tree had been taken possession of by sea-birds for a roosting-place, and being suddenly alarmed by the close approach of the ship, the birds took flight, flapping their wings, and running along the surface of the water, making considerable noise before they were fairly on the wing. The sleeping Sooloo men were aroused just in time to distinguish the black mass on the water, fading away into the darkness astern. This phenomenon effectually disposed of further sleep that night. In the morning several of the elder men came to their master, and gravely, and with timidity, enquired whether "that were Satan they saw last night!"

In Macassar, Mr. Chippindall again joined the ship, and took charge; he and Mr. Haynes proceeding to Australia, and the mate leaving the ship.

Cossack, the headquarters of the West Australian pearling fleet, was reached in due time. Here a new mate joined, and work was begun at the head of the Exmouth Gulf. From April to October it is fine, calm, clear water, but too cold for naked diving. Even in November the water in the Gulf was standing at 68° Fahr., and the atmosphere at 72° Fahr., while all the boats were necessarily idle. Such cold would be sufficient to kill men if they dived.

There was one other schooner with Solorese on board, but all the others working West-Australian aborigines. These men dive feet first, and turn in the water; such a method being far less exhausting than plunging head foremost. The Solorese imitated the Australian men, but the Sooloo men would not give up their old habits, and they treated the latter with the utmost contempt as unclean animals. The Australians, however, proved themselves by far the best shell-getters.

In order to avoid the excessive cold, the " Sree Pas-Sair" and another boat went north, to the Montebello group, where the water was quite warm and clear. This was the first time the group had ever been dived, and magnificent shells were found averaging 380 pairs to the ton. (The West Australian technical term is "a pair of shells," *i.e.* one oyster). Six weeks of steady diving went on, and after "their ears were broken," the Sooloo men did fairly well. If a man ceases to dive for a few months, he experiences great pain in his ears on again commencing, and this is slightly alleviated by oil and laudanum. After persevering from four to six days, something suddenly appears to give way in the ears when under water, and then all pain disappears; the man can at once proceed to greater depths, and will suffer no inconvenience for the rest of the season. There is no discharge of blood, neither is the sense of hearing impaired.

Christmas day was spent at the Montebellos; and on Boxing day a magnificent Pearl weighing 40 grains was found. This is the finest and best-shaped Pearl yet obtained from this coast. As the fresh water was now running short, a likely

M

spot was decided upon, and a well was sunk through 20 feet of rock, below which a fair supply of good water was fortunately found. A beacon has now been erected to guide vessels into the group and to the well of fresh water.

Early in January the two ships returned to the Gulf, finding the water warm at last, and all the other pearlers doing fairly well, but the ground did not suit the Sooloo men.

In February all the fleet went into a creek and beached for shelter, the barometer having fallen unusually low, and the weather looking very threatening, but they escaped without a " blow " and returned to work after four days. As stinging weed and fishes were plentiful, and the water was very thick, the " Sree Pas-Sair " and the " Ivy " returned to the Montebellos. Beautiful weather set in, and every morning the water was as smooth as oil, the shell being seen from the top. The daily work was performed with ease and profit ; but unfortunately " Beri-beri " commenced to show itself amongst the Sooloo men. A dropsical tendency appeared, and half the men had to stop work. A house was built ashore, and flour substituted for rice, and to this is attributed the unusually low mortality. Four men died, and to save the others, a premature return had to be made. Cossack was again visited, to obtain the ship's papers, and to pay the duty of £4 per ton on the shells obtained.

A course was then laid for Macassar, and a fair run made to Sapie Straits, but three more poor fellows died on the way across, two of them within twelve hours of their first complaining of illness. This brought the total number of deaths up to seven, and happily then all sickness disappeared. Strange to say, these Sooloo men showed great apathy at the loss of their comrades ; they made no noisy lamentations over them, and as soon as a body was committed to the deep, the occurrence was apparently forgotten. Had there been a panic amongst them, the deaths would probably have been trebled, as many of the men showed symptoms of the disease. Fortunately, there was a deck-load of cows and sheep, which kept the men employed and interested. The boxing gloves were also got up, and the men were instructed in the art of self-defence, in order to distract their attention, great merriment being caused by many of the combats.

At the entrance to the Sapie Straits the ship was becalmed for six days, and the men had very hard work towing the ship all day. Every afternoon a little wind sprang up, and the unfathomable straits were entered ; but after a couple of miles the wind died away, and the ship being caught by the furious ebb tide, was sent helpless out to sea again, the tide rips and whirlpools spinning her round and round. On the sixth day the last tank of fresh water was broached, and the unsurveyed Western passage was that night attempted and successfully made. Water and grass were obtained from one of the islands, and Macassar was soon reached.

Here the Sooloo men were paid their wages, so that they might invest in goods, thereby greatly increasing their earnings by selling their purchases in their own country. It spoke well for their acquired habits of confidence and discipline, that they accepted their master's statement as to the amount due to each, with silent approval and without question.

A rule had been made that no wages should be paid for days lost by sickness, in order to deter the lazier men from feigning illness; and the justice of this rule is highly appreciated by the industrious men themselves. It is often difficult to determine whether a complaining man is, or is not, skulking, but it is much safer, if in doubt, to permit him to remain on board though well, than to order him out to dive, even at the risk of creating discontent among the more honest and industrious of the ship's company.

Two days' liberty were given to the men, who

quickly exchanged their wages for goods. An English acrobatic company happened to be in Macassar at the time, and all the hands were taken to see the performance, to the intense delight of all, but especially of the younger men.

Unfortunately the possession of so much money and the excitement of being in a large town proved too much for the mind of one of the divers, Akalal by name, who had hitherto been a slave in his own country, but was now a free man for life, with all a free man's privileges. Impressed with the idea that everybody wanted to rob him of his riches, he became greatly excited; at night he swam off to the ship, clambered up the side, and knocking down the Malay sailor at the cabin door with a belaying pin, he entered the vacant cabin, and there seizing two large krisses, attacked his comrades asleep on deck. Fortunately he was secured before doing much harm, and soon became quieter.

Two days afterwards, Mr. Haynes left Macassar in charge of the ship, bound to Sooloo and back again, Mr. Chippindall returning to Singapore. The second day Akalal again broke out, and seriously injured an unoffending Macassar sailor. Mr. Haynes then put him in irons for the remainder of the voyage, and he was kept securely tied up in one of the boats. Indeed, there was considerable difficulty in preserving his life from his comrades, who begged to be allowed to kill him. He gradually became better, but appeared depressed, fearing his probable fate might be to be killed as soon as he left the ship. On the tenth day he was allowed out for two hours for exercise, and then again ironed, but his comrades must have failed to tie him up securely, for that night, the ship being becalmed, and everybody asleep, he managed to get out of the boat, and, ironed as he was, picked up a 9 lb. hand lead, and struck Mr. Haynes on the forehead whilst asleep in a chair on deck, leaving him senseless, covered with blood, and apparently dead, in which state he remained for six hours. The madman then attacked a Sooloo boy also asleep, but was secured before doing much further harm.

The mate then took charge, and the ship was headed for Macassar, where she arrived four days later. Here Mr. Haynes was most hospitably cared for, and kindly tended by a Dutch gentleman for six weeks, and gradually becoming stronger, he recovered his senses of taste and sight, which were temporarily lost. The outer table of the frontal bone was severely fractured, evidence of which will remain visible throughout life; he experiences now but little inconvenience from the injury, beyond that resulting from a permanent loss of the sense of smell.

The Sooloo divers were sent home *via* Singapore, where the madman was sent to prison, but before leaving Macassar the head-men visited Mr. Haynes to bid him farewell, and actually shed tears to think that one of their number had committed such an outrage.

The late Mr. Chippindall eventually rejoined the ship, and introduced several diving dresses for use on the Australian coast during the cold winter months. It is not difficult to teach natives to become proficient in this work: indeed, several of the Sooloo men were successfully and quickly taught. At the first descent they are, like many white men, very nervous; but if no hitch occurs, they soon regain confidence, and all goes well.

Neither is it difficult, with perseverance, to acquire the art of naked diving. A bright little half-caste boy joined the ship, as apprentice, in Singapore, and at that time he could only get down three fathoms—and even that caused his nose to bleed,—yet he persevered steadily, although he was not expected or even asked to dive, and after five months' practice, could accomplish his ten-and-a-half fathoms. He can now find shells as well as any native.

Mr. Chippindall practically proved that diving dresses could be worked satisfactorily on the North-west Australian grounds, and in a systematic manner. This fact being assured, the use of swimming divers will henceforth gradually but surely die out. The "Telephone" and the "Sree Pas-Sair" are now used as floating and moveable stations, for the needs of the fleet. Each vessel carries a diving dress and seven men; thus the fleet now consists of 21 boats carrying 150 divers, and 21 diving dresses. All these men are signed under shipping articles, and are therefore under complete control. The extended nature of the West-Australian pearling grounds, renders this system absolutely necessary, and this will in the future tend to prevent the relations between the masters and the men falling into the state which now exists in Torres Straits.

It speaks well for the discipline of the crew, and the kindness of the officers, that they never have to punish a man, beyond sending him up aloft. Every other night, half of the men come on to the mother ship, to hear the music. The severest punishment the men can receive is not to be allowed to be present at the concert. They work hard and willingly, and being paid so much per pair of shells, no pressing is required to get them to work. By feeding them with flour, mutton, and other food, instead of rice, it is hoped that the dreaded "Beri-beri" disease may be entirely prevented. The Dutch have just appointed a commission of medical men to enquire into the nature of this dreadful disease, and if possible to devise a remedy.

CHAPTER XI.

CEYLON PEARL FISHERIES.

"These spoils of Neptune, th' Indian ocean boasts."
—*Marbodus.*

HE Pearl fisheries of Ceylon — the "Taprobane" of ancient classical writers—are of great antiquity, and were well-known to the Phœnicians, who traded there for ·Pearls. The first Europeans who obtained firm footing in Ceylon were the Portuguese. In 1506 the ruler of the island undertook to pay them a yearly tribute of spices and Pearls, from which they derived a considerable revenue. In 1640 the Dutch obtained power, and seized upon the Pearl fishery. The fishing took place every third year, but in consequence of a dispute between the Dutch and the rajah, the fishing at Manaar was forbidden, and from 1768 to 1796 the beds were left unmolested. Neither had there been any fishing between 1732 and 1746. It is said that in 1797 the fishing right was purchased by a native of Jaffna, named Candappa Chetty, for the sum of £110,000, and that in 1798 he again rented the fishery, paying on this occasion £140,000 ; but the author, after much experience in the value of Pearl-fisheries, is inclined to doubt this statement: perhaps it does not refer to pounds sterling.

With reference to the famous fishery of 1797, and the rent paid for it, reference may be made to an interesting paper published by Mr. Le Beck, in the volume of *Asiatic Researches* for the following year :—

"From the accounts of the former Pearl-fisheries at Ceylon, it will be found" says the writer, "that none have ever been so productive as this year's. It was generally supposed that the renter would be infallibly ruined, as the sum he paid for the present fishery was thought exorbitant, when compared with what had been formerly given ; but this conjecture in the event, appeared ill-founded, as it proved extremely profitable and lucrative.

" The farmer this time was a Tamul merchant, who for the privilege of fishing with more than the usual number of donies or boats, paid between two and three thousand Porto Novo pagodas, a sum nearly double the usual rent. These boats he farmed out again to individuals in the best manner he could, but for want of a sufficient number of divers, some of them could not be employed.

"The fishing, which commonly began about the middle of February, if wind and weather allowed, was this year for various reasons, delayed till the end of the month; yet so favourable was the weather, that the renter was able to take advantage of the permission granted by the agreement, to fish a little longer than the usual period of thirty days."

The following extract from "An Account of the Island of Ceylon," by Mr. Robert Percival, in 1803, gives a graphic description of the animated scene which took place during the Pearl-fishing season in the Bay of Condatchy. The writer says: "This desert and barren spot is at that time converted into a scene which exceeds in novelty and variety anything that I have ever witnessed. Several thousands of people of different colours, countries, castes and occupations, continually passing and repassing in a busy crowd; the vast numbers of small tents and huts erected on the shore, with the bazaar or market-place before each; the multitude of boats returning in the afternoon from the Pearl banks,

some of them laden with riches; the anxious ex-
pecting countenances of the boat-owners while the
boats are approaching the shore; the eagerness
and avidity with which they run to them when
arrived, in hopes of a rich cargo; the vast numbers
of jewellers, brokers, merchants of all colours and
all descriptions, both natives and foreigners, who
are occupied in some way or other with the Pearls,
some separating and assorting them, others weighing
and ascertaining their number and value, while
others are hawking them about, or drilling or
boring them for future use,—all these circumstances
tend to impress the mind with the value and importance of that object which can of itself create
the same."

The mode of fishing is described as follows:—
A fleet of boats, sometimes as many as 150, put
out, but not before they have gone through num-
berless ceremonies, which the natives will on no
account forego. Under the command of the "*ada-
napar*," or head pilot, each boat is manned with twenty
men and a steersman, ten being rowers and ten
divers, besides a "*pillal barras*" or shark charmer.
The government keep the charmers in regular pay,
as no diver would descend without their presence.
Other conjurors remain on the shore, mumbling in-
cantations until the boat returns. The men go

down into the sea five at a time; when the first
five come up the other five go down, and by this
method of alternately diving, they give each other
time to recruit themselves for a fresh plunge.

In order to accelerate the descent of the divers,
large stones are employed, five of these being taken
in each boat for the purpose; they are of a reddish
granite, common in the country, and of a pyramidal
shape, round at the top and bottom, with a hole
in the smaller end, sufficient to admit a rope. Some
of the divers use a stone shaped like a half moon,
which they fasten round their middle when they
wish to descend, and thus keep their feet free. The
stones generally weigh from 20 to 25 lbs. each.
The diver, when he is about to plunge, seizes the
rope to which one of the stones previously described
is attached, with the toes of his right foot, while he
takes hold of a bag of network with those of his
left, it being customary with all the natives to use
their toes as well as their fingers in working or
holding, and such is the power of habit, that they
can pick up even the smallest object from the
ground with their toes, almost as nimbly as a
European can do so with his fingers. The diver
thus prepared, seizes another rope with his right
hand, and holding his nostrils shut with the left,
plunges into the water, and by the assistance of the

stone, speedily reaches the bottom. Then throwing himself flat on the bottom, and relinquishing the stone, the diver with much dexterity and all possible dispatch, collects as many oysters as he can while he is able to remain under water, which is usually half-a-minute or a little longer. This done, he resumes his former position, makes a signal to those above by pulling the rope in his right hand, and is immediately drawn up into the boat.

The great dread of the divers is the ground shark, a common inhabitant of the seas in those latitudes. During the time of the fishery conjurors stand on the shore till the boats return in the afternoon, muttering prayers, twisting their bodies into strange attitudes, and performing various ceremonies in order to divert the sharks. All this time they ought to abstain from food and drink, but they occasionally regale themselves with toddy until they are no longer able to stand at their devotions.

If an alarm be given by one diver none of the others will descend that day. The diving dress has been occasionally adopted, and if brought into general use would of course much diminish the danger.

On the return of the boats they are unloaded, and the oysters deposited in sheds or "kottoos;"

sometimes they are left to putrefy in pits or closed vessels, and when these are opened the decomposing oysters are put into troughs, and the Pearls are washed with sea-water. On other occasions however, the shells are opened immediately, and the Pearls forthwith extracted. The oysters, however, are generally sold unopened, and as their contents are alike unknown to both buyer and seller the transaction takes more the form of a lottery than a commercial exchange, — in fact the trade has in it much of the spirit of gambling : many oysters may be opened without yielding a single Pearl, whilst on the other hand, one pair of shells may contain a Pearl worth £20 or £30, but very seldom of higher value.

The government has derived a large income from this fishery, and it is protected by the strictest regulations. Those places to be fished are marked out with buoys carefully before the boats leave the land, and are examined from time to time by experienced divers.

Vincent, in his "Commerce and Navigation of the Ancients," (1807), speaks of Manaar, which was the island of Epidorus, as the centre of the Pearl fishery. According to the " Periplus of the Erythrean Sea," the Pearl-oysters are found only at this locality. The banks are situated off the north-west coast of the island, at a distance of about eight or ten miles from the shore. According to Vincent, the different powers—Kandyan, Portuguese, Dutch, or English—who have presided over the fishery at different times, always took up their abode at Tutacorin, on the Indian coast, but carried on the fishery on the Ceylon side of the Straits of Manaar, at Chilao, Seewel, Condatchey, etc. From fifty to sixty thousand persons would assemble to take part in the fishery—merchants, tradesmen, divers, mariners, etc. The sovereign of the coast, the Naygue of Madura, received the result of one day's fishing; the wife of the governor of Manaar (under the Portuguese), the proceeds of another day's fishing, afterwards given to the Jesuits, and the owner of the fishing vessel received one draught every fishing day. When the fishing was ended the fair was held at Tutacorin. The brokerage and duty amounted to 4 per cent., paid by the seller.

From 1820 to 1827 there was no fishing, and in 1834 it was again a blank. The fishery of 1837 too, was a conspicuous failure. Lady William Norton, being about to leave Ceylon in that year, the inhabitants, to testify their esteem and affection for her, unanimously subscribed for a set of Pearl ornaments as the most appropriate testimonial to their benefactress; but in consequence of the exhaustion of the beds by yearly fishing, sufficient Pearls could not be found in Ceylon, and the order had to be executed in London. Between 1837 and 1855 there were no fisheries.

It is said that 150 Pearls, mostly small ones, have been found in one oyster. This would, no doubt, be a group of seed Pearls, clustered together like a bunch of grapes. At the fishery of 1828, Captain Stewart counted 67, taken from one of the oysters which fell to him as his official privilege; but the vast proportion of the oysters contained no Pearls. He also saw ten Pearls and some crushed oyster-shells taken from the stomach of a fish called the " chartree."

In order to extract the Pearls from the oysters, the molluscs are allowed to putrefy, and are then washed in water, whereby the decaying organic matter is removed, and the coveted Pearl, if present, readily found. During this operation, the decomposing molluscs exhale " an ancient and fish-like smell," which is in the highest degree repulsive. A writer in *Fraser's Magazine*, for 1860, who had visited the fishery at Aripu, says that " a more disgusting spectacle can hardly be conceived than that of a crowd of women and children, employed upon this loathsome work, nor can human nature be viewed in a much more repulsive aspect, than in that of an old coloured woman, almost destitute of clothing, her hair tangled and dishevelled, her eyes gleaming with cupidity, and her skinny arms half buried in a hideous mass of corruption, that would appal an analytical chemist."

At the present time the government claim as royalty two-thirds of the oysters. At the fishery of 1881, which was the last successful fishery in Ceylon, the government share realized £59,900. The yield of the fishery is very uncertain. The young Pearl-oysters on the banks at Aripu have sometimes disappeared in a remarkable manner, having probably been either buried under shifting sands or washed away by strong currents. The young of the Pearl-oyster are devoured in vast numbers by skate and other voracious fish. The Ceylon oyster attains maturity in about six years but after the sixth year its life is very uncertain.

It is predicted by those best able to judge that the Ceylon banks will yield good Pearl-fishing in the years 1888 and 1889.

It should be mentioned, that a small Pearl-fishery is carried on in the bay at Tamblegam, near Trincomalee, on the North-east coast of Ceylon.

Here the Pearls are obtained, not from the ordinary Pearl oyster, but from the *Placuna placenta*—a mollusc which is popularly known as the "Window-oyster," in consequence of its thin flat shell being sufficiently translucent to admit of its use in China as a substitute for glass in windows. The Pearls from this species are usually small, irregular in shape, and of bad colour. Specimens of the Tamblegam Pearls were exhibited in the Colonial and Indian Exhibition of 1886, but their insignificance is sufficiently indicated by the statement in the official handbook that the Tamblegam Pearl-fishery is now let for 500 rupees.

The experience of Mr. Streeter's Agent at the Ceylon Pearl Fisheries.

After a number of unsuccessful Pearl Fisheries, the attention of the Ceylon Government was called to the considerable decrease in the revenue, arising from this particular department, and a special officer was appointed to inspect the banks periodically, and report upon the condition of the various beds. A most able and zealous officer was appointed-namely, Captain Donnan, the master - attendant of the harbour of Colombo. This gentleman made frequent surveys, and at proper periods he employed for temporary purposes certain divers, who brought up samples of the oysters. These oysters were carefully washed, and the Pearls found were catalogued, so as to arrive at an average result in preparing for a more extensive fishery. In the year 1879, such a preliminary fishery had been attempted, and in consequence of the general good average of the yield of Pearls, the Ceylon Government decided to organize the following year a much more extensive fishery, so as to embrace a large number of of previously explored banks, which had been reported as having yielded a high per-centage of fine Pearls.

The usual notices were circulated throughout Ceylon and India, and created considerable excitement amongst the natives, as for many years the fisheries had yielded such poor results that Pearls were becoming exceedingly scarce, as indeed they still are.

Previously to this fishery, no European had ever ventured upon the speculation of buying oysters on a large scale ; although for many years, as each successive fishery had been conducted by the government, a few Europeans, such as the military officers and merchants of Ceylon, had speculated in a small number of oysters, to the extent of £2 or £3, just as they might venture on a Derby sweepstake. But no regular organized washing of Pearl oysters had ever been attempted by any European. The whole business had for generations been monopolized` by the native merchants from the bazaars of India and Ceylon.

The report of the survey being encouraging, and the sample of Pearls found in the preliminary diving having been above the average, both in yield and in quality, the author of this work determined upon speculating, and accordingly an agent was commissioned in Colombo to attend the public auction, and bid for the whole of the yield of the fisheries. But the Ceylon Government refused to entertain any single private offer or tender, and determined to put the oysters up in lots in the usual way.

The fisheries were held off the N.W. coast of Ceylon, at a district called Silavatorrai, or Silvatura, a most inaccessible place, the only means of transport being by common fishing canoes, or by chartering a special steamer.

The fleet consisted of two divisions alternately working the banks, which were situated at a distance of about 10 to 15 miles from the shore. The agent had arranged for native brokers to purchase at market rates as many lots as possible, and the prices varied each day, according to the reports of successful finding of Pearls. In rough numbers a quarter of a million of oysters were purchased. As the distance from Silavatorrai to Colombo was not only very great, but bare of all means of transport, a fleet of boats was kept constantly employed in sailing between the fishery station and Colombo, until all the oysters purchased had been brought to the capital.

The preparation of a place to receive the oysters, and to carry on the washing and search for Pearls, proved a most difficult undertaking. The first journey of the small fleet landed about 12,000 oysters, each boat being capable of carrying a thousand. The sacks containing the oysters were sealed at Silavatorrai, whilst the oysters were alive, and were conveyed to a large building on the beach at Colombo. Preparations were at once made for immediate washing but unfortunately the difficult passage from Silavatorrai to Colombo, with contrary winds, had so delayed the arrival of the boats, that by the time they had reached the capital, the sacks of oysters emitted a most unpleasant odour. The Superintendent of Police, Captain Hansard, upon receiving a complaint from the residents in the neighbourhood, at once communicated with the agent, and threatened confiscation of the whole cargo, if not immediately removed. On receipt of this communication from the police, the agent immediately prepared four large tin-lined cases, in which were packed a sample of 10,000 oysters. These were to be shipped at once to England, in order to ascertain by personal knowledge, the most satisfactory method of securing the Pearls. It was intended that the washing should take place at Buxted, on the river Ouse, near the Crowborough Hills, in Sussex, where plenty of running water could be obtained for the purpose.

In the meantime the boats had been arriving at Colombo with fresh lots of oysters, and it became imperatively necessary to provide a suitable place wherein to warehouse them, especially as they were fast decomposing. A second place was therefore, engaged, about nine miles from Colombo, in a very sparsely - populated native village. Here, whilst erecting temporary huts and buildings for warehousing the oysters, and making the necessary arrangements for washing them, a second notice from the police arrived, forbidding any attempt to commence operations. The inhabitants refused to allow the erection of buildings to proceed, and after considerable delay, the authorities suggested a district several miles away from the village, in the

Ratnapura road. By bribing the few inhabitants who were within a mile of the locality, permission was at last given to conduct the washing at this spot.

By this time the accumulation of several boatloads was causing considerable indignation in Colombo, and a general protest was being made against the offending oysters. It must be admitted that there was ample cause for this interference, inasmuch as the horrible odour threatened some fearful plague. As speedily therefore, as possible— bullock carts being the only available means of transport—the oysters were packed and despatched under guard, to the place appointed, and a large native hut was hired in the neighbourhood where the sacks were deposited as the different cartloads arrived. To make this hut more secure, it was boarded up with planks, and every means of entry stopped, except a door, which was protected by stout padlocks. At special request, the authorities had told off for private duty four policemen, who in turns guarded the hut and its valuable contents, by night and day for a month.

Much preparation of the ground had to be made, and hence there was necessarily some delay before operations could be commenced. A deep cutting in connection with a neighbouring stream had to be effected, in order to get a continuous flow of water. The staff numbered about 40, including four native inspectors, selected from the moormen community, who represent almost exclusively the precious stone and gem merchants of Ceylon. The rest consisted of coolie labourers, both Tamil and Cingalese, who were to work and search for the hidden Pearls.

It may occur to certain persons that the washing of the oyster is an easy task, and the subsequent finding—or chance of finding—a valuable Pearl, is sufficient reward for the labour. Possibly it may sometimes be so, but in this case matters were entirely different, for the oysters had arrived at such a state of decomposition that they had generated small larvæ in such incredible quantities, that only natives of the lowest caste could be induced to enter the hut. When the sacks were brought into the open, the contents were emptied into large barrels or tubs; when these were about half full of oysters, the water was turned on and flowed in continuously. Around each tub four coolies were stationed, each under the inspector, and as each oyster was fished up the shell was washed clean, and if it contained no Pearl, was thrown on one side.

As a rule the larger Pearls were invariably

found in the hinge of the oyster, often imbedded in the decayed matter, and required some effort to dislodge them. In a few instances they were slightly adhering to the shell and almost required cutting away, but as a rule, the Pearl was so loosely fixed in the oyster itself, that it fell out readily as the mollusc was washed. The greater number of Pearls, however, were discovered lying amongst the sandy deposit at the bottom of the tub, mixed with shining portions of broken shell. As fast as each lot was inspected, the Pearls that were found were bottled and carefully sealed preparatory to their final washing and cleaning in rice, which effectually prepared them for the London Market.

During the time of washing, large bonfires were kept continually burning; but notwithstanding all precautions it was impossible to prevent disastrous effects on some of the men employed, especially the Europeans: the coolies alone seemed able to endure the horrible surroundings.

Every possible care was, of course, taken to guard against robbery. Orders had been issued that every man engaged in the washing was to be stripped, with the exception of the scantiest loin cloth. Moreover, the chewing of betel and other masticatories commonly used by the natives was prohibited while they were at this work, for it is not an uncommon thing, when such orders are not insisted upon, that under the pretence of chewing the betel, they adroitly slip into the mouth any rare Pearl, and effectually hide it from the owner; indeed, cases have been known in which the more adventurous have swallowed several Pearls. However, such precautions were taken that the chance of their so cunningly disposing of the gems could only occur on any occasional absence or slight inattention of the overseers.

Considering the magnitude of the undertaking, it was impossible to entirely control the thievish propensities of the native coolies, who have a very low standard of morality. Robbery is considered by no means a disgrace, or even a wrong, unless detected. Nevertheless a satisfactory result was obtained as regards the actual net receipt of Pearls. It is true that not many large or fine gems were found, but the quantity of small ordinary Pearls was very good, and reached a total of some thousands of grains. The largest Pearls, which attained an average weight of about 9 or ten grains each, were very round and well-shaped, but unfortunately were not of the best colour.

The most unfortunate condition of the Pearl fishery was the avarice of the government, who in order to secure an increase to their yearly revenue, had opened the fishery before the oysters were of mature age. The result of this short sightedness was that the Pearls found were of smaller size and less in number than would probably have been the case had the fishery been longer delayed. Of this there was unmistakeable proof in the opinion of native experts, inasmuch as very many of the shells contained large unformed Pearls, which, if longer time had been given, would probably have developed into valuable and perfect gems, but which in their immature state were useless. Some two or three hundred of these shells had as many as from twenty to thirty massed together, but most of these were imperfectly formed and useless for ornamentation.

It is held by some authorities that when oysters are left in a decaying condition, the skin of the Pearl is seriously impaired. This is so in the Australian fisheries, but was certainly not the case in Ceylon, for experience has shewn that equally good Pearls have been found in the shells which have been immediately washed while the oyster is alive, and in those which have been buried for weeks, and generated larvæ.

Whilst the early washing of the oysters just described was proceeding, the four cases already mentioned, containing several thousand of originally sealed sacks from Silavatorrai, had been shipped by the W. W. Co. to the harbour for putting on board the steamer in order to be forwarded for examination to the author in London ; but owing to a few days' delay, decomposition proceeded so rapidly, that a foul gas was generated, which burst open the tin-lined cases, and polluted the atmosphere for miles round. The inhabitants of the Fort district of Colombo naturally complained to the authorities, who thereupon seized the cases, and threatened confiscation if they were not immediately removed. But the difficulty was to dispose of them, as no place could be found in which the authorities would permit them to be buried. Ultimately they were taken in bullock-carts to the bungalow of the agent, who had been sent for in haste from the scene of the washing operations, and he at once had pits dug to receive them. In support of the view that decaying matter does not injure the Pearl, the fact may be stated that two months afterwards the pits were opened, and Pearls were found equal in quality to those which the earlier and less polluted oyster had yielded.

In all the more recent fisheries, great competition has existed between local Ceylon native dealers, chetties, and others who come over from India, more especially from Madras and Bombay. As a consequence of such competition, the price has risen considerably for the oyster, although the yield of the oyster in fine Pearls has been less. Formerly at the public auction, 15 rupees was a fair average price for a thousand oysters, but in the fishery of 1880, the competition was so keen that several lots reached 60 and 70 rupees a thousand. To this must be added the great expense of transfer to Colombo, and the many changes necessary before the final washing was undertaken; considering the uncertain chances of the yield of Pearls, the speculation becomes as risky as a gambling table.

No doubt if the business were conducted entirely by natives much of the expense could be saved, as the Pearls might then be washed at the fishing station; but from the intense heat and discomfort of a tropical country, residence in a temporary hut and exposure for weeks to a dangerous atmosphere, scarcely any European could live there, and, indeed, very few of the natives care to undertake operations on the spot. The enterprize is a most speculative one, and is scarcely ever found to be a profitable transaction, even when pursued entirely by the natives.

For the purchaser of oysters a much safer and more lucrative result could be obtained by purchasing of the small dealers the little lots of Pearls that each derives from his oysters. This has been proved by personal experience. The government agent, in payment of the boatmen and divers who engage in the fishery, allot one fourth of the yield of each boatful of oysters to them; and these lots are allowed to be put up separately, and in many cases are sold in small and convenient quantities to suit all purchasers.

In some instances the boatmen wash the oysters themselves, but in either case a good judge of Pearls can with much greater safety buy the gems themselves than venture upon large quantities of oysters, with their attendant trouble and expense, and the chance of perhaps after all realizing an insufficient quantity of Pearls to reimburse him for the outlay.

Most of the Pearls from these fisheries are secured by the Indian chetties, as Bombay is considered a much better market for them than Ceylon or even London; much higher prices are paid by the wealthy Rajahs of India direct to the Pearl merchants, than could ever be got from London dealers. Notwithstanding the frequent fisheries and finds of Pearls, it is nearly impossible to buy any really fine ones in Ceylon.

Immediately after the famous Pearl fishery of 1880, scarcely a Pearl of any size or value was to be obtained in Colombo. Several orders were received by the agent from persons who were unable to buy oysters, or who had been unsuccessful in finding Pearls. As these orders could not be executed there, the Pearls were procured from the London market. Some of the wealthy natives, resident in Ceylon, succeeded in collecting a few Pearls of fair size and value, but only a very limited number; indeed, as a depôt for Pearls, Ceylon was as inferior in supply a month after the fishery, as any small provincial town in England could have been. It may be confidently asserted that if the Pearls which had been sent to London had been kept in Ceylon, and sold when the excitement and demand were at their height, far higher prices would have been realized.

The Pearl Fishery of Southern India.

While the waters which wash the island of Ceylon are studded in certain localities with banks of Pearl-oyster, as described in the preceding pages, it is only natural that the opposite coast of Southern India should in like manner possess its beds of Pearl-producing molluscs. From times beyond the reach of our western records, Pearls have been obtained by the natives of the southern extremity of the Indian peninsula. The oyster-banks are situated off the coast of Tinnevelly, especially opposite to Tuticorin, but the improvement of the Paumben Channel has of late years created currents, which are inimical to the development of the Pearl-oyster.

Mr. Clements Markham inspected the Tinnevelly fishing grounds in 1866, and in the spring of the following year, read an interesting paper on the subject before the Society of Arts. After discussing the position of the localities where this industry was formerly carried on, as described by Ptolemy, and afterwards by various mediæval writers, Mr. Markham concludes that "the true locality which was the head-quarters of the Indian Pearl-fishery from time immemorial, is to be found at, or near, the modern salt station of Coilnapatam, on the coast between Tuticorin and Trichendoor."

Friar Jordanus, a missionary bishop who visited India about the year 1330, tells us that as many as 8,000 boats were then engaged in the Pearl-fisheries of Tinnevelly and Ceylon ; the value of these fisheries in the middle ages is also attested by several other travellers, such as Friar Odoric, Ludovico de Varthema and the Portuguese Duarte Barbosa. For the last two centuries the head-quarters of the fishery, successively conducted by the Portuguese, the Dutch, and the English, have been at Tuticorin.

In 1822, after the English occupation of Tuticorin, there was a fishery which yielded a profit of £13,000 to the Indian revenue; and another in 1830 yielded £10,000. The Tinnevelly banks afterwards passed into an unsatisfactory condition, and were not profitably worked for many years. But Capt. Robertson, and his successor Capt. Phipps, who officially examined the fishing grounds between 1856 and 1859, reported favourably on their condition, and in March, 1860, a fishery was commenced—the first which had been attempted since 1830.

The Pearl-banks off Tuticorin and Trichendoor, lie at a distance of about six or eight miles from the shore, and at a depth of from five-and-a-half to eight-and-a-half fathoms. From time immemorial this fishing has been conducted by "a caste called Parawas, who are met with along the Tinnevelly coast, from Cape Cormorin to the Paumben Channel. They were all converted and baptized wholesale by St. Francis Xavier, and are now Roman Catholics, the ancient church at Tuticorin being the freehold of the caste." The divers are described as an honest set of men, but readily yielding to intemperate habits. "They cross themselves before plunging into the water; and I was told," says Mr. Markham, " that the longest time any of them has been known to keep under, is one minute and eight seconds. They get a rupee a day in ordinary times."

The following is given as the native classification of these Indian Pearls :—

1. *Anie*—Pearls of perfect sphericity and lùstre.
2. *Anathorie*—failing in one of the above two points.
3. *Masengoe*—failing slightly in both points.
4. *Kalippo*—failing still more.
5. *Korowel*—or double Pearls.
6. *Peesal*—or mis-shapen Pearls.
7. *Oodwoe*—beauty.
8. *Kural*—very small and mis-shapen.
9. *Thool*—seed Pearls.

Mr. Markham has given an interesting account of the attempts to form a nursery for the culture and development of Pearl-oysters at Tuticorin.

CHAPTER XII.

" Heaps of Pearl,
Inestimable stones, unvalued jewels,
All scattered in the bottom of the sea."
—*Richard III. Act I., Scene IV.*

EARLS have been found from time immemorial in the waters that wash . the shores of " Araby the blest." The Persian Gulf, which separates Arabia from Persia, has been the scene of Pearling operations certainly for more than two thousand years, and probably for a much longer period. Isidorus of Charax, a Greek historian, who is said to have lived three centuries before the Christian era, tells us in his description of Parthia, that "in the Persian sea is a certain island where abundance of the Pearl-oyster is to be found. · Wherefore rafts of reeds are stationed all around the island, from off ·which the divers, jumping into the sea to the depth of twenty fathoms, bring up two shells at a time." Then follows a fanciful story about the influence of thunderstorms on the breeding of Pearls; and much importance is attached to the depth at which the Pearl-producing mollusc lives, as a factor in determining the character of its secretion. "The pinna of the deep water produces the most lustrous and clear and large Pearl; that which swims near the surface, is spoilt by the rays of the sun, and gives those of bad colour and smaller size."

An interesting account of the Pearl-fisheries of the Persian Gulf, as carried on two centuries ago, may be found in a curious anonymous work, entitled "The History of Jewels," printed at the sign of "The Ship," in the Upper Walk of the New Exchange, A.D. 1671 :—

"Before we speak of the manner how they fish for Pearl, and of their different qualities" says our unknown author, "we must make report of the divers places of the world where they are found.

"First of all they have discovered four fishing places for Pearl in the East, the most considerable is performed in the isle of Bahren, in the Persian Gulph; the which appertains to the Sophy of Persia, who receives thence a great revenue.

While the Portuguese were masters of Ormuz and
Mascati, every vessel which went to fish was
obliged to take a passport from them at a dear
rate ; and they maintained always five or six small
galleys in the gulph, to sink those barks which
took no passports ; but at present they have no
further power upon those coasts, and each fisher
forfeits to the king of Persia, not above one third
of what they gave to the Portugals.

"The second fishing is over against Bahren,
upon the coast of Arabia Felix, near to the city
of Catif, which belongeth to an Arabian prince
who commandeth that province. The most part of
the Pearls which are fished in these two places,
are carried into India, because that the Indians
are not so hard, but give a better price for them
than we ; they are therefore carried thither, the
unequal as well as the round, the yellow as well
as the white, every one according to its rate : some
of them also are sold at Balfora, and those which
are transported into Persia and Moscovy, are sold
at Bandarcongue, two days' journey from Ormuz.
They fish twice in a year, in the months of
March and April, and in the months of August and
September ; the depth where they fish is from four
to twelve fathoms, and the deeper the oyster is
found the Pearls are the whiter, because the water

is not so hot there, the sun not being able to
penetrate so deep."

Rather more than fifty years ago, Lieut. J. R.
Wellsted, an officer in the Indian navy, undertook
the exploration of part of Arabia; and in the
record of his travels he published an interesting
description of Pearl-fishing as then conducted. in
the Persian Gulf. He describes the Pearl-banks as
extending from Sharja to Biddulph's Group, the
bottom being composed of shelly sand and broken
coral, and the depth varying from 5 to 15 fathoms.
It is found in the fisheries of the North-western
coast of Australia, that the finest Pearls occur in
association with coral. The season for Pearl-fishing
in the Persian Gulf extends only from June to
September. The boats employed in the fishery
are of various sizes, "averaging from 10 to 50 tons.
During the season it is computed that the island
of Bahrein furnishes, of all sizes, 3,500; the Persian
coast 100; and the space between Bahrein and the
entrance of the gulf, including the pirate coast, 700.
The value of the Pearls obtained at these several
ports is estimated at forty lacs of dollars, or
£400,000. Their boats carry a crew varying from
8 to 40 men, and the number of mariners thus
employed at the height of the season is rather above
30, 000. None receive any definite wages, but each

has a share of the profits upon the whole. A small tax is also levied on each boat by the sheikh of the port to which it belongs. During this period they live on dates and fish.

Wellsted's description of the manner in which the divers in the Persian Gulf carry on their occupation is worth quotation, inasmuch as it embodies the results of personal observation. " When about to proceed to business, they divide themselves into two parties, one of which remains in the boat to haul up the others, who are engaged in diving. The latter, having provided themselves with a small basket, jump overboard, and place their feet on a stone, to which a line is attached. Upon a given signal this is let go, and they sink with it to the bottom. When the oysters are thickly clustered, eight or ten may be procured at each descent; the line is then jerked, and the person stationed in the boat hauls the diver up with as much rapidity as possible. The period during which they can remain under water has been much over-rated; one minute is the average, and I never knew them but on one occasion, to exceed a minute and a half."

Among the dangers of the pearler in the Persian Gulf, the dreaded saw-fish may be mentioned as the chief enemy. This shark-like creature is furnished

with a formidable weapon in the shape of a flat
projecting snout, reaching a length of perhaps six
feet, and armed along its edges with strong tooth-
like spines. In the presence of such a terrific weapon
the diver is almost powerless, and instances are
recorded in which the poor fellows have been completely cut in two. Nor are the attacks of saw-fishes
and sharks the only sources of danger. " Diving is
considered very detrimental to health, and without
doubt it shortens the life of those who much practice
it. In order to aid the retention of breath, the diver
places a piece of elastic horn over his nostrils, which
binds them closely together. He does not enter
the boat each time he rises to the surface, ropes
being attached to the sides, to which he clings, until
he has obtained breath for another attempt."

In 1853 these fisheries were described by
Colonel Wilson; and in 1865 an official report
on the Bahrein Pearl-fishery was prepared by
Colonel Pelly, the political resident at the Persian
Gulf. According to this latter document the richest
banks for Pearl-fishing are those of the island of
Bahrein, where the oysters are found at all depths,
from a little below high-water mark down to eight-
teen fathoms. The Arabs, who monopolize the right
of fishing on all the banks along the Arabian coast
of the Persian Gulf, cling to the old belief that the

lustre of the Pearl depends on the depth of water in which the oyster lives. The most productive banks are formed of fine light-coloured sand, over-lying coral-rocks. Bahrein alone employs about 1,500 boats in this industry. The fishing takes place annually, and is said to yield a profit of about £400,000 a year. This agrees with the estimates previously cited by Wellsted. Bombay receives most of the Persian Pearls, and Bagdad offers a market for the rest. As the Pearl shells from the fisheries of the Persian Gulf commonly pass through Bombay, they reach England under the name of "Bombay shells." At the present time (October, 1886), the price of Bombay shell varies between 22s. 6d. and £5. 5s. per cwt., according to the quality.

The Red Sea Fisheries.

Although in the time of the Ptolemies the Red Sea produced the chief supply of Pearls, this fishery has long since sunk into insignificance, and is now hardly worth working.

When Wellsted visited the Pearl banks half-a-century ago, he described them even then as furnishing but a scanty supply of Pearls, and these of poor quality. " Probably the most convincing

proof which can be given of the insignificance of
this trade is that it has escaped the notice, or is
deemed unworthy the attention of the pasha's
officers. A few boats are occasionally despatched
by the Jeddah merchants to search for Pearls, but
the precarious and ill-paid task of collecting them
is left mostly to the Tuwal and Huteimi tribes.
The former have about forty boats engaged in the
trade, which are mostly employed upon the Abyssinian
coast. Their mode of collecting Pearls differs entirely from that adopted in the Persian Gulf, where
they are found in nine or ten fathoms of water.
The fishermen wait for a calm day, when they pull
along the outer edge of a single reef, until they
discover the oyster from the boat in three or four
fathoms."

The Pearl-shells from the Red Sea were formerly sent to Alexandria, and being shipped thence to
Europe were known commercially as " Egyptians,"—
a designation which they still retain. At one
time large supplies were sent to Trieste, and thence
by rail to Vienna, where the Mother-of-Pearl was
worked into a variety of ornamental objects, chiefly
for the American market. A good deal of the
Red Sea produce also finds its way directly to
London. The little Pearl-fishing that is still prosecuted in the Red Sea is not now a government

monopoly, but when the goods are landed, the customary import duty of eight per cent. must be paid on their value. The fishing is almost exclusively carried on by Bedouin Arabs, who have settled on the Asiatic and African sides of the coast. The chief places where the trade in Pearls is conducted are Jeddah and Kosseir. The lofty Bedouins refuse to dive themselves, but train their young slave-boys to the art. The slave while training, will be shown a shell at the bottom, and told to fetch it. If he fails to bring it up, he is bound to be flogged, and his very life is jeopardized ; and even when he brings up the most valuable shells, scanty food is his only reward. The Red Sea fishery formerly exhibited slavery under one of its worst aspects. In return for the barbarity of man, mother Nature appears to yield but a scanty supply of Pearls, and indeed, the Pearl-fisheries of the Red Sea may now be regarded as practically extinct. The shell however is still imported. The price of Egyptian shell at the present time (October, 1886), ranges according to its quality, from 52s. 6d. to £4. 10s. per cwt.

CHAPTER XIII.

THE AMERICAN PEARL-FISHERIES.

"The floor is of sand like the mountain drift,
   And the Pearl-shells spangle the flinty snow;
From coral-rocks the sea-plants lift
   Their boughs where the tides and billows flow."
                    —*James Percival* (*American Poet*).

MONG the treasures of the Western Hemisphere, which were first brought to the notice of Europeans by the discovery of America, at the close of the fifteenth century, not the least remarkable were the vast hordes of Pearls. Garcilaso de la Vega and other old Spanish chroniclers, make frequent mention of the surprising number of Pearls which they found in the possession of the various tribes of Indians, who used them as personal ornaments.

But we have evidence that ages prior to the

Columbian discovery of the New World—long before the written history of America begins—the ancient inhabitants who built the huge mounds that are so widely spread through the Mississippi Valley, were in the habit of collecting and treasuring Pearls. Messrs Squier and Davis, the explorers of so many of these pre-historic tumuli, discovered in some of the Ohio mounds great numbers of Pearls that had been perforated for use as beads, but were rendered friable by the partial calcination to which they had been subjected on the hearths of the ancient mounds. The explorers were led to believe that most of these beads were not fresh-water Pearls, derived from the neighbouring rivers, but were true marine Pearls which must have been obtained, directly or indirectly, from the sea coast.

When Columbus visited for the first time some of the islands in the Gulf of Mexico, he found the natives fishing for Pearls, which they used as beads for necklaces. It is curious to note that the views of the Indians as to the origin of Pearls, were identical with those which obtained for ages such wide credence in the old world; and which have been set forth in the early chapters of this work. The Indians of America regarded them, in fact, as congealed dew-drops, which had been caught by the gaping oysters.

During one of the expeditions of Ferdinand

de Soto, which Garcilaso de la Vega accompanied, in the early part of the sixteenth century, the cacique of the province of Ichiaha not only presented the general with a very long string of fine Pearls, but offered him a selection from the stores which had accumulated at the shrine of his ancestors in the temple of Ichiaha. He also ordered some Indians to fish for the oysters, and afterwards, opening them in the presence of De Soto, extracted a number of fine Pearls, which however were much impaired in lustre by the crude method which he employed of opening the shells in hot ashes.

Here it may be interesting to quote some remarks from an old work by Mons. P. de Rosnel, respecting the large quantities of Pearls which had been brought to Europe from South America during the latter part of the sixteenth century. Pierre de Rosnel was jeweller to Louis XIV. and in 1672, published a work entitled "Le Mercure Indien, ou le Tresor des Indes," in which he gives this information :—

"On remarque que depuis que les Espagnols ont esté maistres du Perou, il s'est apporté dans l'Europe une telle quantité de Perles, et si fort surprenante, qu'en l'année mil cinq cens quatre-vingt sept, on fit compte sur les memoires des Indes, qu'il avoit pour le Roy d'Espagne dix huit à vingt

marcs de Perles de differentes sortes, et toutes d'une
beauté parfaite, outre trois cassettes pleines de
menuës, c'est à dire de Perles que nous appellons
Perles à l'once ; et que pour les Marchands parti-
culiers d'Espagne et de Portugal, il y en avoit plus de
treize cens marcs, sans plusieurs sachets appartenans
à plusieurs passagers qui n'avoient point esté pesées,
ce qu'on prendroit à present pour une chose imaginée
à plaisir."

From a curious old work on jewels, printed in
London in 1671, from which a quotation has already
been made in a preceding chapter, we extract the
following description of the Pearl-fisheries of the
Western world, as known two centuries ago :—

" In the West are discovered five Pearl Fishings,
the first is in the island of Margarita, two-and-
twenty leagues from the firm land ; this isle is
thirty-five leagues about, and hath a good haven
towards the south, at the east point it is all
encompassed with rocks ; it is fruitful enough, but
there is want of water ; and the inhabitants go up
into the country to furnish themselves with it, yet
there are great store of cattle, and it beareth maize
and other things necessary for those who live there.

" The second Fishing was discovered in the
year 1496, by the isle of Cubagua, a league from

the former, in the Gulph of Mexico, it is in ten degrees-and-a-half of northern latitude, an hundred and threescore leagues from St. Domingo in Hispaniola, and an hundred from Santa Cruz, one of the Careeby islands, and four leagues from the Province of Aria, which is part of the continent; it is much less than Margarita, without cattle, or any other thing which may serve for the sustenance of man, particularly it wanteth water, but the inhabitants are furnished from the continent, from a river called Comana, 'seven leagues from New Cadis. This island Cubagua was discovered by that famous Genoese, Christopher Columbus, who having perceived a small boat with some fishers in it and a woman who had three rows of fair Pearls about her neck, said to his companions that he thanked God he had now discovered the most rich country in the world. He broke an earthenware plate of divers colours, and for a piece or two of it this woman gave him very willingly a row of these Pearls, and for another plate he received many others, and learned of the Indians the place and manner of their fishing for Pearls.

"The third is at Comana, near the continent.
"The fourth is called Comangote, twelve leagues from the former.

"The fifth and last is at the isle of S. Martha, three-score leagues from the river La Hache.

"All the Pearls of these five fishings are of a white water, weak, dry, faint, milky, or leady; not but that they find some fair ones, but they have not so live a water as those of the East: in recompence they are great ones, in weight from eighteen to forty-two carats, and are almost all of the shape of a pear.

"These five fishings of which I have spoken, are all in the North sea, but they find also great quantities in the South sea near to Panama, they are long rather than round, but not so fair as the others, and ordinarily are somewhat black, for the Indians opened the oyster by fire, till Vasques Dugnez taught the Cacique to open them without it, and since they find the Pearls whiter. Experience teacheth us that oysters change their places as well as other fish, and that they pass sometimes to one side of the island, and sometimes to the other.

"It is a considerable curiosity to know how they fish for Pearls; seven, eight or nine men at most go in one bark, two of which descend to the bottom of the sea, six, nine, or twelve fathoms deep. About the isles of Margarita and Cubagua the water is very cold, but the greatest difficulty in fishing is

holding the breath under water, sometimes a quarter
of an hour or longer, and that these poor slaves
may the better endure it, they feed them with dry
meats and in a little quantity, avarice putting them
upon these abstinences, but besides this, they put
upon their nose little pincers made of buffalo's horn,
which stoppeth their nostrils, they stuffe their ears
with cotton wool. Others hold oil in their mouths,
especially those who cannot hold their breath long.
Others hold their mouth under their armpits, and
after that manner breathe two or three times under
water. There is a sack of stones or sand tied to
each of their feet to make them sink straight to
the bottom, and another bag tied to their waist, to
put their oysters in. There is a cord fastened under
their armpits held by them who remain in the boat,
and they under water hold another cord in their
hands, which they draw to give notice to those in
the boat that they can now hold their breath no
longer, and that they must draw them up quickly.

"When they have found a thousand or two of
these oysters, they sell them at adventure, without
knowing what is within them. The meat of the
oyster is without relish, and of very ill digestion, and
is so far from being so good to eat as the meat of
our oysters from Spain, or those of England, that the
very fisherman disdain them, and seldom eat any

of them. Acosta, in the fourth book of his history, glorieth that he had eat of these oysters, and found Pearls in the middle of them. When the night cometh, the fishermen retire to the island and carry the oysters home to him that employeth them. Upon the opening they find in some none, in others from one to six Pearls, more or less, and in some great numbers of grains, which we call seed Pearl. These oyster shells are within of a lively colour, towards an azure, they make spoons of them and other toys, such as we call Mother-of-Pearl. The Pearls are of very different forms, bigness, figure, colour and polish, and differ also much in their price."

The principal fisheries or Pearl-producing centres on the West coast of America, are those of Panama and California. It is believed that Pearl-banks extend with more or less interruption, from the Gulf of Darien to the Gulf of California, though generally at too great depths to be reached by the ordinary methods of fishing. The Pearls from the Western coast of America are obtained from the *Meleagrina Californica*, a mollusc which has a smaller and thinner shell than the common Pearl-oyster — *M. Margaritifera*. The Mother-of-Pearl shell of this species is known in commerce as " Panama " or " bullock-shell," but the principal

fisheries are now in the Gulf of California rather
than the Bay of Panama. The present price of
Panama shell (October, 1886), is from 36*s*. to
37*s*. 6*d*. per cwt.

After these American fisheries had, by continued
fishing, become exhausted they were practically
abandoned for many years, but attention has of
late been directed again to their development, and
many [fine Pearls have recently been obtained.
Mr. W. H. Dall writing on Pearl-fishing in the
"American Naturalist" in 1883, says,—"Of late
years it has looked up again, and the Mexican
Government has farmed out the beds to private
parties, who have been in the habit of granting
licenses to persons provided with the equipment for
fishing. This method ignores the preservation of
the beds as such, and each licensee endeavours
to strip them as thoroughly as possible. Rubber
armour is used, and natives of Central America
are employed as divers. Even with these appliances
the work is attended with risk, and deaths are not
uncommon. About three tons of fresh shells are
obtained by an ordinary party per day, from water
about forty feet deep when the weather is fair.
About one shell in a thousand contains a Pearl,
but these are often of excellent quality. The natives
work on shares of the Pearls; the shells go to the

vessel's account. The working season is about three months."

Unusually fine Pearls have at various times been recorded from the Bay of Mulege, near Los Coyetes, in the Gulf of California. It is not only, however, along the Western coasts of North and Central America that Pearls occur; they are also to be found on certain parts of the Western shores of South America, especially off Ecuador. Mr. P. L. Simmonds states that in 1871 an American schooner was engaged in Pearling near Guayaquil, the government receiving one-fifth of the produce. On the Eastern side of South America they are found to a limited extent, in the waters off the coast of Brazil.

Several of the West Indian islands, especially St. Thomas and those on the North coast of South America, have at various times produced large quantities of Pearls. The island of Margarita off the Venezuelian coast, takes its name from the Pearls which it has yielded. In 1574, a Pearl found here weighed 250 carats.

It is said that in 1597, as much as 350 lbs. weight of Pearls were brought into Spain, from the fisheries of the Caribbean Sea. It appears that the earliest connections with the American fisheries, were by far the most profitable, for although in the seventeenth century they were very productive, nothing since then has anything like approached these figures.

The West Indian Pearls are yielded by *Meleagrina squamulosa,* Lam., the shells of which pass in commerce under the names of "blue-edged" or "black-lipped" shells, and it is these shells that furnish most of the so-called "smoked Pearl." One method of obtaining the shells in the Caribbean waters, is by dragging over the rocky sea-bottom a rake or wooden frame set with curved spikes, whereby the shells are torn from their bed.

In 1856, there were imported into England Pearls valued at about £25,000 from the fishery in the Caribbean seas. But our connection with this fishery has lately been anything but satisfactory: indeed we have known a considerable sum of money lost upon trying to revive the industry in this area. The author hoped to obtain further authentic information with regard to the present condition of the American Pearl-fisheries, and the publication of the present work has been delayed on that account; but as the expected information has not yet arrived, the work cannot be kept back any longer, and any additional matter must therefore be reserved for insertion in a future edition.

WITH PEARL ON ONE VALVE.

CHAPTER XIV.

RIVER-PEARLS; BRITISH AND FOREIGN.

"She meets with Conway first, which lyeth next at hand
  Whose precious orient *Pearle* that breedeth in her sand,
  Above the other floods of Britaine doth her grace."
                    —*Drayton's Polyolbion.*

English Pearls.

IT seems proved beyond doubt that Pearl-fishing in the rivers of Britain was an established industry long before the Roman Conquest. According to the historian, Suetonius, who wrote the lives of the Cæsars in the early part of the second century, one of the inducements for undertaking the expedition against Britain, under the "divine Julius," was to obtain possession of the Pearls, so coveted by the luxurious ladies of ancient Rome. It appears, however, that the Roman conquerors after ransacking our rivers, were rather disappointed with the Pearls which they obtained, and condemned them not only as being small but especially as lacking lustre.

Pliny, as rendered by old Dr. Holland in the phraseology of the seventeenth century, refers to the British Pearls in these terms:—"In Brittaine it is certaine that some do grow; but they bee small, dim of colour, and nothing orient. For Julius Cæsar (late Emperour of famous memorie) doth not dissimule, that the cuirace or brest-plate which hee dedicated to Venus Mother within her Temple, was made of English Pearles."

Mr. L. E. Adams in a recent conchological work, reminds us that Tacitus refers to a theory current in his time, to the effect that the dull reddish colour of our Pearls was due to their being collected from cast-up shells instead of being gathered from living shells from the bottom of the sea; but he adds with characteristic dry humour that the fault probably lay in the Pearls themselves, as otherwise his avaricious countrymen would have been sure to discover the best method of obtaining them. It thus appears that some at least of the

Roman writers regarded the British Pearls as of marine origin.

Of all the rivers of Britain the most famous for Pearls in ancient times was the Conway, or Conwy, in North Wales. This river — the Toisobius of Ptolemy—flows through some of the most picturesque scenery of Carnarvonshire, and has been described not inaptly as the "Welsh Rhine." It is in the higher reaches of the river, above Trefriw, that the best Pearls have been found. Mr. Robert Garner, in a paper read before the British Association in 1856, says that "The true Pearl-mussel must be searched for a good many miles up the river, and the writer found it plentiful about a mile above the ancient bridge of Llanrwst, near the domain of Gwydir, where the water is beautifully clear, rapid and deep, and it may be had thence up to Bettws-y-Coed."

Of late years, however, fewer Pearls have been found than formerly. Thomas Pennant, writing in the latter part of the last century, speaks of as many as sixteen Pearls having been taken in a single shell, in the Conway; and he then proceeds to explain the origin of these bodies, according to the lights of his day. He regarded them as nacreous calculi. "They are," says he, "the diseases of the fish, analogous to the stone in the human body. On being squeezed they will eject the Pearl, and often cast it spontaneously in the sand of the stream."

The fame of the Conway as a source of Pearls, led Spencer, writing in the sixteenth century, to describe the river, in his *Faerie Queen*, in these terms :—

> " Conway, which out of his streame doth send
> Plenty of *Pearles* to deck his dames withall."

The Welsh Pearls are mostly of a dull colour, and indeed River-Pearls not unfrequently present a dim leaden hue. The author recently received a Pearl from the mouth of the Conway, which was quite black.

The Pearl mussels are known to the Welsh as *Cragen-y-duliw.* They are referred by most naturalists, as stated in an early chapter of this work, to the *Unio margaritifer*, though some conchologists place them in Say's sub-genus *Alasmodonta*, and others in Schumacher's sub-genus *Margaritana*. It appears that in addition to the Pearls obtained from these fresh-water mussels, there are many Welsh Pearls of inferior quality yielded by the common marine mussel—the edible species, *Mytilus edulis*—which is found abundantly at the mouth of the Conway, where it is largely gathered at low water as bait and as food for swine. These shells are known locally as *Cragen las.* The Pearl-bearers are confined to the bar of the river, no Pearls being found either in those mussels that are collected higher up or in those found on the sea shore. Each Pearl usually presents in its centre a dark-coloured hard granular nucleus; and on careful microscopic examination of the mussels from the bar of the Conway, Mr. Garner came to the conclusion that the Pearls had usually been concreted around a small parasitical *Distomus.*

Fresh-water Pearls have been often found in mussels from the mountain-streams of Cumberland, especially in the Irt and the Esk. In Camden's *Britannia* we read that "At the mouth of the little brook Irt, on the sea coast, are bred a sort of shell-fish or mussel, which gaping there, and sucking in its dewy streams, conceive and bring forth Pearls, or (as the Poets call them) Shell-berries. The inhabitants gather them up at low water, and sell them to the jewellers at London for a trifle, who make a considerable gain of them . . . . . . Those that are not bright and shining, commonly called Sand-Pearl (and such are those found in these parts usually) are as useful in physick as the finest, tho' not so beautiful. Dr. Lister says he has found sixteen of them in one mussel, and asserts them to be "*Senescentium Musculorum Vitia*"—

(that is to say, diseases of the old mussels). There is a patent lately granted to some gentleman and others for Pearl-fishing in this river; but it is uncertain whether it will turn to any account." The person here referred to was Sir John Hawkins, the famous circum-navigator of the sixteenth century.

Hutchinson in his " History of Cumberland," written in 1794, duly records the fact that " Pearls are found in the river Irt, which discharges itself into the ocean a few miles North of Ravenglas." But in a foot note, in another part of the work, he adds " None have been seen for many years past." He quotes, however, from Nicholson and Burn, who say " That Mr. Thomas Patuckson, late of How, in this country, having employed divers poor inhabitants to gather these Pearls, obtained such a quantity, as he sold to the jewellers in London for above £800."

The Pearls of Southern Britain are not confined to the rivers of North Wales and Cumberland, but have occasionally been found in the streams of less mountainous districts, such as Buckinghamshire. When Sir Hugh Plat published in 1653, his curious " Jewel House of Art and Nature," he introduced into his book an interesting account of various minerals, which he entitled " A rare and excellent Discourse of Minerals, Stones, Gems and Rosins,

with the virtues and use thereof, by *D. B. Gent."*
This worthy gentleman devotes a section to the
subject of Pearls, or as he calls them *Margarites*,
and gives some information on the subject of
British Pearls well worth quotation :—

"I have seen," says the writer, "very fair
Margarites taken out of a shell-fish called a horse-
mussel, and on the inside of the said shell remains
the true Mother-of-Pearl. I knew an honourable
lady, which by the employing three or four men
to catch these fish out of the waters, took with a
little charge so many ripe Oriental Margarites, as
made a very rich double necklace. Also I knew
one Mr. Primas Davis (a very ingenious gentleman)
who by making use of some vacant hours in taking
up these shells, in a short time got so many
Margarites of an even size and good colour, as
made him a choice hat-band. The shells of these
fish are on the outside very black, and not so
great as other horse-mussels. I have seen some in
Buckinghamshire, and other countries, and they are
so plentiful in some parts of the river Clun (which
cometh out of Montgomeryshire, through some part
of Shropshire) that they do more than cover the
bottome of that river, and were it not for the
deepnesse of the water, there would be no difficulty
in taking of them. I have some few of the said

Margarites, which I took out of the shell myself
to see the experiment, and I further gained this
knowledge thereby, that all such that have Margarites
in them are rough and craggy on the outside, the
rest are all plain; by which observation I soon
avoided fruitlesse labour in opening of such as had
nothing in them. I found also many fair ones which
were not fully ripe, and so came short of that bright
Oriental colour which others have."

The late Mr. Gwyn Jeffreys, an eminent English
conchologist, writing of the two common species of
British Unios—*U. tumidus* and *U. pictorum*—says:
"Both of these species produce Pearls, though of
very small size and inferior lustre. A consolidated
mass of Pearl is sometimes formed inside the right
valve near the margin of the posterior side."

Scotch Pearls.

In Tytler's "History of Scotland," we read that
as far back as the twelfth century, considerable commerce in Scotch Pearls was carried on. A fishery
existed up to the end of the last century, in the river
Tay, which is alluded to in Goldsmith's "Natural
History." In the river Earn, a tributary of the Tay,
and in the river Doon, Pearl-mussel gathering found

among certain families not only a trade, but their sole means of livelihood. A more agreeable pursuit of the manual order can scarcely be imagined, and is, in point of fact, as pleasant as trout-fishing on a hot day, and infinitely more profitable in the worst of times. Elaborate apparatus is not needed, all the skill necessary may be acquired in an hour, and experience avails little where there are no rules, and scarcely any dogma, to guide the manipulator. During the years 1761 to 1764, Pearls to the value of £10,000 were sent to London from the rivers Tay and Isla.

The following curious extract from "An Accompt current betwixt Scotland and England," by John Spruel (Edinburgh, 1705), will give an idea of the opinions then entertained of their value and importance:—

"If a Scotch Pearl be of a fine transparent colour, and perfectly round, and of any great bigness, it may be worth 15, 20, 30, 40 to 50 rix dollars : yea, I have given 100 rix dollars (£16 9s. 2d.) for one, but that is rarely to get such. . . . I have dealt in Pearls these forty years and more, and yet to this day I could never sell a necklace of fine Scots Pearl in Scotland, nor yet fine pendants, the generality seeking for Oriental Pearls, because farther

Q

fetched. At this very day I can show some of our
own Scots Pearls as fine, more hard and transparent
than any Oriental. It is true that the Oriental can
be easier matched, because they are all of a yellow
water, yet foreigners covet Scots Pearls."

The revenue from this industry shortly afterwards began to decline, and the fishing was almost
abandoned until the year 1860, when it was revived
by a German, who prosecuted the almost forgotten
trade for a while with such success that in 1865,
the value of the Pearls found was computed at
£12,000 for that year alone,—an assertion, however,
that requires confirmation.

Mr. John Gibson, of the Edinburgh Museum of
Science and Art, writing in 1885, in the new
Ordnance Gazetteer, of Scotland, says that:—"Of
fresh-water bivalves the most important Scottish
species is the Pearl-mussel. It is found in most of
the mountain streams, but the Scottish Pearl-fishery
has been chiefly prosecuted in the rivers Forth,
Tay, Earn, and Doon."

We believe that at the present time very little
is done in the way of fishing for Pearl-mussels in
any of the rivers of Scotland, and that the search
which is occasionally made by fishermen in the most

favourable localities rarely proves remunerative. The industry has been rather discouraged, in consequence of its reputed interference with ordinary fishing.

Irish Pearls.

The earliest reference which we have found on the subject of Irish Pearls occurs in the " Philosophical Transactions " for the month of March, 1693, which contains a curious letter from Sir Robert Redding, "Concerning Pearl-fishing in the North of Ireland." It appears that the writer had visited the fisheries in the preceding August, and obtained specimens of the shells and Pearls for transmission to the famous Dr. Lister. " I have sent you," he says, "four or five of the shells, and a few of the Pearls, though clouded and little worth, taken out of the river, near Omagh, in the county of Tyrone, in which county are four rivers abounding with these mussels, all emptying themselves into Lough Foyle, whereon stands the town of Derry, and so into the sea. There are also other rivers in the county of Donegal, a river near Dundalk, the shore running by Waterford, the lough called Lough Lean in Kerry, which afford the like fish." After describing the primitive method of obtaining the Pearls, the writer says that : "Although by common estimate not above one shell in a hundred may have a Pearl, and of those Pearls not above one in a hundred be tolerably clean, yet a vast number of fair merchantable Pearls, and too good for the apothecary, are offered to sale by these people every summer assize. Some gentlemen of the country make good advantage thereof, and myself whilst there, saw one Pearl bought for £2 10s. that weighed 36 caràts, and was valued at £40, and had it been as clear as some others produced therewith, would certainly have been very valuable. Everybody abounds with stories of the good Pennyworths of the country, but I will add but one more : A miller took out a Pearl which he sold for £4 10s. to a man that sold it for £10, who sold it to the late Lady Glenanly for £30, with whom I saw it in a necklace ; she refused £80 for it from the late Duchess of Ormond."

Thomas Pennant in his "British Zoology" refers to the Pearls found in the rivers of Tyrone and Donegal, but he evidently derived most of his information from Sir R. Redding's paper, to which he adds nothing of importance.

In the river Slaney, Co. Wexford, during the summer months when the water is low, some ten or fifteen men are (or were) in the habit of fishing for Pearls. They take the mussels from the bed of the river by a net, or slit at the end of a pole, the shells are then opened, and are subsequently either left on the banks or returned to the river. Sometimes from two to three hundred may be opened and no Pearl found. It is in the large deformed shells that the Pearls generally occur, and these are mostly buried in deep water, the Pearls being worth from £4 to £10 each.

European Pearls.

Many of the rivers of the Continent are the home of the Pearl-mussel. It is found widely distributed in the streams of Northern Europe, being especially abundant in Norway, Sweden, Finland, Saxony, and Bohemia; and even as far south as Bavaria.

The attention of scientific men in this country was called to the River-Pearls of Norway as far back as the year 1673; in a letter from Hamburgh, "By the learned Christopher Sandius," translated in the "Philosophical Transactions of the Royal Society" for 1674. We are there told that "The Pearl-shells in Norway do breed in sweet waters: their shells are like mussels, but larger." The writer then asserts that it sometimes happens that the eggs of the mollusc instead of being voided adhere to the

matrix, and lead to the production of Pearls.
" These (eggs) are fed by the oyster against her
will, and they do grow according to the length of
time into Pearls of different bignesses, and imprint
a mark both on the fish and the shell." This curious
bit of information was obtained from a certain Dane,
named Henricus Arnoldi, described as "an ingenious
and veracious person," who had himself studied the
subject in Christiania ; "and with great seriousness,"
says the writer, "assured me of the truth thereof."

The famous Swedish naturalist, Linnæus, or
Carl Von Linné, paid much attention to the Pearl-
mussels of the rivers of Sweden, and about the
middle of the last century, devised a plan for in-
ducing the artificial production of Pearls, by the
insertion of a foreign body into the shell of the
mollusc. Believing that his process might be profitably carried out, he offered, in 1761, to sell his
secret to the government, but his proposal was not
entertained ; and it is recorded that he afterwards
disposed of it to a merchant of Gothenburg, named
Bagge, for the sum of 18,000 copper dollars. It
seems, however, that no attempt was ever seriously
made to found an industry of this curious character
in Sweden. "In the year 1763," says Beckmann,
in his *History of Inventions*, "it was said in the
German newspapers that Linnæus was ennobled on

account of this discovery, and that he bore a Pearl in his coat of arms : but both these assertions are false, though Professor Fabricius conjectures that the first may be true." What was taken for a Pearl, in the arms of Linnæus, was really an egg— a symbol of Nature.

Pearl-mussels are found in considerable numbers in some of the rivers of Saxony and Bohemia. The principal, or perhaps we should rather say, the only Bohemian locality in which the Pearl-fishery has of late years been conducted, is the Horazdiowitz district, in the beautiful valley of the river Wotawa, between Pilsen and Budweis. Much more important, however, are the fisheries in certain rivers in Saxony.

The Pearl-fisheries of Saxony are chiefly located in the basin of the White Elster and its tributary streams, in the Saxon Voigtland. The industry, from very ancient times, has been under the control of the State. In 1621, Duke Johann Georg I., appointed Moritz Schmirler as Conservator of the Crown Pearl-fisheries, and the successive incumbents of the office have been—with only a single exception— direct descendants of Abraham Schmirler, who succeeded his brother Moritz in 1643. We read that in 1649, this Abraham obtained 93 clear Pearls, of which 51 were large and 42 small; 32 semi-clear Pearls; 59 refuse and 42 black Pearls.

Formerly the Pearls were made over to the Royal Museum of Natural History in Dresden, but at the present day they pass under the control of the Ministry of Finance. In 1802 the Royal Museum sold local Pearls for the sum of seven thousand thalers (£1,050), and with the proceeds purchased the Rachnitz collection of minerals. Some of the finest Elster Pearls are preserved in the Green Vaults at Dresden. The method of fishing is thus described by Mr. Dall, who derived his information from a report by Dr. Nitsche, on the Pearl-fishery as illustrated in the Berlin Exhibition of 1880. "The waters are inspected in spring, to see if the mussel-beds have been disturbed by ice or *débris* during the freshets. The area over which the fisheries extend is not searched every year, but is divided into 313 tracts, of which each tract is considered as equal to one day's work for three Pearl-seekers; and only 20 or 30 tracts are fished over in any one year, so after fishing, each tract has 10 or 15 years' rest before it it fished over again. The Pearl-seekers who appear to be quite at home in the water, gather the mussels with a peculiarly-formed piece of iron, which is sharpened at one end. With this they pry open the valves, and search the animal for Pearls.

If any are detected, they cut the muscles which hold the two valves together, and extract the Pearls ; but if none are found, the creature is restored un-injured to the water. The Pearls are put into a bottle of water on the spot, and afterwards dried and sorted in the house, Sometimes a mussel will be found with small Pearls in it, which give promise of better growth. Such shells are marked with the point of the iron and put back. Sometimes excel-lent Pearls have been obtained from mussels which have been so treated."

In Bavaria the principal rivers which yield Pearl-bearing mussels are those of the Bayrische Wald, or Bavarian Forest, between Regensburg (Ratisbon), and Passau, and some others which take their rise further north, in the Fichtelgebirge. The most celebrated rivers are the Ilz and the Regen. At the Nuremberg Exhibition of Bavarian Products in 1882, there was displayed a large collection of the shells and Pearls, together with examples of the artificial production of Pearls by causing the mol-lusc to deposit nacre on small moulds of fanciful shapes, after the Chinese method, which will be explained below. The Bavarian Pearls have been carefully studied by Dr. Theodor Von Hessling, who has written an elaborate monograph on the subject.

River-Pearls are also found occasionally in the

fresh-water mussels of Russia and of France. In 1849, Dr. Adolphe de Bauran performed numerous experiments on the production of Pearls by the mussels (*Unio margaritifer*) of the torrential stream of Vianz, near Rhoder, in the department of Aveyron. His experiments were not followed by any striking success. Even less successful were the attempts to produce Pearls in the *Unio littoralis*, of the Touch, near Toulouse, as conducted by MM. Mouquin-Tandon and Jules Cloquet, who, in 1858, read a paper on this subject before the *Société d'Acclimatation* of Paris.

American River Pearls.

In many of the rivers flowing through the northern part of the American Continent, the Pearl-mussel is abundant. Dr. Isaac Lea, of Philadelphia, has catalogued many hundreds of species of American river-mussels belonging to the genera *Unio, Margaritana* and *Anadon*. Yet the occurrence of good Pearls in these shells does not appear to be frequent. At any rate, the business of Pearl-fishing, involving as it does, great expense in a country where the value of labour is high, has not hitherto been a very remunerative industry.

River-Pearls have been systematically fished in the Miami river, in Warren county, Ohio. The

season extends from June to October, and some
fine specimens have occasionally been brought to
light. A remarkable Pearl weighing 46½ grains,
was found in this river some few years ago, and
passed into the cabinet of Mr. Israel Harris, a
banker in Waynesville, Ohio, who has formed a very
large collection of Miami Pearls. This specimen
was described as an " agatised Pearl," in consequence
of its displaying a curious agate-like structure, and
was christened by Mr. Harris the " Koh-i-noor
Pearl." One of the finest Pearls ever found in this
district was accidentally discovered by a little boy
of eleven years, named Morton L. Roberts, who,
while on a visit in the neighbourhood, was amusing
himself by collecting mussel-shells from the river,
to border a flower-bed in his aunt's garden. In one
of the shells, lying among a heap that had been
thrown aside by the fishers as useless, the keen eye
of the boy detected a Pearl, which turned out to
be one of unusual value ; being equally fine in size,
form and lustre.

Many good Pearls have been found from time
to time, in the rivers of New England, in the
north-eastern part of the United States, and it is
said that one obtained from a stream in New Jersey
was sold in Paris for as much as £400. According
to Mr. Dall, some fine Pink Pearls have occasionally

been procured from a species of Pearl-mussel inhabiting the rivers of Florida.

Crossing from the United States into Canada,
we find ourselves in a country which has yielded
fresh-water Pearls of considerable size and beauty. It
appears that the Pearls occur more or less abundantly
in most of the small streams in the Province of
Quebec, especially in the country to the north of the
City of Quebec, and also in the districts bordering
on the lower part of the river St. Lawrence. Some
fine Canadian Pearls, varying in weight from three
to seventy grains, were exhibited at the Colonial
Exhibiton of 1886, by a jeweller, of Quebec. The
exhibitor tells us that being desirous of making
himself practically acquainted with the occurrence of
the Pearls, he took a trip through the chief Pearl-
producing districts, in the month of August, 1885.
This trip occupied three weeks, of which time seventeen days were passed in kneeling and paddling in
a bark canoe, and in portaging through a primitive
region of very wild character. The streams which
are richest in Pearl-mussels are but little known,
except to the Indians and backwoodsmen, who take
care to keep the localities as secret as possible.
Mr. Seifert's exploring party "prosecuted the toilsome
task of Pearl-fishing with the greatest perseverance,
and after opening several thousand mussels, succeeded

in securing only two good Pearls." Such at present is the rarity of the River-Pearls of Canada! The author believes, however, that there is a great future for Canadian Pearls : many of them are of large size, and in beauty they approach nearer to the Oriental than any other River-Pearls yet discovered.

Chinese River-Pearls.

Pearls have been highly valued in China, for purposes of personal adornment, from a very early period. Many of the Pearls frequently mentioned by Chinese historians, as remarkable for size and brilliancy, were no doubt marine Pearls; but nevertheless it seems certain that the most ancient Chinese Pearls were of fresh-water origin. Thus, the earliest dictionary, which was compiled eleven centuries before our era, by Chan, the inventor of the compass, makes mention of Pearls as one of the precious productions of Shensi. Now as Shensi is an inland province, in the very heart of China, it is evident that the Pearls of this country must have been obtained from the rivers by which it is watered.

Fresh-water Pearls are largely used by the Chinese at the present day; and these ingenious people, not content with the Pearls which the mussels naturally produce, are in the habit of stimulating their growth by artificial means. This method of Pearl production has already been incidentally alluded to in an earlier chapter of this work (p. 119), but as it constitutes a very ancient and important industry in China, it may be well in this place, to describe the process more minutely. The industry is confined to a district within a few days' journey of Ningpo, and some years ago Mr. Consul Hague and Dr. Macgowan despatched an intelligent native to the locality, with a view of drawing up a complete report on the methods employed, and of procuring illustrative specimens. In 1853, the late Sir John Bowring communicated to the Society of Arts a valuable paper on this subject, prepared by Dr. Macgowan, and from this communication, we extract the following interesting account of this curious art :—

"The practice of the art is confined to two conterminous villages, near the district city of Tehtsing, in the northern part of Chihkiang, in a silk-producing region. In the month of May or June, large quantities of the mussel (*Mytilus cygnus*), are brought in baskets from the Táhú, a lake in Kiangsú, about thirty miles distant, the largest among the full-grown being specially selected. As their health suffers on the journey, they are allowed a few days' respite in bamboo cages in water, before being tortured for the gratification of human vanity, when they are taken out to receive the matrices. These are various in form and material, the most common being pellets made of mud, taken from the bottom of water-courses, dried, powdered with the juice of camphor-tree seeds, and formed into pills which, when dry, are fit for introduction into the unfortunate subject. Moulds which best exhibit the nacreous deposit are brought from Canton, and appear to be made from the shell of the Pearl-oyster. The irregular fragments thus procured are triturated with sand in an iron mortar, until they become smooth and globular. Another class of moulds consists of small images, generally of Buddha, in the usual sitting posture, or sometimes of a fish ; they are made of lead, cast very thin, by pouring on a board having the impression. Pearls having these forms have excited much surprise, since they first attracted the attention of foreigners a few years back.

The introduction of the Pearl nuclei is an operation of considerable delicacy. The shell is generally opened with a spatula of Mother-of-Pearl, and the free portion of the mollusc is carefully separated from one surface of the shell with an iron probe ; the foreign bodies are then successively introduced at the point of a bifurcated bamboo stick, and placed in two parallel rows upon the mantle or fleshy surface of the animal. A sufficient number having been placed on one side, the operation is repeated on the other. Stimulated by the irritating bodies, the suffering animal spasmodically presses against both sides of its testaceous skeleton, keeping the matrices in place. This being done, the mussels are deposited one by one in canals, or streams or pools connected therewith, five or six inches apart, at depths of from two to five feet, in lots of from five to fifty thousand.

If taken up in a few days after the introduction of the mould, they will be found attached to the shell by a membraneous secretion, which at a later period appears as if impregnated with calcareous matter, and finally layers of nacre are deposited around each neucleus, the process being analogous to the formation of calculary concretions in animals of a higher development. A ridge of marl generally extends from one pearly tumour to another, connecting them all together.

About six times in the course of the season, several tubs of night-soil are thrown into the reservoir for the nourishment of the animals, Great care is taken to prevent goat manure from falling in, as it is highly detrimental to the mussels, preventing the secretion of good nacre, or killing them, according as the quantity may be great or small.

In November the shells are carefully collected by the hand, the muscular portion removed, and the Pearls detached by a sharp knife. If the basis of the Pearl be of nacre it is not removed, but the earthen and metallic matrices are cut away, melted yellow resin poured into the cavity, and the orifice artfully covered by a piece of Mother-of-Pearl. In this state these more than semi-orbicular pearly pellicles have much of the lustre and beauty of the solid gem, and are furnished at a rate so cheap as to be procurable by all who care to possess them: they are generally purchased by jewellers and others, who set them in tiaras, circlets, and various ornaments of female attire. Those formed on the image of Buddha, are finished in the same manner, and are used as ornaments and amulets on the caps of young children. A few shells are retained with their adhering Pearls, for sale to the curious or superstitious, specimens of which have by this time found their way into the principal public and private cabinets of Europe and America. They are generally about 7 inches long and 5 broad; containing a double or triple row of Pearls or images; as many as 25 of the former and 16 of the latter

R

to each valve. That the animal should survive the
introduction of so many irritating bodies, and in
such a brief period secrete a covering of nacre over
them all, is certainly a striking physiological fact.
Some naturalists, indeed, have expressed strong
doubts as to its possibility, supposing the Pearls
were made to adhere to the shell by some composition; but the examination of living specimens in
different stages of growth, having both valves studded
with Pearls, has fully demonstrated its truth. A
tinge of yellow is found over the whole inner surface
of some shells, shewing that the more recent secretion of nacre by the suffering animal was unnatural;
the flesh of all, however, is eaten.

Above five thousand families are represented
as being engaged in this singular branch of industry
in the villages of Chung-kwan and Siau-chang-
ngan; they, however, mainly derive their support
from cultivating the mulberry, and in rearing silk-
worms, and other agricultural occupations. Those
who are not expert in the management of the shells
lose ten to fifteen per cent. by deaths; others lose
none in a whole season.

The invention is attributed by the villagers to
a native of the place, ancestor of many of them,
named Yu Shun-yang, to whom a temple has been
erected, in which divine honours are paid to his

image. He lived about the close of the fourteenth century. The topography of Chih-kiang mentions a Pearl sent to Court in 490 A.D., which resembled Buddha, being three inches in size. The resemblance was probably fanciful, being but an irregular form of Pearl, produced in the usual manner. Those now made are but half-an-inch long, and while in the shell have a bluish tint, which disappears with its removal from the matrix."

It will be observed that Dr. Macgowan, in the above extract, refers the Chinese Pearl-mussel to the *Mytilus Cygnus.* Possibly more than one species may be used ; the specimens of Buddha Pearls in the British Museum are on shells described as *Dipsas plicata.*

The fresh-water Pearl-mussels of Japan have been briefly referred to at p. 81 of this volume. We shall be glad to learn more of the history of Japanese Pearls, and to introduce the information into a future edition of our work.

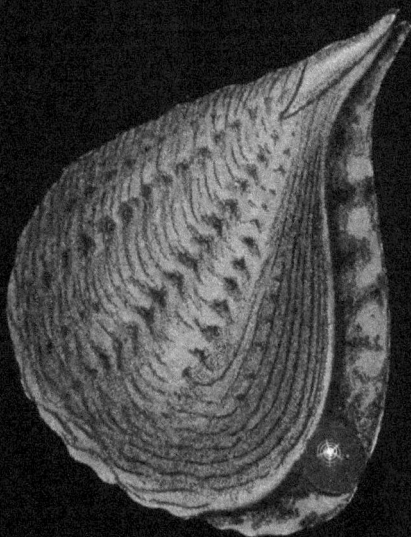

BLACK PEARL ON PINNA.

CHAPTER XV.

COLOURED PEARLS.

"Brighter the offspring of the morning dew,
The evening yields a duskier birth to view;
The younger shells produce a whiter race,
We greater age in darker colours trace."
—*Marbodus.*

IN the above quotation from the curious old "Lapidarium" of Marbodus, following the translation given by the Rev. C. W. King, we have an exposition in brief of the views of the ancients respecting the cause of the various tints which are assumed by certain Pearls.

It was commonly held by the early naturalists, that the dark-coloured Pearls had been formed either under the gloomy influence of the shades of evening, or by an aged oyster. Dismissing these

fancies, however, we may refer to the opinion so often expressed and still entertained in some quarters, that the black colour of a Pearl is traceable to some disease in the Pearl-bearing mollusc.

Although the origin of the colour is in the deepest degree obscure, it seems probable that it is in some cases due to the presence of certain pigments in the medium in which the molluscs live. The subject of the colouring matter of the nacre in the shells of the genus *Unio*, afforded matter for an interesting discussion at the meeting of the Academy of Natural Sciences of Philadelphia, on March 20, 1860. If we know the nature of the pigment which colours the nacreous lining of the shell, we may safely conclude that we know also the character of the colouring matter in the tinted Pearl; inasmuch as a Pearl is of precisely the same nature as the nacre of its shell. Here we refer not to the pearly hue of a nacreous shell, which, as explained in an early chapter (p. 87), is a purely optical phenomenon, but to the substantive colour of the carbonate of lime which constitutes both the nacre and the Pearl, and which colour is, no doubt, due to the presence of some material pigment. The late Dr. James Lewis, of Mohawk, New York, suggested that the colour of many freshwater shells might be caused by certain salts of gold, minute quantities of the precious metal, probably in the state of a chloride, being held in solution in the stream, and received into the system of the mollusc. " I notice," said Dr. Lewis, "that colours are most brilliant in regions where gold may be suspected. In the lake regions of the western States, minerals are abundant, and the conditions are not incompatible with the supposition that gold is sparingly disseminated among them, in quantities too small perhaps, to be available. . . . Of two streams producing identically the same species, one will give a large proportion of white nacres, and the other will present coloured nacres ; and usually we also notice another phenomenon — a greater *brilliancy* of nacre where rich colours abound. In this case I have my private opinion that gold produces its peculiar tonic effect, for tonic it is, under certain circumstances, by increasing the secretion."

Dr. Isaac Lea, the great authority on the genus *Unio*, was not disposed to attribute the colour to any auriferous compound ; and remarked that Dr. Draper had calcined purple shells, and could not detect in the white calx any metallic substance. According to Dr. Lea, the colours of many of the American *Unionidæ* with purple, pink, and salmon-coloured nacre, are probably due to the presence of some organic compound, such as is supposed to produce the colour of certain kinds of fluor-spar and quartz. It is a curious fact that the *Unio rectus* is usually white in the Ohio river, while in the more northern waters it is generally of a fine rich purple or salmon colour. Again, the *Unio ligamentinus* has probably never been found, either pink or purple in the Ohio, while at Grand Rapids, in Michigan, the pink and salmon shells are quite common. In like manner the *Margaritana margaritifera*—or common Pearl-mussel—has usually a fine purple nacre in the Columbia river and its tributaries, while it is almost universally white in the rivers of Pennsylvania, Connecticut, and Massachusetts, as is also the case in Northern Europe. Instances like those seem to prove that the colour is caused by certain foreign substances, which are present in some streams and not in others.

It seems probable that the gold theory of Dr. Lewis may explain the origin of the purple and violet colours of certain Pearls, inasmuch as it is well known that such tints are readily yielded by salts of gold : thus the magnificent dye termed "purple of Cassius" is a compound of the chlorides of gold and tin. According to the American conchologist, Mr. Tryon, jun., the Pearls found occasionally in *Anomia cepa* are purple, while those in *Arca Noæ* are violet. These, however, are of no commercial value.

Black Pearls.

When we turn to the true *Black* Pearls, which of late are to be reckoned among the most valued of the jeweller's resources, we must probably seek some other pigment as the colouring agent ; and some authorities have suggested that in this case, the carbonate of lime is coloured with certain compounds of silver.

Mexico is the great centre for Black Pearls, and it is said that the oyster-beds yielding such Pearls lie near to the washings from certain silver mines. Hence it has been suggested that some salt of silver exists in the water, and that the presence of this body causes the nacre inside the shell to assume a black colour. Any Pearl that may be formed will necessarily have the same composition as the nacreous deposits lining the shell, and will, consequently, be black instead of white. This conclusion is partly based on the fact that of late years certain fresh water Pearls have been artificially dyed black by means of argentiferous pigments ; but the colour of these dyed Pearls is not constant ;

it lasts only for a few months, and then gradually fades, leaving the Pearl ultimately of a dull brownish hue, and the original delicate tint never returning.

Here it may be well to record an incident which occurred to a genuine black Pearl. The Pearl, mounted with diamonds, was displayed in a jeweller's shop window, but upon exposure to sunshine, the beautiful black sheen gradually disappeared, apparently leaving the Pearl of a dull leaden colour. The jewel was then returned to the original setter, and after consultation it was decided to withdraw the Pearl from its setting. When removed, it was found that the part of the Pearl which had been hidden from the light had not been affected, but remained as black as when the gem was first taken from the shell. Upon further examination, it was deemed advisable to peel off the outer layer of the Pearl, and when this had been accomplished, it was discovered, to the great joy of the owner, that the Pearl, after losing only a few grains in weight, was as bright and as black as in its original condition ; thus shewing that the light had affected only the outer skin.

Among a consignment of Pearls from Koepang, and some other localities, a curious *lusus naturæ*

was once found, in the shape of a parti-coloured
Pearl, the top or upper half of which was perfectly

FIG, 10, PARTI-COLOURED PEARL, BLACK AND WHITE.

white, while the other half was perfectly black; the
two parts being separated by a sharp line of demar-
cation. It is difficult to explain with satisfaction
the cause of so unusual a phenomenon. Some who
examined it supposed that the oyster, having been
at one time diseased, had first formed a black Pearl,
and then on regaining its normal condition, was proceeding to cover the morbid concretion with a layer
of healthy white nacre, but was taken from the sea
when the work had been only half accomplished.
Others have suggested that a part of the Pearl had
been coloured by the inky secretion of the squid or
cuttle-fish. These cuttle-fishes abound in the waters
where the Pearl-oysters find their home, and it is
highly probable that the murky pigment, if ejected
in the neighbourhood of the oyster, might affect the
colour of the nacre and of the Pearl.

The dark-coloured secretion, or "ink," of the
squid and other cephalopods, was formerly used for
writing, and is employed in the preparation of sepia
and true Indian ink. It is a body of intense

tinctorial power, and if shed near a Pearl-oyster, might determine the colour of the carbonate of lime, which the mollusc was secreting. The organic pigment would be decomposed by heat, and this would agree with the behaviour of the black Pearl when exposed to a high temperature.

When the palace at Alexandria was burnt down during the bombardment a few years ago, many of the Khedive's jewels were utterly destroyed. When the English had landed, and the fires were extinguished, the *débris* was examined, and among the rubbish were found two black Pearls, so burnt as to be scarcely recognizable. One of these was a round black Pearl, worth when perfect, about £2000; the other being a smaller one of the value of about £200. The author bought these two burnt Pearls as a curiosity, from a Paris merchant for a sovereign! This shews how readily valuable Pearls are lost or rendered useless by a conflagration, and may in some measure account for the disappearance of many historical Pearls. It is known for instance, that vast numbers of Pearls once existed in the possession of the great families of Italy, and in the treasures of the Church, of which no trace now remains. Many ancient Eastern cities, which, in the vicissitudes of time, have been destroyed by fire and revolution, must have contained, when in a flourishing condition, extensive treasures of Pearls, collected in the course of ages, and surpassing in magnificence anything likely to have reached the hands of collectors in the west of Europe. Yet no vestige of their wealth has come down to us.

It would seem that black Pearls were not regarded as objects of value by the ancients. At any rate, we have not met with any mention of them by mediæval writers. Even thirty years ago they were but little esteemed. A perfect round black Pearl weighing eight grains was bought for £4, for which at the present day £100 would be gladly given. The great increase in value of these Pearls dates from the time of the Empress Eugénie, the wife of Napoleon III., who set the fashion of wearing black in preference to white Pearls. The Empress possessed a famous necklace, consisting of a row of matchless black Pearls, for which the large sum of £4000 was obtained when it was sold at Messrs. Christie's, after the overthrow of the Imperial dynasty. The Pearl forming the snap was subsequently sold at Christie's to the Marquis of Bath for 1000 guineas, to form the centre of a bracelet. The demand then began to be greater than the supply, and the market price has continued to rise until the present time.

Another instance may be given of the low esteem in which the black Pearl was held abroad, even as late as the year 1870. The author was asked by a member of a London Syndicate to proceed to the East, to value a large quantity of jewels, as a heavy sum of money was about to be advanced to a certain Power, to carry on the sinews of war. On his way he was requested to stop at one of the principal towns in Germany, to purchase some jewels which had been valued for probate, but were not easy of sale in that market. The valuation paper was shown to him, and after examining the jewels, he agreed to take them at the prices named. Amongst them was an old gold brooch of Russian manufacture, valued at £4; in the centre of this brooch was what appeared to be a piece of hematite, but which was in reality a fine round black Pearl, weighing 77 grains. The colour had faded from exposure to the sun, as explained before. This Pearl was brought to London, and the outer layer was taken off, when a perfect black Pearl of 67 grains remained. This was sold to a manufacturing jeweller in London for £400, but having heard that in Paris, there was a Pearl that would exactly match it, the author bought it back again for £600, and then sold it at a large profit to one of the Paris crown jewellers who, in his turn, sold the pair to a rich iron merchant for 50,000 francs (£2000). Since then the sum of 100,000 francs (£4000), has been refused for this pair of matchless black Pearls.

Mexico, Tahiti and Fiji supply the principal markets of the world with black Pearls. A few come from Japan and other islands, and very few indeed from Panama, the Pacific, and Western Australia. Black Pearls of inferior quality are occasionally found in the *Pinna,* a genus of wedge-shaped shells, with a thin dark nacreous lining. Very fine ones are also occasionally yielded by the curious shells which are known from their shape as "Hammer" oysters, belonging to the genus *Malleus.* This constituted a genus of the Blainville family of *Margaritacea,* and is placed by later writers amongst the *Aviculidæ,* or the principal Pearl-producing group of molluscs; whilst it has also been made the typical shell of a family to which it gives its name. It consists of about six species, inhabitating the East and West Indies.

Various attempts, more or less successful, have been made to imitate the black Pearl. The material commonly used is a compact variety of hematite or native peroxide of iron, which is sometimes used under the name of "iron-stone jewellery."

At Sherm-el Dahab, or "Creek of Gold," in the Gulf of Akabah (Red Sea), a beautiful kind of hematite is said to be found, and to be worked up so as to represent black Pearls. Such imitations, however, do not in the least mislead a practised eye, for they lack the true sheen and lustre of a natural Pearl, and are immediately distinguished by their weight, the density of hematite being considerably greater than that of carbonate of lime—the substance of the Pearl.

Pink Pearls.

It has sometimes been assumed that the ancients were familiar with pink Pearls—the assumption being based on the slender evidence of a passage in Pliny, which refers to Pearls of a ruddy hue. In Dr. Holland's quaint translation we read that "Pearles were wont to be found in our seas of Italie ; but they were small and ruddie, in certain little shell-fishes which they called Myæ."

The origin of the pink colour is as obscure as that of the black referred to in the previous section of this chapter. Chemists are aware that carbonate of lime assumes a pink tint by the presence of manganese, and a red colour by that of oxide of iron but it seems more likely that the delicate roseate hues of the pink Pearl are referable to some subtle organic pigment.

Pink Pearls are found in the rivers of South

America, in the Bahama Islands, in the Yagni river, and at Acapulco, in Mexico, and also in the Gulf of California. It is seen, therefore, that fresh-water as well as marine shells may yield pink Pearls, but those of fresh-water origin are of a more rosy pink colour. The principal shell which produces these beautiful objects is the great *Strombus gigas*.

The genus *Strombus* represents the typical form of the family of *Strombidæ*, and consists of about sixty species, which inhabit the West Indies, Mediterranean, Red Sea, India, Mauritius, China, New Zealand, the Pacific and Western America.

The *Strombus gigas*,—the "fountain shell" or "conch shell" of the West Indies—is one of the largest living shells, some specimens weighing as much as four or five pounds. Immense quantities are annually imported from the Bahamas, for the manufacture of cameos, and for use in porcelain manufacture. According to the late Prof. Archer, 300,000 were brought to Liverpool alone in one year. This enormous scale of importation will account for our familiarity with the shell as a household ornament.

It is this shell also which is generally used by carvers of Italian shell cameos—for which purpose it is admirably adapted by its delicate tints. The

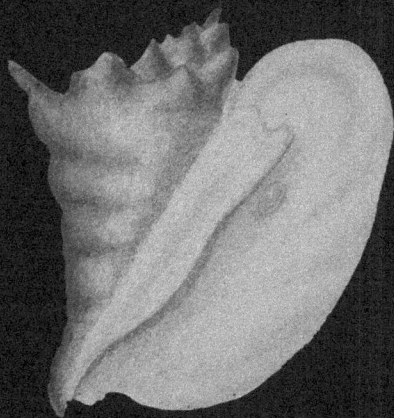

PINK PEARL ON CONCH SHELL *(Strombus)*

inner face of the shell presents a lovely pink colour, and occasionally a Pearl is found which possesses a similar rosy hue. The pink conch Pearl displays a wavy appearance and peculiar sheen, something like that of watered silk. To be perfect, it should be quite spherical, but this shape very seldom occurs, and a round and rosy Pearl is a gem of excessive rarity. A writer on conch Pearls in " The Scientific American " in 1880, says with truth, that " It is a very rare circumstance to find a Pearl which possesses all the requirements that constitute a perfect gem, and when such does happen, it proves an exceedingly valuable prize to its fortunate finder. A good Pearl is very valuable indeed, some having been sold in Nassau for no less a sum than four hundred dollars. Although many of these Pearls are annually obtained by the fishermen in the Bahamas, not more than one in twenty proves to be a really good gem, and hence probably their high price.

" Pink is the most common and only desirable colour, although white, yellow and brown Pearls are occasionally found. Even among the pink ones there is usually some defect which mars their beauty and materially injures them ; some are very irregular in shape and covered apparently with knobs or pro-tuberances ; others are too small, while many lack

S

the silky sheen, which gives them their great value and chief beauty.

"The conch abounds in the waters of the Bahamas, and thousands of them are annually obtained and destroyed for their shells, which form quite an article of commerce, but in not one conch in a thousand is a Pearl found. When this is taken into account, and the other fact, that not more than one in twenty of the Pearls found turns out to be perfect, it will at once be seen that a good conch Pearl will always be a rare and costly gem.

"Most of the conch Pearls found in the Bahamas are exported to London, where they are readily sold. A few have been sent to New York, having been purchased in Nassau by an agent of Messrs. Tiffany & Co., the well-known jewellers.

"Like everything else that is valuable, the conch Pearl has been imitated, and some of the imitations have been sold as the genuine article. Many years ago an ingenious American visited Nassau and conceived the idea of making conch Pearl. He succeeded admirably in cutting out of the pink portion of the shell some very creditable imitations. To make success doubly sure, he procured a number of the live shell fish, carefully inserted his spurious Pearls in the position in which the genuine Pearl is usually found, and placed the fish in an enclosed place in the water. At the expiration of a month or more, the fish were again removed, and, of course, Pearls found in them, several of which were sold to inexperienced persons· before the fraud was detected. It was found out, however, and the perpetrator received prompt and deserved punishment."

Mr. Wood, in his "Zoography" relates that he saw a pink Pearl, which was taken from the body of the animal of the great West Indian conch shell, which is fished for the table off the Island of Barbadoes. The Pearl was discovered by chance, while the men were cleaning the fish. Its weight was 24 grains, but it lacked perfection of shape. The same author states that only four of these Pearls had been discovered in the vast number of shell fish that are annually brought to market in that part of the world, though he has reason to believe that this is in some measure owing to the carelessness of the negroes, who clean their fish without consideration, and have probably in their hurry returned many a Pearl to the sea. Once there, sand, by continuous washing against the Pearl, would soon reduce it to powder, the carbonate of lime of the Pearl being not so hard as the sand.

Pink Pearls have one great drawback, namely, that ninety per cent. of them are irregular in shape,

and present so ungraceful a form, as to preclude their
use for personal adornment. This may be accounted
for in the following manner. The Pearl in the
course of formation, is twisted into various forms
by the efforts made by the mollusc to unroll itself
to get out of its spiral shell. The fish naturally
often changes its position, and the disturbed Pearl
becomes ill-shapen. When a pink Pearl is found
perfectly round, it is most likely due to the mollusc
having been less energetic than most of its species.
It is not generally known what difficulty is experienced in getting the great conch out of its shell,
but it is affirmed upon reliable authority that the
shells have to be placed in a certain hanging position,
with a weight attached to the mollusc. Some time
elapses before the fish is drawn out, and often by
this means the Pearl is entirely lost. The conch,
although the commonest, is not the only shell that
produces Pearls of a rosy tint. For instance, a
specimen in the British Museum shews a fine pink
Pearl attached to the *Turbinella scolymus*, a porcellanous univalve shell. (See plate.)

It is not unusual to find specimens of pale
pink coral cut and shaped like pink Pearls, and
offered for sale as such ; but an experienced eye
will not fail to detect the absence of the peculiar
silky sheen of the concentric layers of which

PINK PEARL ON TURBINELLA.

the Pearl is composed, which is widely different from the lustre and cellular texture of the coral. In no instance has the coral ever been found to possess the same lines as the pink Pearl. It is true that some Pearls themselves lack this beauty, but they then fall considerably in value. At the present time the pink Pearl is not so much in request as formerly. Some few years back, from 1857 to 1860, the supply was not equal to the demand, as may be seen by the following instance : an officer in the 1st Life Guards on his marriage, wished to present his bride with a necklace of pink Pearls and diamonds, but Pearls of the first quality could not be obtained, and in order that it might be finished in time, the necklace had to be made up with some inferior pink Pearls. It is the same with these as with all other commodities, excepting specimen-gems, which always fetch their value : according to the supply and demand, so the prices rise and fall. While black Pearls are highly appreciated and eagerly sought after, pink Pearls are now but little in request, and are therefore, not of great value in the market.

In the " Hope " collection, there was a curious cameo pink Pearl, representing two hands mounted on a gold ring, with a device of forget-me-nots in diamonds. The collection also contained a cream-coloured Pearl, obtained from Polynesia. This was

in appearance very like an opal; the summit displaying a radiating lustre. Probably this Pearl was
obtained from the great clam shell—a shell which
occasionally produces Pearls, but of no value, being
lustreless, and not to be compared even with a
common fresh-water Pearl.

Pearls of various other Colours.

Respecting Pearls of other colours than black
and pink, very little need be said. The *greenish-
black* is probably of all tints most coveted; it occurs,
however, but rarely, and when a Pearl of this particular hue, possesses the right orient, it exceeds in
value all other coloured Pearls. A *bluish-black*
Pearl, if of fine orient, is almost as valuable as a
true black one. The Pearls from the *Placuna
placenta* are often of a dull leaden colour, while those
occasionally found in the outer coat of the *Pinna
squamosa* are commonly of a brown tint. *Brown*
Pearls are of very little value; neither are those
of *plum-colour* much sought after. *Red* Pearls are
worth only about one shilling per grain. *Yellow*
Pearls again do not generally realize more than a
few shillings per grain, and those of *gamboge* tint
are practically of no value in this country. When,
however, a Pearl is of a very fine bright *golden*
colour, it may be worth from twenty to forty
shillings per grain.

CHAPTER XVI.

FAMOUS PEARLS.

" The fair Pearl Necklace of the Queen,
That burst in dancing, and the Pearls were spilt ;
Some lost, some stolen, some as relics kept,
But nevermore the same two Sister Pearls,
Ran down the silken thread to kiss each other
On her white neck."
    —*Tennyson's " Merlin and Vivien."*

T seems desirable to introduce here a
short account of the most famous Pearls
that have figured in history. Many
of these great historical jewels have contributed in
no small degree to the adornment of royalty in
various ages, and have been the subject of strange
stories connected with the fortunes of the great.
It has been said by Miss Landon, with reference to
historical diamonds, that " Fresh from the merchant,
diamonds convey no sentiment but that of wealth ;

while these hereditary diamonds recall whole generations of stately beauties." With equal, or perhaps
with even more truth, may this be said of Pearls.
The Pearls which we are about to describe have
been possessed by some of the most eminent
historical personages, and have been prized for
personal decoration by the most admired beauties
of all ages. The subject is one of peculiar fasci-
nation, but it is to be regretted that in many
cases, the information that has come down to us
from antiquity, respecting those exceptional Pearls,
is only of a meagre character. In the following
descriptions an attempt is made to arrange them
roughly in chronological sequence, but it will be
understood that many of the dates are mere ap-
proximations. The most ancient Pearl of which
we have found any record may be termed .the
" Servilia Pearl."

The Servilia Pearl—circa B.C. 44.

After the Roman conquests in the East, particularly when Mithridates, the great king of Pontus,
distinguished for his knowledge of languages and
far-reaching schemes of policy, had been overthrown
by Lucullus and Pompey—the Pearl became highly
valued, not only in Rome, but throughout the Roman
empire. The ladies wore them in profusion, as

already mentioned (p. 36 *et seq.*). Julius Cæsar, after his return from his Egyptian campaign, presented to Servilia—the mother of his murderer, Brutus—a magnificent Pearl, which he had retained as part of the spoils of war. The value of this gem was estimated at a sum equivalent to £35,600 of our present money.

The Cleopatra Pearls.—circa B.C. 30.

These celebrated Pearls were possessed by the famous Cleopatra, queen of Egypt and last of the Ptolemies. According to the well-known story, one of these gems was dissolved in vinegar, and drunk by the queen at a banquet given by her in honour of Antony, one of the second triumvirate, and *de facto* ruler of the East.

This is how Pliny tells the tale, according to old Dr. Holland's version : "Two onely Pearles there were together, the fairest and richest that ever have been knowne in the world, and those possessed at one time by Cleopatra, the last queene of Egypt, which came into her hands by the means of the great kings of the East, and were left unto her by descent. This princesse, when M. Antonius had strained himselfe to doe her all the pleasure he possibly could, and had feasted her day by day most sumptuously, and spared for no cost, in the

height of her pride and wanton braverie (as being
a noble curtezan, and a queene withall), began to
debase the expense and provision of Antonie, and
made no reckoning of all his costly fare. When he
thereat demaunded againe how it was possible to
goe beyond this magnificence of his; she answered
againe, that she would spend upon him in one
supper 100 hundred thousand sestertij. Antonie,
who would needs know how that might bee (for
hee thought it was unpossible), laid a great wager
with her about it, and she bound it againe and
made it good. The morrow after, when this was to
be tried, and the wager either to bee won or lost,
Cleopatra made Antonie a supper (because she
would not make default, and let the day appointed
to passe), which was sumptuous and roiall ynough;
howbeit, there was no extraordinarie service seene
upon the bourd, whereat Antonie laughed her to
scorne, and by way of mockerie, required to see a
bill with the account of the particulars. She againe
said, that whatsoever had been served up alreadie,
was but the overplus above the rate and proportion
in question, affirming still that shee would yet in
that supper make up the full summe that she was
seazed at; yea, herselfe alone would eat above that
reckoning, and her owne supper should cost 600
hundred thousand sestertij: and with that commanded
the second service to be brought in. The servitours

that waited at her trencher (as they had in charge before) set before her one onely crewer of sharpe vinegar, the strength whereof is able to resolve Pearles. Now she had at her eares hanging those two most precious Pearles, the singular and onely jewels of the world, and even Nature's wonder. As Antonie looked wistfully upon her, and expected what she would doe, shee tooke one of them from her eare, steeped it in vinegar, and so soon as it was liquified, dranke it off. And as she was about to do the like by the other, L. Plancius, the judge of that wager, laid fast hold upon it with his hand, and pronounced withall that Antonie had lost the wager. Whereat the man fell into a passion of anger."

The other Pearl of Cleopatra's pair which was thus preserved from a like fate, passed into the possession of the Roman emperor, and was afterwards sawn asunder and made into earrings, by Agrippa, for the statue of the goddess Venus, in the Pantheon. Pliny remarks that the statue was satisfied with one half of Cleopatra's banquet.

With reference to the solution of Pearls, we may add that Cleopatra was not the only personage who performed the costly experiment, but that the Emperor Caligula is likewise said to have drunk Pearls dissolved in vinegar. It is related too that Clodius, the son of Æsop, the tragic actor, a man of great wealth, but noted for gluttony, perpetrated a similar act of folly. Indeed the story runs that he not only dissolved two valuable Pearls and drank off the solution himself, but gave to each guest at his table a Pearl to be drunk in like manner. It is also recorded that a valuable Pearl was similarly destroyed by Sir Thomas Gresham, as will be explained a few pages further on. In connexion with this subject we may remind the reader that in " Hamlet," Shakespeare introduces the idea of dissolving a Pearl, or as he calls it "an Union," in a cup of wine :

> "The King shall drink to Hamlet's better health,
> And in the cup an *Union* shall be thrown,
> Richer than that which four successive kings
> In Denmark's crown have worn."

Let us add that a sceptical age is disposed, not without good reason, to cast doubt upon all the old stories of Pearl drinking. Barbot, the French jeweller, having macerated a Pearl in the strongest vinegar, found that the outer layer was reduced to a gelatinous condition, while the deeper part of the Pearl remained unaffected.

The Lollia Paulina Pearls, c. A.D. 50.

In an early chapter of this work (pp. 37, 38) we have quoted Pliny's description of the extravagant decoration of Lollia Paulina, the wife of the Emperor Caligula, whose parure of Pearls and Emeralds was valued at a sum equivalent to £400,000. " Yet were not these jewels the gifts and presents of the prodigall prince her husband, but the goods and ornaments from her owne house, fallen unto her by way of inheritance from her grandfather, which hee had gotten together even by the robbing and spoiling of whole provinces. See what the issue and end was of those extortions and outrageous exactions of his: this was it; that M. Lollius, slandered and defamed for receiving bribes and presents of the kings in the east, and being out of favor with C. Cæsar, sonne of Augustus, and having lost his amitie, drank a cup of poyson, and prevented his judicial trial; that forsooth his niece Lollia, all to be hanged with jewels of 400 hundred thousand sestertij, should bee seene glittering and looked at of every man, by candle-light, all a supper time." So runs Holland's Translation of Pliny.

The Pliny Pearl, c. A.D. 50.

The largest Pearl known to Pliny, the elder, who was born A.D. 23, and lost his life during the first recorded eruption of Vesuvius, when Pompeii and Herculaneum were destroyed, A.D. 79, weighed half a Roman ounce, equal to 302 grains of our present weight. It was probably a baroque.

The Sassanian Pearl. c. A.D. 500.

It has been mentioned in an early chapter

(p. 30), that in the portraits of the Sassanian kings, a huge Pearl is represented as hanging from the right ear. This was worn by the monarch as a fitting mark of sovereignty. The Sassanian dynasty reigned in Persia from the year 226 to 641 A.D. Procopius who lived in the reign of Justinian, relates in his History of the Persian wars that a daring diver obtained, by the sacrifice of his life, a .Pearl of great size from the custody of a shark. This Pearl, considered a miracle of nature, was worn by King Perozes, who ultimately lost it in an engagement with the Huns. Charging their flying hordes, he was lured by their feigned retreat into a vast pitfall, but to prevent the enemy from possessing such a precious trophy of their victory, he tore the Pearl from his right ear, and cast it before him. This noble jewel was never recovered, although the Huns were stimulated to the search by his Byzantine rival, who promised an enormous reward to the discoverer (see p. 31).

The Gresham Pearl, 1560.

Sir Thomas Gresham, the wealthy and munificent London merchant of Queen Elizabeth's period, was hardly the man to be led into acts of foolish ostentation. Yet it is related that on one occasion his loyalty so far got the better of his judgment, that this sober citizen was induced to imitate the absurdity of Cleopatra, by wantonly destroying a Pearl of great price. In Lawson's "History of Banking" the incident is narrated in the following words :—"The Spanish ambassador to the English court, having extolled the great riches of the king his master, and of the grandees of his master, before Queen Elizabeth, Sir Thomas, who was present, told him that the queen had subjects who, at one meal, expended not only as much as the daily revenues of his kingdom, but also of all his grandees; and added 'this I will prove any day, and lay you a considerable sum on the result.'

" The Spanish ambassador soon afterwards came unawares to the house of Sir Thomas, and dined with him ; and finding only an ordinary meal, said 'Well, sir, you have lost your wager.' 'Not at all,' replied Sir Thomas ; 'and this you shall presently see.' He then pulled out a box from his pocket, and taking one of the largest and finest eastern Pearls out of it, exhibited it to the ambassador, and then ground it, and drank the powder of it in a glass of wine to the health of his mistress. 'My lord ambassador,' said Sir Thomas, 'you know I have often refused £15,000 for that Pearl: have I lost or won ?' 'I yield the wager as lost' said the ambassador, 'and I do not think there are four

subjects in the world that would do as much for
their sovereign,' "

La Peregrina, 1579.

Philip II. of Spain possessed this famous Pearl
which is described as being as large as the biggest
pigeon's egg, and weighing 134 grains. It· was
valued by the jewellers at 14,000 ducats, but pronounced beyond all valuation by the engraver, Freco.
This remarkable Pearl was pear-shaped, and came
from the Panama fisheries. The oyster from which
this Pearl was derived had been found by a negro
boy, but the shell was so small that the fishermen,
regarding it as of no value, were about to throw it
back into the sea, without opening it; second thoughts
prevailed however, and to the surprise of all, this
magnificent Pearl was discovered. The slave was
rewarded with his liberty and his master with the
post of alcalde of Panama. The Pearl was presented
to Philip II, by Don Diego de Têmês. It was
exhibited at Seville as an unparalleled curiosity.

The Rudolf Pearl, 1609.

Anselmus De Boot, a native of Antwerp, who
was physician to Rudolf II., published in the year
1609, a learned treatise, entitled "De Gemmis et

Lapidibus." In this work he mentions a Pearl, belonging to his patron Rudolf, which weighed 120 grains, and cost as much as 120,000 gold pieces. Rudolf also possessed another Pearl that weighed as much as 180 grains,

---

The Youssoupoff Pearl, 1620.

One of the largest Pearls known in Europe, a pear-shaped Pearl weighing 524 grains, was brought from India in 1620, by Gongibus of Calais, and sold by him to Philip IV. of Spain, for 80,000 ducats, a sum equivalent to about £18,000. The merchant when asked by the king how he could have been bold enough to risk all his fortune in a single little article, replied " Because he knew there was a King of Spain to buy it!" It is believed that this magnificent Pearl is now in possession of the Russian Princess Youssoupoff.

The Shah Pearls, 1633—1635.

The Shah of Persia possessed in 1633, a Pearl an inch in diameter, which was valued at £64,coo. It is said that two years later he bought another beautiful Pearl from an Arab, coming from the Catifa fishery. The price paid for this was 32,000 tomanas, or £56,000. It weighed 672 grains, and the shape was an almost perfect heart. At the present

T

day this shape would considerably detract from its value. It is believed that one of these is the Pearl which is known in modern times to have been in possession of Fateh Ali Shah.

The Aurungzeb Pearl, 1650.

The only jewel ever purchased by Aurungzeb, the great Mogul, who affected a pious contempt for all such pomps and vanities, was a perfect round Pearl, weighing 127½ grains. No value is given to this fine Pearl, but it is related, with reference to other Pearls, that there were in India certain persons who would give higher prices than could be obtained from Aurungzeb.

The Conway Pearl, 1662.

History has recorded that Sir Richard Wynn, of Gwydir, who was chamberlain to Catherine of Braganza, the Queen of Charles II., presented to her Majesty a Pearl of unusual beauty and magnitude, which had been found in the river Conway, in North Wales. This Pearl is said to be still preserved in the Imperial State Crown. It is recorded that the Pearl was accidentally found by a lady who carelessly opened a mussel which she happened to pick up, without the slightest expectation of its disclosing a Pearl; it was probably derived from that part of the river which flows near the domain of Gwydir.

The Arabian Pearl, 1689.

Aceph Ben Ali, prince of Nolenna, Arabia, possessed a Pearl to which Tavernier awards the palm for perfection in beauty, but not in magnitude. Its weight was only $12\frac{1}{16}$ carats, $48\frac{1}{4}$ grains, so that many others far surpassed it in that respect. But such was the fame of its perfection that £140,000 is said to have been offered in vain for it by Aurungzeb.

La Pellegrina, 1830.

There is in the Zosima Museum at Moscow, a Pearl of exceptional beauty, which has been called " La Pellegrina," and is sometimes confounded with "La Peregrina" already described. It is said that the Moscow Pearl was purchased by Zosima in the early part of this century from the captain of an Indian ship, at Leghorn, in Italy. The Pearl weighs about 90 grains, and is described as being perfectly spherical and of surpassing lustre.

The Hope Pearl, 1839.

In the collection formed by the late Mr. Henry Philip Hope, and arranged by Hertz, were several Pearls of unusual magnitude and beauty. The largest was a baroque Pearl weighing 1,800 grains, which is thus described in the catalogue of the Hope collection, published in 1839 :—

"A most extraordinary large specimen of an Oriental Pearl, of an irregular pear shape, measuring 2 inches in length, 4½ inches in circumference at the broadest end, and 3¼ inches at the narrower end ; weighing 3 ounces, or 1,800 grains. About 1½ inches of the Pearl are of a fine bright orient ; the bottom part is of a fine bronze tint, or dark green shaded with copper colour. This gigantic Pearl was detached from the shell, but it was deemed necessary to leave a small portion of the shell adhering to it, but which is of so fine an orient, and so well polished, that it is not distinctly perceived to be of the nature of shell.

"Considering the growth of Pearls in general, that they are a morbid secretion of a species of oyster, which is of small size, it is surprising to behold, in the present specimen, a mass of Pearl which must surpass the fish which formed it at least six times in weight ; and we may presume that it is the largest Pearl ever found. It is surmounted with a royal crown of red enamelled gold, and studded with fine brilliants, rubies, and emeralds."

This specimen was for many years exhibited at the South Kensington Museum, by permission of A. J. Beresford-Hope, Esq., and was sold this year

(1886), at Messrs. Christie & Manson's with the rest of the Hope collection of precious stones.

<hr>

The Russian Pearl, 1840.

"Sometime before I went to Moscow," observes the traveller, J. G. Kohl, in his work on Russia, "there died in a convent, whither he had retreated after the manner of the wealthy pious ones of his nation, a rich merchant, whose house had large establishments in Moscow, Constantinople, and Alexandria, and extensive connexions throughout the East. Feeling the approach of age, he had by degrees given up the toils of business to his sons. His wife was dead and the only beloved object, which even in the cloister, was not divided from him, was one large, beautiful Oriental *Pearl.* This precious object had been purchased for him by some Persian or Arabian friend at a high price, and enchanted by its water, magnificent size and colour, its perfect shape and lustre, he would never part with it, however enormous the sum offered for it. Perhaps in the contemplation of its peerless beauty, as it lay before him in his leisure hours, he recalled the events of his early life, and the glories of the East, as he had formerly beheld them with his own eyes. He fairly worshipped the costly globule. He himself inhabited an ordinary cell in the convent; but this object of his love was bedded on silk in a golden casket. It was shown to few; many favorable circumstances and powerful recommendations were necessary to obtain such a favor. One of my Moscow friends who had succeeded in introducing himself, and had received a promise that he should behold the *Pearl of Pearls*, informed me of the style and manner of the ceremony. On the appointed day he went with his friends to the convent, and found the old man awaiting his guests at a splendidly covered breakfast, in his holiday clothes. Their reception had something of solemnity about it. The old man afterwards went into his cell and brought out the casket in its rich covering. He first spread a piece of white satin on the table, and then unlocking the casket, let the precious Pearl roll out before the enchanted eyes of the spectators. No one dared to touch it, but all burst into acclamations, and the old man's eyes gleamed like his Pearl. It was, after a short time, carried back to its hiding-place. During his last illness, the old humourist never let his Pearl out of his hand, and after his death it was with difficulty taken from his stiffened fingers. It found its way afterwards to the Imperial Treasury."

The Paris Pearls, 1878.

It may be doubted whether any of the famous Pearls of antiquity were equal in beauty, perfection, and rarity to the marvellous pair, weighing 227 grains, exhibited in the French Exhibition of 1878.

One of these Pearls, weighing in its then condition 116 grains, was purchased by the author in 1877, of a private customer, and sold to one of our leading London merchants who, with great skill removed a blister that then disfigured it on one side, and made of it a perfect Pearl of 113¾ grains. This gentleman held it for some time without being able to sell it. In the beginning of 1878, it occurred to him, the merchant, to suggest to Messrs. Hunt and Roskell that it would probably match a famous Pearl of 113¼ grains, sold by them to Prince Dhuleep Singh some fifteen years previously, and that the prince might consequently like to purchase it. It was submitted by Messrs. Hunt and Roskell to the prince, and on being compared with his Pearl, was found to match it exactly, and to form with it a pair probably unique in the history of such jewels. The one weighs 113¼ grains, the other 113¾ grains: both are absolutely round, like a marble, perfect in whiteness and skin, and very lustrous (orienté). The one originally bought, having been mounted in a brooch, and in the usual manner fastened on a peg, has a small hole drilled on one side, but this, of course, in no way detracts from its beauty or value ; the other, not having been mounted, was intact. Early in 1878, Messrs. Hunt and Roskell purchased both Pearls,—the one from Prince Dhuleep Singh, and the other from the merchant, — and shortly afterwards sold them back as a pair to the above-mentioned merchant for £4,800, which was even then much below their value, and to-day they would be worth £10,000. They were almost immediately re-sold to Messrs. Bapst, jewellers, of Paris, and by them exhibited suspended on wires in their case in the great Paris exhibition, 1878. There they attracted universal attention and were pronounced by connoisseurs to be the most extraordinary pair of Pearls ever seen in Europe. They were sold from the Exhibition to a private individual for a very large sum.

Other Famous Pearls.

Among the list of monies received by the Earl of Craven as executor to Prince Rupert, we find mention of Mrs. Ellen Gwynne, £4,520 for the great Pearl necklace.

In a curious and characteristic letter of Lady Compton to her husband, apparently written at the end of the sixteenth century, we find among other items which she terms "reasonable," the following remark :—"I would have £6,000 to buy me jewels, and £4,000 to buy me a Pearl chain or necklace."

In the time of James I. (1617), the chamberlain consoles himself with the reflection, that "the choice of Pearls and other rare jewels is not touched, among which there is a carquenet of round and long Pearls, rated at £40,000, in the judgment of Lord Digby and others, the fairest that are to be found in Christendom."

The following is a valuation of the Pearls in the Crown Treasury of France (1791).

	Grains	Value
A perfect white round virgin Pearl, weighing	388—	£8,000
2 pear shaped Pearls each ...	214	12,000
4 „ „ „ together	399	2,560
6 round Pearls, together ...	772½	2,400
3 „ „ „ ...	232	880
5 „ „ „ ...	408 1/16	1,200
7 „ „ „ ...	464 5/16	1,320
8 „ „ ·, ...	628½	960
6 „ „ „ ...	392½	728
11 „ „ „ ...	712⅛	448

At the present day these Pearls, which doubtless were of the purest and finest description, would be worth a far larger sum than the amounts named.

It is said that Napoleon I. possessed a Pearl of about 160 grains weight, but no trace of it has ever been found.

The Municipality of Florence possessed for a long time a magnificent single row of Pearls. After the restoration in 1849, this was borrowed by the Grand Duchess, who having once obtained possession of this prize, was in no hurry to return it.

The Crown Prince of Germany gave the Princess Royal of England, on their marriage, a Pearl necklace valued at £20,000, but the Pearls are not all round, and some are *baroque*.

The Devonshire Cabinet contains an enormous Pearl, of the finest lustre, but singularly mis-shapen. This Pearl has been skilfully converted into the body of a very graceful mermaid. It was at one time valued at £2,000, but at the present day, large ill-shapen Pearls are of comparatively little value. North-Western Australia having yielded several examples, their value has dropped fully 75 per cent.

Among other Pearls of unusual magnitude and beauty, mention may be made of the magnificent Pearl of 40 grains weight, found on December 26, 1884, in the Montebello Archipelago, as narrated at p. 177. The necklace of matchless black Pearls, belonging to the Empress Eugénie has been referred to at p. 268 ; and the curious history of the pair of fine black Pearls, weighing 77 and 67 grains, will be found at p. 269. There are no doubt, other famous Pearls worthy of description, and some of these we hope to describe in a future edition of this work. The author will always be glad to receive information respecting any Pearls of exceptional interest, with the view of rendering the subject, in a future edition, as perfect as possible.

CHAPTER XVII.

THE SOUTHERN CROSS PEARL.

" To thee as thy loadstars resplendently burn,
  In their clear depths of blue, with devotion I turn,
Bright *Cross of the South!* and beholding thee shine,
  Scarce regret the loved land of the olive and vine."

—Mrs. Hemans.

THE extraordinary Pearl, or rather cluster of Pearls, known as "The Southern Cross," is probably the most remarkable production of its kind, that Nature has ever produced. So far as is known, it occupies an absolutely unique position in the history of Pearls.

It consists of a group of nine Pearls, naturally grown together in so regular a manner, as to form an almost perfect Latin Cross. Seven Pearls

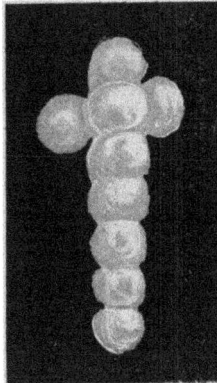

FIG. II.—THE GREAT SOUTHERN CROSS PEARL.

compose the shaft, which measures an inch-and-a-half in length, while the two arms of the cross are formed by one Pearl on each side, almost opposite to the second Pearl, reckoning from the top downwards. The component Pearls are of fine orient, and would be of good shape were it not that by mutual compression during growth, they have become slightly flattened on their opposed sides, while some of them, though round in front, are distorted into drop shapes at the back.

For the following account of the discovery of this remarkable Cross, the author is indebted to Mr. F. H. Cheesewright, by whom the Pearl was brought to this country :—" I learn from the Hon. Maitland

Browne," writes Mr. Cheesewright, under date August 7, 1886, "that the Pearl was discovered by a man named Clark, while Pearl-fishing at Roeburn, in Western Australia, in the schooner 'Ethel,' the owner being a Roman Catholic, called 'Shiner Kelly.' When the shell was opened, Clark senior, Shiner Kelly, and more especially young Clark, were filled with amazement and awe. Kelly regarding it as some Heaven-wrought miracle, with a certain amount of superstitious dread, buried it— for how long it is not known. The Pearl was discovered in 1874, and in 1879 the great Australian explorer, Alexander Forrest, saw it in Roeburn, just before he commenced his journey to Kimberley. The Pearl has changed hands many times, and each time it has done so, the person parting with it has made a hundred per cent. on the price he paid for it. It is now the property of a syndicate of gentlemen in Western Australia, and it was at the solicitation of these gentlemen that I was induced to bring it home."

This extraordinary Pearl Cross was exhibited in a prominent position in the Western Australian Court of the Colonial and Indian Exhibition of 1886. The cluster of Pearls was set in a simple gold mount, leaving the back of the Cross as well as the front face perfectly free. In consideration of the unique character of the Pearl, it was valued by the owners at £10,000 ; but this price is unreasonably high.

At first sight it might be supposed that the component Pearls, or at least some of them, had been artificially grouped together ; and it was natural that many visitors, who had not had the opportunity of closely inspecting the cross, should be disposed to entertain this opinion. Considering the almost geometrical regularity in the grouping of the Pearls, such an attitude of scepticism was pardonable enough. But minute examination of the Cross under high magnifying power is sufficient to dispel any notion of its artificial character.

It is notable that when any natural object of striking novelty is presented to a scientific observer, he is, by force of training, disposed to hesitate before assenting to its genuineness. This is not the first time that Australia has puzzled our cautious men of science by the singularity of its native products. For instance, when the duck-billed platypus (*Ornithorhynchus paradoxicus*) was originally brought to this country, zoologists hesitated to believe that so strange a creature could be natural, and were led to conclude that a hoax must have been perpetrated, by cunningly grafting the bill of a duck on to the body of a small

mammal. Yet it was soon found that this para-
doxical creature was no manufactured monster, but
a veritable product of the great island-continent,—
a curious union of bird and beast, which in our
limited knowledge we might be led to regard as a
strange "freak of nature."

In somewhat like manner, the great Southern
Cross Pearl might be regarded on a cursory view,
as having been manufactured by art, or at least
improved artificially. The author was therefore
anxious to submit it to severe scrutiny, and was
indebted for an opportunity of doing so to the
courtesy of Mr. A. F. Thompson, of the West-
Australian Court. On the 29th of July, 1886, the
Cross was exhibited, with a collection of choice
diamonds and other objects of value, at 18, New
Bond Street. A large number of scientific and literary
men, with many Colonists and Indians, availed themselves of the invitations which had been sent to
them, to inspect this strange curiosity. In order
that the fullest opportunity might be given for a
thorough examination, the Pearl was freely handled
by the visitors; and to make the scrutiny more
severe, a powerful lime-light was projected on to the
Cross, while magnifying glasses of high power were
provided to assist in the criticism. Under these
circumstances of strong illumination and close

examination, any artificial junction between the Pearls, or any trace of an artificial cementing medium, must have been detected by some of the acute critics who handled the gem. It is satisfactory however, to state that the Cross came out from the ordeal without shadow of suspicion, and was pronounced to be a *lusus naturæ* of unique character.

How it came about that these Pearls should be so regularly grouped together, no one has yet been able to explain with satisfaction. Dr. MacLarty has suggested, with some feasibility, that a fragment of serrated sea-weed may have gained access to the shell, and that the succession of teeth along the margin of the frond, may have determined the deposition of nacre at regular intervals, so as to form a string of Pearls running in a straight line. Whatever may have been the determining cause, it seems clear that it was a perfectly natural one, in no way resembling that artificial production of Pearls, which is practised on the fresh-water mussels of China. The Cross was found in the oyster, just as it was taken from its native element, without any possibility of its having been subjected to human manipulation.

As this remarkable cruciform group of Pearls was found in the southern hemisphere, it has very appropriately received the name of the Southern Cross, in allusion to the famous constellation of that name. This constellation is of course unknown, by observation, to dwellers in the northern hemisphere : and hence a description of it may be acceptable to the English reader. The author has therefore applied for information to the Right Hon. the Earl of Crawford and Balcarres, whose observations at the Dun Echt observatory, in Aberdeenshire; are known in every part of the world where science is cultivated. His lordship, with characteristic courtesy, has most obligingly favoured us with the following interesting letter :—

> CARLTON CLUB,
> PALL MALL, S.W.
> *24th June,* 1886.

DEAR SIR,

As I promised, I send you a few notes on the constellation known as *Crux Australis*, or " Southern Cross," and I hope that they may be of service to you.

The existence of this group of stars was not recognized as a separate constellation by the ancients, and they were placed by Ptolemy and 'As-Sufi, the Arabian astronomer, as forming a foot of the *Centaur.*

The Arabic globes and catalogues of stars were known in early mediæval times in Europe, and I think that there is little doubt but that Dante was acquainted with them when he used the following lines in the *Purgatorio*, canto i., lines 22-4.

> " Io mi volsi a man'destra, e posi mente
> Ali'altro polo, e vidi quatro stelle
> Non viste mai fuor' ch'alla prima gente."

The last line would probably allude to the few travellers who had gone so far to the south that the group was seen by them.

The first notice of it in modern times occurs in the letters of the great Florentine traveller, Corsali, where he speaks of it as the "Croce maravigliosa," in 1515. Again, Pigafetta notices it in his account of the voyage to South America, under the leadership of Magellan, in 1520-22.

It was considered then to be of a good omen, and had much mystic effect on the crew of the ship. It was first *figured* as a separate constellation by Bayer, in his atlas engraved in 1648, and is there noted as a new constellation.

It has gained its reputation solely on account of its form, as its component stars are small, and it is insignificant in comparison with others in the southern heavens. Only eight stars are visible to the naked eye. One of these, however, though barely visible to unaided vision, offers a most lovely object to the telescope. It is then found to consist of a cluster of no less than 110 stars, very small, but of the most vivid colours. Two are ruby red, two emerald green, three of an aquamarine tint, another of sapphire blue, while others range from dark orange to delicate lemon colour. Those which are white seem to shine out more vividly from the contrast.

It may truly be considered to form a tray of the jeweller's finest gems.

I enclose a little sketch of the stars, and am,

Yours faithfully,

CRAWFORD.

Mr. EDWIN W. STREETER.

CHAPTER XVIII.

ON THE VALUE OF PEARLS.

" So pray you add my
Diamonds to her Pearls."—
Tennyson's Elaine.

IN order to shew how the value of Pearls has varied in this country at different periods, the following extracts are given from the writings of recognized authorities. It is interesting to compare the several estimates, and mark the rise and fall at different times within the last two centuries.

Value of Pearls, A.D. 1671.

The following Table is extracted from " The History of Jewels," printed by T. N., for Hobart Kemp, at the sign of " The Ship," in the New Exchange, 1671. The author, who does not give his name says :—" One curious and intelligent in these matters furnished me with the following rule for the price of Pearls according to their weight."

Pearls.

A round Pearl weighing

1 grain	...	... *is worth*		1	Crown
2 grains	...	...	„	4	Crowns
3 „	...	...	„	9	„
4 „	...	...	„	16	„
5 „	...	...	„	25	„
6 „	...	...	.,	36	„
7 „	...	...	,,	49	„
8 „	...	...	„	64	„
9 „	...	...	„	81	„
10 „	...	...	„	100	„
11 „	...	...	„	121	„
12 „	...	...	,,	144	„
13 „	...	...	„	169	„
14 „	...	...	„	196	„
15 „	...	...	„	225	„
16 „	...	...	„	256	„
17 „	...	...	„	289	„
18 „	...	...	„	324	„
19 „	...	...	„	361	„
20 „	...	...	„	400	„
21 „	...	...	„	441	„
22 „	...	...	„	484	„
23 „	...	...	„	529	„
24 „	...	...	„	576	„
25 „	...	...	„	625	„
26 „	...	...	.,	675	„
27 „	..	...	„	729	„
28 „	...	...	„	784	„

29 grains	...	... *is worth*	841 Crowns
30 „	...	... „	900 „
31 „	...	... „	960 „
32 „	...	.. „	1,024 „

It is remarkable that this "curious and intelligent" man, by the very simple method of multiplying the number of grains by its own number, approached nearer to the true value of the Pearl than is done, so far as we know, in any other published table. It should be mentioned that in the greater part of the original table, the weights are given in carats, and that in the above extract they have been reduced to grains, in accordance with modern practice ; 4 grains making one carat, and $151\frac{1}{2}$ carats making one ounce, by which weight seed Pearl and baroque Pearls are bought by the trade.

Value of Pearls, A.D. 1753.

The next Table is extracted from a "Treatise on Pearls," by David Jeffries, printed at "The Rose," in Paternoster Row, 1753, and therefore 82 years later than the date of the preceding Table. Although the author gives the following value of Pearls, it is most probable that the large ones existed only on paper, inasmuch as not half-a-dozen fine round Pearls of over 50 grains each come into the market in the course of a year. The Table is, therefore, to

a large extent, imaginary. A drop or bouton is
of considerable less value than here stated, and an
ill-shaped Pearl is of hardly any value.

					£	s.	d.
A	4 grain Pearl is valued at				o	8	o
,,	8	,,	,,	,,	1	12	o
,,	12	,,	,,	,,	3	12	o
,,	16	,,	,,	,,	6	8	o.
,,	20	,,	,,	,,	10	o	o
,,	24	,,	,,	,,	14	8	o
,,	28	,,	,,	,,	19	12	o
,,	32	,,	,,	,,	25	12	o
,,	36	,,	,,	,,	32	8	o
,,	40	,,	,,	,,	40	o	o
,,	44	,,	,,	,,	48	8	o
,,	48	,,	,,	,,	57	12	o
,,	52	,,	,,	,	67	12	o
,,	56	,,	,,	,,	78	8	o
,,	60	,,	,,	,,	90	o	o
,,	64	,,	,,	,,	102	8	o
,,	68	,,	,,	,,	115	12	o
,,	72	,,	,,	,,	127	12	o
,,	76	,,	,,	,,	144	8	o
,,	80	,,	,,	,,	160	o	o
,,	84	,,	,,	,,			
,,	88	,,	,,	,,	193	12	o
,,	92	,,	,,	,,	211	12	o
,,	96	,,	,,	,,	230	8	o
,,	100	,,	,,	,,	250	o	o

				£	s.	d.
A 104 grain Pearl is valued at				270	8	0
,, 108	,,	,,	,,	291	12	0
,, 112	,,	,,	,,	313	12	0
,, 116	,,	,,	,,	336	8	0
,, 120	,,	,,	,,	360	0	0
,, 124	,,	,,	,,	384	8	0
,, 128	,,	,,	,,	409	12	0
,, 132	,,	,,	,,	435	12	0
,, 136	,,	,,	,,	462	8	0
,, 140	,,	,,	,,	490	0	0
,, 144	,,	,,	,,	518	8	0
,, 148	,,	,,	,,	547	12	0
,, 152	,,	,,	,,	577	12	0
,, 156	,,	,,	,,	608	8	0
,, 160	,,	,,	,,	640	0	0
,, 164	,,	,,	,,	672	8	0
,, 168	,,	,,	,,	705	12	0
,, 172	,,	,,	,,	739	12	0
,, 176	,,	,,	,,	774	0	0
,, 180	,,	,,	,,	810	0	0
,, 184	,,	,,	,,	846	8	0
,, 188	,,	,,	,,	883	12	0
,, 192	,,	,,	,,	921	12	0
,, 196	,,	,,	,,	960	8	0
,, 200	,,	,,	,,	1,000	0	0
,, 204	,,	,,	,,	1,040	8	0
,, 208	,,	,,	,,	1,081	12	0
,, 212	,,	,,	,,	1,123	12	0

						£	s.	d.
A	216	grain Pearl	is	valued	at	1,166	8	0
,,	220	,,	,,	,,		1,210	0	0
,,	224	,,	,,	,,		1,254	8	0
,,	228	,,	,,	,,		1,299	12	0
,,	232	,,	,,	,,		1,345	12	0
,,	236	,,	,,	,,		1,392	8	0
,,	240	,,	,,	,,		1,440	0	0
,,	244	,,	,,	,,		1,488	8	0
,,	248	,,	,,	,,		1,537	12	0
,,	252	,,	,,	,,		1,587	12	0

Value of Pearls, A.D. 1865 *and* 1867.

The following Tables are extracted from a work on "Diamonds and Precious Stones," by my predecessor, Mr. Harry Emanuel. The values mentioned in the two different Tables given below shew the increase between the publication of the first edition in 1865, and that of the second in 1867.

A round Pearl of		3	grains	each		12/-	to	16/-
,,	,,	,, 4	,,		,,	22/-	,,	28/-
,,	,,	,, 5	,,		,,	35/-	,,	45/-
,,	,,	,, 6	,,		,,	55/-	,,	65/-
,,	,,	,, 8	,,		,,	90/-	,,	110/-
,,	,,	,, 10	,,		,,	£8	,,	£9
,,	,,	,, 12	,,		,,	12	,,	15
,,	,,	,, 14	,,		,,	15	,,	18
,,	,,	,, 16	,,		,,	20	,,	30

A round Pearl of	18 grains	each £30	to £40
,, ,,	,, 20 ,,	,, 40 ,,	50
,, ,,	,, 24 ,,	,, 60 ,,	72
,, ,,	,, 30 ,,	,, 80 ,,	100

It is probable that during the whole time the author of the preceding Table was in business—from 1845 to 1870—he did not have a dozen really fine round Pearls of over 50 grains, pass through his hands.

The above Table was published in 1865. The same author gives in 1867 the following estimates—

A round Pearl of	3 grains	each 18/-	to 20/-
,, ,,	,, 4 ,,	,, 28/- ,,	35/-
,, ,,	,, 5 ,,	,, 40/- ,,	50/-
,, ,,	,, 6 ,,	,, 70/- ,,	80/-
,, ,,	,, 8 ,,	,, 100/- ,,	120/-
,, ,,	,, 10 ,,	,, £10 ,,	£11
·, ,,	,, 12 ,,	,, 14 ,,	16
,, ,,	,, 14 ,,	,, 18 ,,	20
,, ,,	,, 16 ,,	,, 20 ,,	30
,, ,,	,, 18 ,,	,, 30 ,,	40
,, ,,	,, 20 ,,	,, 40 ,,	50
,, ,,	,, 24 ,,	,, 60 ,,	72
,, ,,	,, 30 ,,	,, 80 ,,	100

These prices seem to-day ridiculously low. It may interest the reader to know that the author recently sold a fine round Pearl of a little under 30 grains, for a sum considerably higher than that quoted in the preceding table.

Value of Pearls, A.D. 1886.

The author of the present work has not attempted to give a Table of the present value of Pearls, because in forming an estimate, so many circumstances have to be taken into consideration, such as the shape, the colour, and the brilliancy of the Pearl. For instance, a perfectly round white Pearl of 40 grains may realize a fancy price, while a spot or dent will lessen the value to one-half; and if the Pearl be a little out of the round it may fall to even one-fourth. A bouton of equal weight will not be worth more than a quarter the price of a round Pearl of equal weight; and a Pearl of pear or drop shape only half the value of a bouton. Ear-rings of Pearl drops are not at present in fashion, round Pearls having taken their place, and as there is consequently little or no demand for drop-shaped Pearls, the price of such Pearls has fallen considerably. This example sufficiently shews what a difference in price is caused by fashion, or by any circumstance that detracts from the perfection of the Pearl in either shape or quality. At the present day black Pearls, if of the finest quality, are more valuable than white.

CHART OF THE PRINCIPAL PEARLING REGIONS.

Scale in miles

NORTH PACIFIC OCEAN

Caroline Islands

Pelew

NEW GUINEA

Admiralty I.

Gulf Papua

Flinders

Barrier Reef

Cook Peninsula

TORRES STRAITS

GULF OF CARPENTARIA

ARAFURA SEA

BANDA SEA

CERAM

GILOLO

CELEBES SEA

SULU SEA

PARAGUA

BORNEO

Labuan

MACASSAR STR.

CELEBES

TIMOR

Melville I.

Bathurst I.

AUSTRALIA

Longitude East 120° from Greenwich

Christmas I.

TRUE MERIDIAN

JAVA SEA

JAVA

SUMATRA

Lombok

Bali

N.W. Cape

MALAY PENINSULA

GULF OF SIAM

Singapore

INDIAN OCEAN

APPENDIX.

BIBLIOGRAPHY OF PEARLS.

THE following list of Works which have been consulted in the preparation of the present treatise may be useful, as forming a Bibliography of the subject of Pearls. It is not to be supposed that such a list can be complete, for, notwithstanding the vigilance of the writer in collecting, for many years, all literature within his reach, bearing upon the subject of Pearls, there are, no doubt, many writings, especially articles scattered through various journals, that have escaped his notice. At the same time he confidently believes that no work of importance is omitted from the following list.

ADAMS, L. E. "The Collector's Manual of British Land and Freshwater Shells." London, 1884.

AITKEN, W. G. Papier Mâché Manufacture. In Timmin's " Resources, Products and Industrial History of Birmingham." London, 1866.

BARBOT, CHARLES. "Traité complet des Pierres Précieuses." Paris, 1858.

BARRERA, MADAME DE. "Gems and Jewels." London, 1860.

BECK, HENRY J. LE. An Account of the Pearl Fishery in the Gulph of Manâr in March and April, 1797. *Asiatick Researches*. Vol. V., 1798, p. 393.

318

Appendix.

BERTRAM, J. G. "The Harvest of the Sea." 3rd
Edition. London, 1873.

BOHLEN, J. P. "Das Alte Indien." Königsberg, 1830.

BREWSTER, SIR DAVID. "On New Properties of
Light, exhibited in the Optical Phenomena of
Mother-of-Pearl." *Philosophical Transactions*, 1814.
Part II., p. 397.

———— "Observations on the peculiar Lustre of Pearls."
Edinburgh Journal of Science.. Vol. VI.,· 1827,
p. 277.

———— "A Treatise on Optics." Lardner's Cabinet
Cyclopædia. London, 1831.

BROCKENHAUS'S "Conversations-Lexikon." (Article,
Perlen). 13th Edition. Leipzig, 1885.

BURNHAM, S. M. "Precious Stones in Nature, Art and
Literature." Boston, 1886.

CAMDEN, WILLIAM "Magna Britannia et Hibernia, or
a New Survey of Great Britain." Wherein to the
Topographical account given by W. CAMDEN, is
added a more large history. 6 Vols. London,
1720—1731.

CARPENTER, W.B., M.D., F.R.S. "On the Microscopic
structure of shells." *Report of the British
Association* for 1844. p. 1.

CEYLON. "Official Handbook and Catalogue of the
Ceylon Court." Colonial and Indian Exhibition, 1886.

CEYLON. "Recollections of Ceylon; its Forests and
Pearl Fishery. (Anonymous). *Fraser's Magazine.*
Vol. LXII., 1860, p. 753.

CHARDIN, JEAN. "Voyage en Perse." 10 Vols. Paris, 1811.

CHURCH, A. H., M.A. "Precious Stones." (South
Kensington Museum Handbooks). London, 1883.

COUTANCE. A Chapter, "La Perle" in "Diamants et Pierres Précieuses." By E. JANNETTAZ, E. VANDERHEYM, E. FONTENAY and A. COUTANCE. Paris, 1881.

DALL, W. H. "Pearls and Pearl Fisheries." *American Naturalist.* Vol. XVII., 1883, p. 579, and p. 731.

DIEULAFAIT, LOUIS. "Diamants et Pierres Précieuses." (Bibliothèque des Merveilles). Paris, 1871.

EMANUEL, HARRY. "Diamonds and Precious Stones." London. 1st Edition, 1865; 2nd Edition, 1867.

GARNER, ROBERT. "On the Pearls of the Conway River, North Wales." *British Association Report* for 1856. Part II., p. 92.

GIBSON, JOHN. "Ordnance Gazetteer of Scotland." Edited by FRANCIS H. GROOME. 3 Vols., 1885.

HAGUE, W. F. "On the Natural and Artificial Production of Pearls in China." *Journal of the Royal Asiatic Society.* Vol. XVI., 1856, Part II., Art. XV.

HERSCHEL, SIR J. F. W. "On certain Optical Phenomena exhibited by Mother-of-Pearl." *Edinburgh Philosophical Journal.* 1820. Vol. II. p. 114.

HESSLING, DR. THEODORE VON. "Die Perlmuscheln und ibre Perlen, naturwissenschaftlich und geschichtlich; mit Berücksichtigung der Perlengewässer Bayerns." Leipzig, 1859.

HOME, SIR EVERARD, BART. "On the Production and Formation of Pearls." *Philosophical Transactions.* 1826. Part III.

HUTCHINSON, WILLIAM. "The History of the County of Cumberland." Carlisle, 1794.

IRVING, THEODORE. "Conquest of Florida." London, 1835.

JACKSON, J. R. "Minerals and their Uses." London, 1849.

JEFFRIES, DAVID.   "A Treatise on Diamonds and
    Pearls." 2nd Edition. London, 1751.

JEFFREYS, J. GWYN.   "British Conchology." 5 Vols.
    London, 1862.

JEWELS.   "The History of Jewels, and of the Principal
    Riches of the East and West. Taken from the
    Relation of divers of the most famous Travellers
    of our Age, attended with fair Discoveries conducing
    to the knowledge of the Universe and Trade."
    Printed by T.N., for Hobart Kemp, at the sign of
    "The Ship," in the Upper Walk of the New
    Exchange. 1671.

KING, C. W. M.A.   "The Natural History, Ancient and
    Modern, of Precious Stones and Gems." London,
    1865.

KLUGE, KARL EMILE.   "Handbuch der Edelsteinkunde."
    Leipzig, 1860.

LAWSON, W. J.   "History of Banking." (Sir T. Gresham's
    Pearl). London, 1850.

LEWIS, DR. JAMES.   "On the colouring matter of
    Pearl-shells." *Proceedings of the Academy of Natural
    Sciences of Philadelphia* for 1866. p. 88.

LEWIS, W.   "Experimental History of the Materia
    Medica." 4th Edition. London, 1791.

MACGOWAN, D. T. M.D.   "Pearls and Pearl-making in
    China." *Journal of the Society of Arts.* Vol. II.,
    1853, p. 72.

MARCO POLO'S TRAVELS.   Edited by Col. H. YULE, C.B.
    London, 1871.

MARKHAM, CLEMENTS R., ESQ.   "The Tinnevelly
    Pearl Fishery." *Journal of the Society of Arts.*
    March 1, 1867. Vol. XV., p. 256.

MOEBIUS, KARL.   "Die Echten Perlen." Hamburg, 1858.

OUSELEY, SIR WILLIAM. "Travels in the East." 3 Vols. London, 1819—23.

PENNANT, THOMAS. "British Zoology." 4th Edition, 1777.

PERCIVAL, ROBERT. "An Account of the Island of Ceylon." 2nd Edition. London, 1806. See also *Edinburgh Review.* Vol. II., 1803., p. 136.

PLAT, SIR HUGH. "The Jewel House of Art and Nature." London, 1653.

PLINY. "The Historie of the World. Commonly called The Naturall Historie of C. Plinius Secundus." Translated into English by PHILEMON HOLLAND, Doctor of Physick. London, 1601.

REDDING, SIR R. "A letter from Sir ROBERT REDDING, late Fellow of the R.S., concerning Pearl-Fishing in the North of Ireland; communicated to the Publisher by Dr. LISTER, R.S.S." *Philosophical Transactions*, 1693. Vol. XVII., p. 659.

ROSNEL, PIERRE DE. "Le Mercure Indien, ou Le Tresor des Indes." Paris, 1672.

RUDLER, F. W. Article "Pearl," in "*Encyclopædia Britannica.*" 9th Edition, Vol. XVIII., 1885.

RUSCHENBERGER, W. S. W. "Voyage round the World." 2 Vols., London, 1838.

SIMMONDS, P. L., F.R.C.S., F.S.S. "On the Pearl, Coral, and Amber Fisheries." *Journal of the Society of Arts.* Vol. XVIII., 1870, p. 173.

——— "The Commercial Products of the Sea." London, 1879.

SMITH, W., LL.D. "A Dictionary of the Bible." (Articles "Bdellium" and "Pearls.") London, 1860-3.

SOURINDRO MOHUN TAGORE, RAJA. "Mani-Málá, or a Treatise on Gems." 2 Vols. Calcutta, 1881.

X

Appendix.

Spon's "Encyclopædia of the Industrial Arts, Manufactures, and Raw Commercial Products. Edited by Charles G. Warnford Lock. (Article "Pearl.") London, 1882.

Tavernier, Jean Baptiste. "Les Six Voyages qu'il a fait en Turquie, en Perse et aux Indes." 3 Vols. Paris, 1681-82.

Tryon, George W. Jun. "Structural and Systematic Conchology.' Philadelphia, 1882.

Tytler, P. F. "History of Scotland.' 2nd Edition. London, 1843. (For Scotch Pearls).

Ure's "Dictionary of Arts, Manufactures and Mines." By R. Hunt, f.r.s., and F. W. Rudler, f.g.s. (Article "Pearls") 7th Edition. London, 1875.

Vincent, William, d.d. "The Commerce and Navigation of the Ancients in the Indian Ocean." 2 Vols. London, 1807. (Containing a version of the anonymous work, "The Periplus of the Erythrean Sea.")

Watts, Henry. "A Dictionary of Chemistry." Vol. 3. (Article "Mother of-Pearl.") 1865.

Wellsted, Lieut. J.R., f.r.s. "Travels in Arabia." London, 1838.

———— "Travels to the City of the Caliphs." 2 Vols. London, 1840.

Wilkinson, Sir J. Gardner. "Manners and Customs of the ancient Egyptians." 6 Vols. London, 1840-41.

Woodward, S. P. "A Manual of the Mollusca." 2nd Edition. By Ralph Tate. London, 1877.

Wright, J. S. "The Jewellery and Gilt Toy Trades." In Timmins' "Resources, Products, and Industrial History of Birmingham." London, 1866.

INDEX.

www.ingramcontent.com/pod-product-compliance
Lightning Source LLC
Chambersburg PA
CBHW031437280326
41927CB00038B/433

9781528712811